Lecture Notes in Computer Science 12031

More information about this series at http://www.springer.com/series/7408

Supratik Chakraborty · Jorge A. Navas (Eds.)

Verified Software

Theories, Tools, and Experiments

11th International Conference, VSTTE 2019
New York City, NY, USA, July 13–14, 2019
Revised Selected Papers

 Springer

Editors
Supratik Chakraborty
Indian Institute of Technology Bombay
Mumbai, India

Jorge A. Navas
SRI International
Menlo Park, CA, USA

ISSN 0302-9743   ISSN 1611-3349   (electronic)
Lecture Notes in Computer Science
ISBN 978-3-030-41599-0   ISBN 978-3-030-41600-3   (eBook)
https://doi.org/10.1007/978-3-030-41600-3

LNCS Sublibrary: SL2 – Programming and Software Engineering

This Springer imprint is published by the registered company Springer Nature Switzerland AG
The registered company address is: Gewerbestrasse 11, 6330 Cham, Switzerland

Preface

This volume contains the contributed and invited papers presented at VSTTE 2019, the 11th Working Conference on Verified Software: Theories, Tools, and Experiments held on July 13–14, 2019 in New York City, USA. The working conference was co-located with the 31st International Conference on Computer-Aided Verification (CAV 2019).

The Verified Software Initiative (VSI), spearheaded by Tony Hoare and Jayadev Misra, is an ambitious research program for making large-scale verified software a practical reality. VSTTE is the main forum for advancing the initiative. VSTTE brings together experts spanning the spectrum of software verification in order to foster international collaboration on the critical research challenges.

There were 17 submissions to VSTTE 2019, with authors from 19 countries. The Program Committee consisted of 32 distinguished computer scientists from all over the world. Each submission was reviewed by three Program Committee members in single-blind mode. In order to ensure that topic-specific expert reviews were obtained, help was also sought from five external reviewers. After a comprehensive discussion on the strengths and weaknesses of papers, the committee decided to accept nine papers. The technical program also included four invited talks by Prof. Tevfik Bultan (University of California, Santa Barbara, USA), Prof. Marsha Chechik (University of Toronto, Canada), Prof. Aarti Gupta (Princeton University, USA) and Prof. Antonine Miné (Sorbonne Université, CNRS, LIP6, Paris, France).

Partial funding for the working conference was provided by the CAV 2019 organizers. We greatly acknowledge their help. We are also thankful to EasyChair for providing an easy and efficient mechanism for submission of papers, management of reviews, and eventually in the generation of this volume.

December 2019

Supratik Chakraborty
Jorge A. Navas
Natarajan Shankar

Organization

Program Committee

Aws Albarghouthi	University of Wisconsin-Madison, USA
Supratik Chakraborty	IIT Bombay, India
Xinyu Feng	Nanjing University, People's Republic of China
Graeme Gange	Monash University, Australia
Ashutosh Gupta	IIT Bombay, India
Arie Gurfinkel	University of Waterloo, Canada
Liana Hadarean	Synopsys, USA
Joxan Jaffar	National University of Singapore, Singapore
Dejan Jovanović	SRI International, USA
Aditya Kanade	Indian Institute of Science, India
Yunho Kim	Korea Advanced Institute of Science and Technology, South Korea
Tim King	Google, USA
Yi Li	Nanyang Technological University, Singapore
Nuno P. Lopes	Microsoft, UK
David Monniaux	CNRS and VERIMAG, France
Jose F. Morales	IMDEA Software Research Institute, Spain
Yannick Moy	AdaCore, France
Kedar Namjoshi	Nokia-Bell Laboratories, USA
Nina Narodytska	VMware Research, USA
Jorge Navas	SRI International, USA
Aina Niemetz	Stanford University, USA
Oded Padon	Stanford University, USA
Venkatesh R	Tata Consultancy Services, India
Philipp Ruemmer	Uppsala University, Sweden
Peter Schrammel	University of Sussex, UK
Natarajan Shankar	SRI International, USA
Rahul Sharma	Microsoft, India
Jing Sun	The University of Auckland, New Zealand
Michael Tautschnig	Queen Mary University of London, UK
Tachio Terauchi	Waseda University, Japan
Aditya Thakur	University of California, Davis, USA
Bow-Yaw Wang	Academia Sinica, People's Republic of China (Taiwan)
Valentin Wüstholz	ConsenSys Diligence, Germany

Additional Reviewers

Hajdu, Akos
Maghareh, Rasool
Mukherjee, Suvam
Noetzli, Andres
Reynolds, Andrew

Abstract of Invited Talks

Combinations of Reusable Abstract Domains for a Multilingual Static Analyzer

Matthieu Journault[1], Antoine Miné[1,2], Raphaël Monat[1], and Abdelraouf Ouadjaout[1]

[1] Sorbonne Université, CNRS, LIP6, 75005 Paris, France
{matthieu.journault,antoine.mine,raphael.monat,
abdelraouf.ouadjaout}@lip6.fr
[2] Institut Universitaire de France, 75005 Paris, France

Abstract. We discuss the design of MOPSA, an ongoing effort to design a novel semantic static analyzer by abstract interpretation. MOPSA strives to achieve a high degree of modularity and extensibility by considering value abstractions for numeric, pointer, objects, arrays, etc. as well as syntax-driven iterators and control-flow abstractions uniformly as domain modules, which offer a unified signature and loose coupling, so that they can be combined and reused at will. Moreover, domains can dynamically rewrite expressions, which simplifies the design of relational abstractions, encourages a design based on layered semantics, and enables domain reuse across different analyses and different languages. We present preliminary applications of MOPSA analyzing simple programs in subsets of the C and Python programming languages, checking them for run-time errors and uncaught exceptions.

Uncertainty, Modeling and Safety Assurance: Towards a Unified Framework

Marsha Chechik, Sahar Kokaly, Mona Rahimi, Rick Salay,
and Torin Viger

University of Toronto, Toronto, Canada
{chechik,skokaly,mrahimi,
rsalay,torinviger}@cs.toronto.edu

Abstract. Uncertainty occurs naturally in software systems, including those that are model-based. When such systems are safety-critical, they need to be assured, e.g., by arguing that the system satisfies its safety goals. But how can we rigorously reason about assurance in the presence of uncertainty? In this paper, we propose a vision for a framework for managing uncertainty in assurance cases for software systems, and in particular, for *model-based* software systems, by systematically *identifying*, *assessing* and *addressing* it. We also discuss a set of challenges that need to be addressed to realize this framework.

Verifying Network Control Planes

Aarti Gupta

Princeton University, Princeton, USA
aartig@cs.princeton.edu

Abstract. The last decade has seen tremendous advances in applying formal methods to verification of computer networks. In this talk, I will describe two recent efforts that target network control planes, i.e., the complex distributed systems comprising various protocols for exchanging messages between routers and selecting paths for routing traffic. In the first effort, we develop a general-purpose, symbolic model of the network control and data planes that encodes the stable states of a network as a satisfying assignment to an SMT formula. Using this model, we show how to verify a wide variety of properties including reachability, fault-tolerance, router equivalence, and load balancing. Our second effort focuses on leveraging symmetry in control planes to find network abstractions that achieve compression in size while preserving many properties of interest.

This is joint work with Ryan Beckett, Ratul Mahajan, and David Walker.

Quantifying Information Leakage Using Model Counting Constraint Solvers

Tevfik Bultan

University of California, Santa Barbara, USA
bultan@cs.ucsb.edu

Abstract. This paper provides a brief overview of recent results in quantitative information flow analysis, model counting constraints solvers, side-channel analysis and attack synthesis. By combining model counting constraints solvers with symbolic execution it is possible to quantify the amount of information that a program leaks about a secret input. As discussed below, this type of analysis is crucial for detection and analysis of side channel vulnerabilities.

This material is based on research supported by an Amazon Research Award, by NSF under Grant CCF-1817242, and by DARPA under the agreement number FA8750-15-2-0087. The U.S. Government is authorized to reproduce and distribute reprints for Governmental purposes notwithstanding any copyright notation thereon. The views and conclusions contained herein are those of the authors and should not be interpreted as necessarily representing the official policies or endorsements, either expressed or implied, of DARPA or the U.S. Government.

Contents

Combinations of Reusable Abstract Domains for a Multilingual Static Analyzer

Matthieu Journault[1], Antoine Miné[1,2(✉)], Raphaël Monat[1], and Abdelraouf Ouadjaout[1]

[1] Sorbonne Université, CNRS, LIP6, 75005 Paris, France
{matthieu.journault,antoine.mine,raphael.monat,
abdelraouf.ouadjaout}@lip6.fr
[2] Institut Universitaire de France, 75005 Paris, France

Abstract. We discuss the design of MOPSA, an ongoing effort to design a novel semantic static analyzer by abstract interpretation. MOPSA strives to achieve a high degree of modularity and extensibility by considering value abstractions for numeric, pointer, objects, arrays, etc. as well as syntax-driven iterators and control-flow abstractions uniformly as domain modules, which offer a unified signature and loose coupling, so that they can be combined and reused at will. Moreover, domains can dynamically rewrite expressions, which simplifies the design of relational abstractions, encourages a design based on layered semantics, and enables domain reuse across different analyses and different languages. We present preliminary applications of MOPSA analyzing simple programs in subsets of the C and Python programming languages, checking them for run-time errors and uncaught exceptions.

Keywords: Static analysis · Program verification · Abstract interpretation · Tool design

1 Introduction

Static analysis aims at inferring automatically the behavior of programs in order to prove correctness properties. Abstract interpretation [4], a theory of the approximation of program semantics, helps in designing semantic-based static analyses with formal guarantees: they are sound, in that every property proved by the analyzer indeed holds; but incomplete, in that not all true properties of the program are inferred (due to incompleteness, it may fail to establish that a correct program is correct). One view we hold here, is that an *abstract interpreter* is an interpreter in the usual sense of a program interpreter computing some output and defined by induction on language syntax, except that:

This work is partially supported by the European Research Council under Consolidator Grant Agreement 681393—MOPSA.

S. Chakraborty and J. A. Navas (Eds.): VSTTE 2019, LNCS 12031, pp. 1–18, 2020.
https://doi.org/10.1007/978-3-030-41600-3_1

1. it computes a *collecting semantics*, that collects all possible program executions along all execution paths, for all possible inputs;
2. at an *abstract level*, that forgets semantic details and performs simplifications to achieve an efficient computation in a compact machine representation—a classic example is keeping variable bounds, forgetting which values are reachable within these bounds and any relationship between variable values.

```
int main(int argc, char *argv[]) {
    int i = 0;
    for (char **p = argv; *p; p++) {
    1: printf("%s\n", strlen(*p)); // valid string
        i++; // no overflow
    }
    return 0;
}
```

Fig. 1. Example C program analyzed by MOPSA

Numeric:
$argc \in [1, maxint]$
$size(argv) = argc + 1$
$size(@) \in [1, maxsize]$
$0 \leq offset(p) \leq size(argv) - 1$
$offset(p) = i$

Pointers:
$argv[0 \ldots argc - 1] \mapsto \{@\}$
$argv[argc] \mapsto \{NULL\}$
$p \mapsto \{argv\}$

Memory:
variables: argc, argv, p, i
summary block: @

Strings:
$\exists k \in [0 \ldots size(@) - 1] : @[k] = 0$

Fig. 2. Invariants inferred at label 1 for the program of Fig. 1

An attractive feature of abstract interpretation is the existence of a variety of such abstract domains of interpretation, which target different kinds of properties and various trade-offs between cost, precision, and expressiveness. Abstract interpretation has led in the last two decades to several static analysis tools used in industry: PolySpace, Astrée [13], Sparrow [19], Julia [20], Frama-C [9], Infer [3], etc. We present here our work in progress designing MOPSA [17], a Modular Open Platform for Static Analysis programmed in OCaml. MOPSA differs from existing tools by its highly extensible, modular design, which allows easily defining and combining heterogeneous abstractions, and reusing them to analyze widely different programming languages, such as C and Python.

As a simple example, consider the small C program in Fig. 1, that prints the length of its command-line arguments, a NULL-terminated array of 0-terminated strings. MOPSA is able to prove that the string manipulation does not cause any dereference error and there is no arithmetic overflow. This is established by a combination of collaborating abstractions, as illustrated in Fig. 2: a memory abstraction partitions the memory into variables (`argc`, `argv`, ...) and summary blocks (@) representing possibly unbounded collections of dynamically allocated blocks (here, the command-line arguments pointed to by the elements of the `argv` array); a pointer abstraction maintains points-to information ($p \mapsto \{argv\}$); a string abstraction maintains predicates on the position of the terminating 0 ($\exists k \in [0 \ldots \texttt{size}(@) - 1] : @[k] = 0$); and a numeric abstraction infers ranges and affine inequalities. Despite abstracting very different objects, these domains obey a common signature and are loosely coupled, and so can be easily plugged in and out. Moreover, they collaborate in several ways:

1. Cartesian products, to combine domains discussing about orthogonal semantic objects (such as pointer variables and numeric variables);
2. reduced products, to combine domains abstracting the same semantic object in different ways (such as interval and polyhedra [8]);
3. delegation, for a domain to rely on another one for its computations (*e.g.* the pointer domain relies on numeric domains to maintain offset information).

When combined, these mechanisms allow a powerful interaction between domains. For instance, Fig. 2 shows that it is possible to infer affine relations between integer variables and other integer quantities introduced by the other abstract domains, such as pointer offsets and string sizes.

Section 2 presents our representation of programs in MOPSA, which is close to the source level to avoid losing high-level information and uses extensible abstract syntax trees to support the addition of analysis targets. This is in contrast to traditional analyzers, that translate source programs into a simplified, fixed, low-level representation (such as simplified C, or LLVM bitcode), on which the semantic analysis is performed. Section 3 presents the dynamic simplification of expressions performed during the analysis. This again contrasts to traditional analyzers, where front-ends perform static simplifications, and it is key to achieve a flexible delegation mechanism of domain computations while keeping a fully relational analysis. Section 4 details how the combination of domains is achieved. Section 5 presents our application to analyzing a large subset of the C and Python languages, as well as preliminary experimental results. Although MOPSA is not yet able to analyze large-scale C nor realistic Python programs, we believe that these results are encouraging as few tools have yet shown the ability to analyze languages as dynamic as Python, nor been able to factor the analysis of such different languages as C and Python in the same framework. Moreover, MOPSA is intended as a platform for research, and has been exploited in several exploratory works on analyzing Python [10], strings [11], and trees [12]. We plan to release our implementation as open-source software. Section 6 concludes. This article extends on a short presentation of MOPSA from [17] by giving notably more details and examples on MOPSA's abstractions, dynamic expression simplification, domain compositions, as well as more recent benchmarks.

2   Unified Extensible Language

Classic static analyzers operate on an intermediate language—such as LLVM bitcode [14]—rather than the source language. One benefit is that the semantic analysis needs to handle far less constructions, with a simpler semantics. Supporting a new target language is then only a matter of writing a new front-end that translates it into this fixed intermediate language. However, some information is lost in the translation, which may hurt the subsequent analysis (*e.g.* LLVM forgets whether integer types are signed or unsigned, while transformation to 3-address code puts a strain on relational domains to maintain precision [18]). Additionally, a common intermediate language may not fit all possible language kinds. On the contrary, MOPSA employs an extensible AST data-type to keep as much high-level information as possible and be open for new targets. Each analyzer module can define additional variants for syntactic objects: statements, expressions, types, variables, etc. Currently, MOPSA supports the following:

- Universal, a toy-language that mainly features an unbounded integer data-type and simple control constructs (loops, conditionals, functions);
- most of C, through Clang's parser, and a contract annotation language inspired by ACSL [9] to model library functions (Sect. 5.2);
- a large subset of Python 3 (using a dedicated parser).

Extensible Syntax. Using OCaml's extensible variant types, any OCaml module can extend MOPSA's AST. For instance, MOPSA's abstract syntax for simple `while` loops in Universal is introduced as:

```
type stmt_kind += S_while of expr * stmt
```

Then, the C syntax module defines loops as:

```
type stmt_kind += S_c_for of stmt * expr option * expr option * stmt
               | S_c_do_while of stmt * expr
```

We do not redefine `while` loops for C as they are identical to the ones in Universal. However, we add `for` and `do-while` loops, which have a different syntax, so as to keep separate each kind of loops in the program representation, instead of lowering them to `while` loops. For completeness, Python loops are defined as:

```
type stmt_kind += S_py_for of expr * expr * stmt * stmt
               | S_py_while of expr * stmt * stmt
```

They feature an additional statement, which denotes the else clause of the loops.

Distributed Iterator. The semantic effect is defined by a domain which provides an `exec` function. Like the syntax, the `exec` function can be distributed among several modules. A global iterator will call in turn the `exec` functions until one of them returns a non-`None` value. For instance, the semantics of `while` loops in Universal is defined as a fixpoint as follows, where `flow` represents the flow of abstract information, `lfp` performs classic fixpoint iteration with acceleration, and `join` computes the union of abstract information:

```
let exec stmt man flow = match stmt_kind stmt with
| S_while (cond, body) ->
    let i = lfp (fun f -> Flow.join f (man.exec (S_assume cond) f |>
                                       man.exec body)
                ) flow
    in Some (man.exec (S_assume (E_not cond) i))
| _ ->
    None (* pass-through to the next domain *)
```

The semantics of loops is defined in terms of the semantics of the loop body and conditions (S_assume), hence, its exec function must be able to call the global iterator that will in turn find the proper module to handle these statements; this is the role of the *manager* man passed as argument to all abstract functions.

The semantics of a C for loop can be defined in terms of Universal loops as a simple syntactic transformation, which will be automatically delegated to Universal's loop iterator, after executing the loop initialization statement:

```
let exec stmt man flow = match stmt_kind stmt with
| S_c_for (init, cond, incr, body) ->
    let body' = ... in
    Some (man.exec (mk_block [init; S_while (cond, body')]) flow)
| _ -> None
```

This has the benefit of factoring the logic for fixpoint computation in one place. Such a translation is done at analysis time: it could access information from the abstract state (through flow) and manipulate it (through man). While this is not the case for this simple example, we will see its benefit in Sect. 3.

Domains. Traditional analyzers separate iterators, that work on high-level control structures or control-flow-graphs, from abstract domains, that ultimately handle atomic statements, such as assignments and tests. However, MOPSA uses the same signature for both. The same way the global exec function available through the manager man is composed of exec functions defined in all domains, the abstract flow of information flow is composed of information from each domain (such as intervals, pointers, etc.) and can be manipulated by any domain (*e.g.* to perform joins). A loop iterator happens to be a domain with empty abstract state, and the policy of finding the first domain that handles a specific statement is one example of domain composition, called sequence. Other domain composition operators, such as reduced and Cartesian products, are discussed in Sect. 4. A typical analysis instance contains dozens of domains. This is illustrated in Fig. 3 for the case of the C analyzer (we give more details on these domains in Sects. 4 and 5). Note that many domains defined for Universal are reused in the C analysis.

3 Dynamic Expression Rewriting

When analyzing a program, the original AST goes through successive transformations that reduce its complexity. For instance, an assignment in C can be

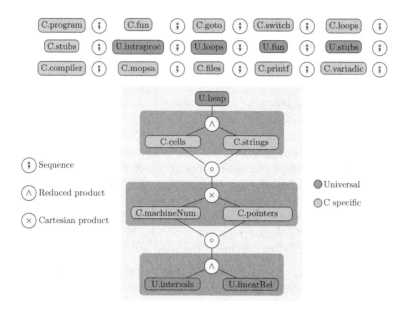

Fig. 3. Domain composition in Mopsa's C analyzer (see also Sect. 5.1)

first translated into a simplified subset of C by flattening all data structures into arrays, before moving to another subset containing only scalar variables by resolving dereferences. These transformations are performed dynamically during the analysis in order to gain in precision by leveraging the inferred constraints.

Evaluating to Expressions. An important particularity of these translations in Mopsa is the evaluation mechanism of expressions. In order to preserve relational constraints present in the original structure of the program, expressions are not evaluated into abstract values, but into other expressions.

As an illustration, consider the assignment `x = a[i] + 1` in the Universal language. The numeric domain is responsible for assignments to integer variables, but can not handle expressions with arrays. Therefore, it delegates, with `eval`, the evaluation of the right-hand-side expression to other domains via the manager:

```
let exec stmt man flow = match skind stmt with
  | S_assign(E_var x, e) ->
    let e' = man.eval e flow in
    ...
  | _ -> None
```

A domain that abstracts arrays as smashed variables implements the evaluation of `a[i]` by providing an `eval` function returning an auxiliary numeric variable, `a*`, introduced by the abstraction to denote the values of all the array elements:

```
let eval exp man flow = match ekind e with
  | E_subscript(E_var a,i) ->
```

```
    let smash = mk_smash a in
    Some (Eval.return smash flow)
  | _ -> None
```

The original statement `x = a[i] + 1` is thus translated into the simplified assignment `x = a* + 1`, which can be handled directly by the numeric domain.

Keeping the right-hand side of the assignment symbolic allows a relational domain to infer relations between program variables. Consider, for instance, a memory domain abstracting arrays by expansion, creating variables `a0, a1, ...` to denote the values of `a[0], a[1], ...` Then, in an environment where $i = 1$, the domain will translate `x = a[i] + 1` into `x = a1 + 1`, allowing a domain such as polyhedra [8] to maintain the relation $x = a1 + 1$.

Note that neither adding an array data-type, nor choosing whether to abstract by smashing or by expansion, required any change to the numeric domain; the new abstraction is conveyed through expression rewriting. This mechanism makes it easy to reuse existing abstractions with novel operators and semantics. As another example, while Universal features arithmetic on mathematical integers, which fits classic numeric domains well, C expressions are evaluated using machine integers. Thus, we added a domain that translates machine arithmetic into integer arithmetic. It checks for overflows in the current abstract state, and exploits the fact that, in the absence of overflow, the two semantics coincide, to output, when possible, expressions that are close to the original ones.

Disjunctions. Evaluations in MOPSA also offer an elegant way to perform a case analysis. Domains can evaluate an expression into a disjunction of different expressions, for different subsets of the abstract state. To manipulate these disjunctive evaluations easily, two mechanisms are provided. Firstly, domains can use a monadic bind operator `>>=` to execute a transfer function on each case of the evaluation. Secondly, abstract versions of common test statements, such as `if` and `switch`, are introduced to express guarded evaluations.

Consider an abstraction of 0-terminated C strings [11] that abstracts strings with their length, *i.e.* the position of the first 0 in the array. To each memory block `b`, the domain associates an integer auxiliary variable b_l such that:

$$b[b_l] = 0 \wedge \forall i \in [0, b_l - 1] : b[b_l] \neq 0$$

Using this auxiliary variable, the evaluation of an access `b[i]` is decomposed into three cases using the abstract operator `switch`. Indeed, depending on the ordering between `i` and b_l, `b[i]` may evaluate to a non-null, a null, or an arbitrary byte value. Each case is a pair containing a guard and the associated expression:

```
let eval exp man flow = match ekind e with
| E_c_subscript(b, i) ->
  (* Evaluate the index expression *)
  man.eval i flow >>= fun i' flow ->

  ...

  (* After checking out-of-bound accesses *)
  let length = mk_length b in
```

```
Some (switch [
  (* Case 1: access before the first 0 *)
  (mk_lt i' length), (* i < length(b) *)
  (fun flow -> Eval.return (mk_interval 1 255) flow); (* [1,255] *)

  (* Case 2: access at the first zero *)
  (mk_eq i' length), (* i = length(b) *)
  (fun flow -> Eval.return zero flow); (* 0 *)

  (* Case 3: access after the first zero *)
  (mk_gt i' length), (* i > length(b) *)
  (fun flow -> Eval.singleton (mk_interval 0 255) flow) (* [0,255] *)
] man flow)

| _ -> None
```

The conditions $i < b_l$, $i = b_l$ and $i > b_l$ are interpreted by numeric domains and refine the abstract environments during the evaluation. Then, an assignment such as x = b[i] will trigger three assignments in the numeric domain, one for each case, after which the cases are merged with an abstract join. When using a relational numeric domain, this allows us to infer easily relations between auxiliary variables, such as b_l, and program variables.

4   Domain Combination

MOPSA provides several combination operators that simplify the construction of complex abstractions, such as the Cartesian product operator $\otimes$, the sequence operator $\odot$, and the reduced product operator $\wedge$. To preserve modularity, domains should be loosely coupled by keeping their abstraction private. On the other hand, domains are not isolated and need to cooperate in order to exploit the available abstractions.

Queries. Similarly to input channels in Astrée [6], domains in MOPSA can request the computation of abstract properties, such as the interval of a numeric expression. This is done by defining a *query*, which is an extensible GADT type encoding the query argument and its result. For instance, the interval query can be defined as follows:

```
type _ query += Q_interval: expr -> (int option * int option) query
```

Answering to queries is done by defining a transfer function ask in the domain:

```
let ask : type r. r query -> t -> r option = fun query state ->
  match query with
  | Q_interval e ->
    let l, u = ... in
    Some (l, u)
  | _ -> None
```

A domain returns `None` for queries it cannot handle. Client domains can retrieve this information via their manager by calling `man.ask (Q_interval e) flow`, and do not need to know which domain(s) can answer. Queries come with lattice operators to combine the replies from several domains.

Reductions. Reduced products [5,6] are a common example of cooperation in abstract interpreters. A reduced product computes the intersection of domains approximating the same concrete semantics, and allows refining the abstract state of a domain by exploiting information computed by the other domains.

To illustrate this form of cooperation, consider the classic example of reducing intervals and congruences [16]. Given an interval $[11, 12]$ and a congruence $2\mathbb{Z}+1$, we can refine both values in two steps. Firstly, using the fact that the value is odd, the interval is refined into $[11, 11]$. After that, since the interval is now a singleton, the congruence is refined into $0\mathbb{Z} + 11$.

Defining reductions in MOPSA is different than in existing analyzers in several ways. Firstly, it is simpler while being powerful enough to define complex reductions. Reduction rules are not part of the transfer functions of domains and do not require using particular communication channels to retrieve required information. Instead, they are defined externally in separate modules with a simplified signature that allows access to the internal representation of abstract elements easily. It is thus easy to design new reductions, or remove them, while keeping the core transfer functions of the abstract domains unchanged. For instance, the reduction between intervals and congruences is defined as:

```
let reduce man pointwise =
  let i = man.get Interval.id pointwise
  and c = man.get Congruence.id pointwise in
  let i', c' = meet_interval_congruence i c in
  man.set Interval.id i' pointwise |>
  man.set Congruence.id c'
```

Secondly, in contrast to Astrée [6], there is no fixed order of computation in a reduced product. Post-conditions are computed independently, before applying reduction rules on the pointwise result. Finally, reduced products in MOPSA are not limited to iterated pairwise reductions, but support n-ary reduction rules, which enables more precision [7].

Sharing. While many abstract interpreters offer the possibility to build reduced products [2,9], a distinctive feature of MOPSA is the ability to define products of abstract domains that share a part of their abstraction. For instance, the C analysis (Fig. 3) features a Cartesian product of a domain `C.machineNum` handling statements over C numeric expressions by rewriting them into mathematical integer expressions, and a domain `C.pointers` handling C pointer expressions and storing points-to information. These domains are assembled in a Cartesian product as their semantics do not overlap: unlike reduced products, they target orthogonal expressions. However, both abstractions delegate a part of their state to an underlying numeric domain: integer C variables for C.machineNum, and pointer offsets for C.pointers. MOPSA offers the possibility for these two domains to share some underlying abstract state (denoted as ⊙ in Fig. 3). We can thus exploit a numeric domain to infer relations between pointer offsets and integer variables. As a consequence of this sharing, the composition of abstract states from individual domains forms a DAG, not a tree.

Logs. As for the Cartesian product, MOPSA allows domains composed in a reduced product to delegate part of their abstraction to another (potentially shared) domain. This is the case for the reduced product between the C.cells and the C.strings domains in the C analysis of Fig. 3. The cell domain [15] is used to represent the C memory: it translates the semantics of all C memory accesses into a semantics over a set of scalar variables. Abstracting the values of these variables is then delegated to an underlying abstraction. Recall that the string domain represents the length of a C string, *i.e.* the position of the first 0, by associating a numeric variable to each memory region [11]. The cell and string domains provide information on common parts of the C memory, hence, they are composed in a reduced product. Sharing the underlying domain allows the discovery of relations between string lengths (managed by the string abstraction), and numeric and pointer variables (managed by the cell abstraction).

In the case of a Cartesian product, a statement is always handled by at most one of the domains in the product. In contrast, in the case of a reduced product, the statements are handled by all the domains. Each domain transforms the shared underlying domain, inducing several different states for the shared component, which must then be merged into a sound post-condition.

As an example, consider a simplified abstraction defined as the reduced product between the cell and string domains delegating to a shared numeric domain. Consider moreover the statement $s \overset{\text{def}}{=}$ a[0] = '\0' executed in the shared numeric abstract state $S^\sharp = \{a_0 = 1, a_l \geq 3\}$, where a_l is the variable encoding the length of string a (managed by the string domain) and a_0 is the variable representing the values of a[0], the first character of the a string (managed by the cell domain). The cell abstraction will translate s into a_0 = 0. The string abstraction will translate s into a_l = 0 (indeed the length of string a will be 0). The execution of the abstract statements on $S^\sharp$ yields the two following abstract states: $S_1^\sharp = \{a_0 = 0, a_l \geq 3\}$ and $S_2^\sharp = \{a_0 = 1, a_l = 0\}$. Neither state is a sound post-condition for statement s. Indeed, the effect of the statement should update both variables, but here each domain instead only updates its own variable. $S_1^\sharp$ and $S_2^\sharp$ must therefore be *merged* into a sound post-condition. In our example, the abstract elements can be merged by forgetting the constraints on the variables modified by the other domain, and then intersecting the two resulting abstract states, yielding $S_r^\sharp = \{a_0 = 0, a_l = 0\}$, which is a sound post-condition containing both the transformations induced by the cell and string domains. In order to know which variables were modified by the other component of the product, we automatically log the list of statements that were applied on each abstract element, and use these two logs to merge together the parts of the abstraction that we want shared.

To sum up, the computation of post-conditions is done independently on each abstract domain as if no sharing was present, then the tree of domains is merged back into a DAG. The process is mostly automated, and does not require any action from the domains in the reduced product. It is sufficient that all shareable domains, such as numeric domains, define a suitable merging function.

5   Implementation and Applications

MOPSA is written in OCaml. Parsers and utilities account for 19,000 lines of code (we used the `cloc` command to measure the length of our files). The framework, describing the structure of abstract domains and the domain combinators, consists in 8,000 LOC. The analysis of Universal takes 3,000 LOC, while the one of C and its stubs takes 7,100 LOC, and the analysis of Python is 7,700 LOC long.

5.1   C Analysis

MOPSA performs a reachability analysis of C programs to infer invariants and report run-time errors, such as arithmetic overflows, invalid pointer uses, or failed assertions. MOPSA first parses the source files using a front-end based on Clang, and converts the AST to OCaml, keeping all C high-level syntax and type information. The files are then linked, *i.e.* merged into a single AST by resolving symbol definitions. The analyzer is then called on the `main` entry-point using the configuration of abstract domains currently described in Fig. 3. This configuration is naturally intended to evolve as new abstractions are introduced.

Iterators. The configuration starts with a long sequence of iterators, `C.program` to `C.variadic`, *i.e.* state-less domains that handle individual parts of the C compound syntax by induction, including loops, `switch`, `goto`, etc. As explained in Sect. 2, the configuration merges domains reused from the Universal toy-language and C-specific domains. C domains often delegate to Universal ones, *e.g.*, in the case of loops (respectively `C.loops` and `U.loops`). As another example, MOPSA currently handles function calls by semantic inlining (*i.e.* calling recursively the iterator on the function body at each call), which is implemented in a Universal domain `U.fun` (although we are experimenting with summary-based modular function analyses [11]). A C-specific domain, `C.fun`, translates C function calls into Universal ones, taking care of C-specific aspects such as calls through function pointers. Additional domains handle special calls, such as variadic arguments (`C.variadic`), calls to builtin analyzer functions (such as `printf` or file operations) or user-defined stubs (Sect. 5.2).

Domains. Following these iterators, the C analysis contains a composition of domains that handle atomic statements such as assignments and tests. Dynamic memory is handled by U.heap using recency abstraction [1]: each allocation site is associated with at most two abstract blocks, one representing the lastly allocated block at this site (on which we can perform strong updates, which is critical for precision), and one representing all the allocated blocks before (on which we must perform weak updates)—this domain could be easily replaced with any domain that partitions the possibly unbounded set of allocated blocks into a bounded set of abstract blocks. Each variable or abstract heap block is then decomposed into a set of virtual variables, called *cells*, of scalar type, by C.cells. In order to handle transparently union types and type-punning, we use the cell abstraction from [15], where the decomposition is adapted dynamically according to the actual access pattern during the execution (rather than based on the static type, which can be deceiving). As explained in Sect. 4, the cell domain is composed using a reduced product with a string abstraction, C.strings, tracking the position of 0 in character arrays. Both domains are able to rewrite expressions into dereference-free expressions on scalar variables. These are handled by a Cartesian product: C.machineNum translates machine integer arithmetic into mathematical arithmetic, handing overflow-checking and wrap-around semantics; while C.pointers translates pointer arithmetic into byte-offset arithmetic while maintaining in its internal abstract state the bases (*i.e.* pointed-to variables) of each pointer. Both these domains collaborate to rewrite scalar expressions into expressions on mathematical integers, which are then handled natively by classic numeric abstract domains, such as integer intervals (U.intervals). MOPSA also features a rational polyhedra domain (U.linearRel), which is a work in progress and was not enabled in our benchmarks. Floating-point arithmetic is also supported, using intervals, but not shown here for simplicity.

Benchmarks. To assess the effectiveness of MOPSA, we have analyzed real-world C programs from the GNU Coreutils package, which is a collection of command-line utilities. MOPSA was easily integrated into the make-based build system, without modifying any source file or build script. We have also tested MOPSA on a part of the Juliet test suite developed by NIST. These programs differ from Coreutils as they are composed of a large number of small functions for testing analyzers on common software weaknesses.

The results are summarized in Table 1. As the analyzer is still a work in progress, not all programs from the benchmarks were analyzed. For Coreutils programs, each analysis terminated under 10 s, while the number of reported alarms was generally high. This imprecision is mainly due to the absence of an adequate abstraction of pointer arrays, which is currently under development. For Juliet, we focused on three kinds of weaknesses relevant to MOPSA: NULL-pointers, integer overflows, and divisions by zero. The results for Juliet tests were more precise, as they do not employ complex data structures. Nevertheless, the analysis of the CWE369 tests for assessing the detection of divisions by zero shows a high imprecision rate due to the absence of a partitioning abstraction.

Table 1. Benchmark results for the analysis of some programs from GNU Coreutils v8.30 and NIST Juliet v1.3

Benchmark	Name	LOC	Time	Alarms
GNU Coreutils v8.30	true	759	6.92 s	20
	printenv	814	6.66 s	20
	getlimits	970	8.83 s	119
	test	1,238	7.06 s	0
	runcon	1,295	7.16 s	11
	comm	2,634	7.63 s	46
	hostid	2,730	7.61 s	31
	id	2,733	7.12 s	31
	logname	2,735	7.58 s	32
	whoami	2,742	4.69 s	36
	link	2,747	7.76 s	42
	nice	2,955	6.92 s	24
	sleep	3,151	7.87 s	35
NIST Juliet v1.3	CWE476	25k	5 min 51 s	0
	CWE369	109k	17 min 00 s	324
	CWE190	440k	1 h 22 min 56 s	0

5.2   C Stub Modeling

To soundly analyze a C program, MOPSA needs to know the semantic effect of every function that can be called, directly or indirectly, from the `main` entry-point, including all library functions. Linking the full source of all libraries is not always possible (low-level functions may be written in assembly or use compiler intrinsics) nor convenient (as they may be large). Solutions include hard-coding in the analyzer the effect of these functions, or writing a *stub*, *i.e.* a C function modeling its effect as done in Astrée [13] and Frama-C [9]. Instead, MOPSA introduces a dedicated modeling language to ease the quick specification of stubs, and ensure a fast and precise analysis. This language is inspired by ACSL: Frama-C's contract language [9] using pre/post-condition directives put in special comments at function declarations. For instance, the specification of `strlen` is:

```
/*$
 * requires: valid_string(s);
 * ensures: return in [0, size(s)-1];
 * ensures: s[return] == 0;
 * ensures: forall unsigned int k in [0, return-1]: s[k] != 0;
 */
size_t strlen (const char *s);
```

where the predicate `valid_string` is defined as:

```
/*$$
 * predicate valid_string(s):
 *    valid_ptr(s) and
 *    exists int i in [0, size(s)-1]: s[i] == 0;
 */
```

Whenever encountering a call to such a specification, MOPSA checks that the pre-condition (here, that s points to a valid string) is satisfied, and reports a run-time error if this is not true.

In MOPSA, the modeling language does not benefit from a special treatment: it is simply another language that extends the global AST with its own syntax, including logic connectors, such as forall or and, built-in functions, such as valid_ptr and size, while reusing the syntax of side-effect free C expressions. Whenever a function with a model available is called, this model AST is interpreted. This is handled by the iterators C.stubs and U.stubs from Fig. 3, which interpret contracts by relying on a translation into assertions (to verify pre-conditions) and assignments (to enforce post-conditions) of C expressions, using the same mechanism as described in Sect. 2. Additionally, the string domain has been enriched to interpret the simple logical expressions found in the model of strlen and valid_string: $\forall k \in [0, r] : s[k] \neq 0$ and $\exists k \in [0, r] : s[k] = 0$. The domain is actually able to analyze either the model of strlen or an actual implementation of strlen with the same degree of precision.

While similar to logical languages used in deductive methods, such as the WP plugin of Frama-C [9], our modeling language is used in quite a different way. Firstly, it is not used to check the implementation of a function with respect to a functional specification, but rather to replace a function having no implementation with this specification. Secondly, while deductive methods rely on powerful, but costly automated theorem provers to check expressive classes of quantified logic formulas, we rely instead on fast abstract domains that are generally only able to process a very restricted subset of logic formulas, with very specific shapes, but do so in a way consistent with the abstract information they encode—for instance, the string domain only matches simple formulas stating the presence or absence of a 0 in a partition of an array. An interesting point is that C and stub modeling employ quite different kinds of languages, respectively an imperative and a logical language. MOPSA thus achieves a form of multi-lingual analysis, analyzing mixed programs by combining abstractions dedicated to each language while sharing common abstractions.

5.3 Python Analysis

Python's configuration (shown in Fig. 4) is currently simpler than its C counterpart, as it focuses on finding type errors rather than low-level numeric properties. Nevertheless, as Python is a very dynamic language, finding statically such type errors is both difficult and useful for programmers. We also plan to add a value analysis in MOPSA [10]. Python's configuration is composed of several parts:

- `Py.program`, which takes care of program parsing.
- A desugarization, focusing on translating Python-specific control-statements into the Universal language.
- `Py.exceptions`, handling the analysis of specific control-flow statements such as exceptions.
- Universal iterators, handling the intraprocedural (`U.intraproc`, `U.loops`) and interprocedural (`U.fun`) analysis of statements in the Universal language.
- A domain implementing the abstract effect for some parts of Python's vast standard library (this modeling is currently hard-coded in OCaml and does not use a modeling language as for C).
- A domain handling Python objects such as classes and functions.
- A description of Python's data model, encoding the semantics of built-in Python operators, such as attribute accesses, arithmetic operations and subscript operators.
- The stateful part of the analysis, composed of the recency abstraction `U.heap` [1] from Universal; an abstract domain of Python types; and, finally, a smashing-based abstraction of data containers, such as lists and dictionaries, while tuples are abstracted by expansion. Note that the data container abstraction is defined independently from the type analysis, and could be reused in a value analysis instead.

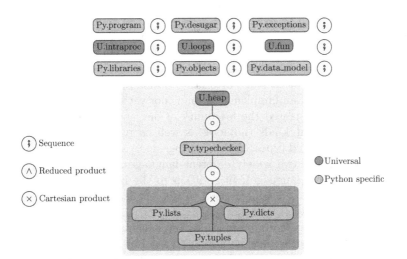

Fig. 4. Domain composition in MOPSA's Python analyzer

We show the results of our analysis in Table 2, on benchmarks used by the standard Python interpreter.[1] We focused on 7 benchmarks, which were chosen for their low number of external dependencies. We found one `TypeError` in `bm_chaos.py`,[2] which was never reached in the actual test, but could be

---

[1] https://github.com/python/pyperformance/.
[2] https://github.com/python/pyperformance/issues/57.

Table 2. Analysis of official Python benchmarks

Name	LOC	Analysis time	# alarms	# false alarms
bm_fannkuch.py	59	0.07 s	0	0
bm_float.py	63	0.06 s	0	0
bm_spectral_norm.py	74	0.33 s	0	1
bm_nbody.py	157	1.5 s	0	1
bm_chaos.py	324	5.6 s	1	0
bm_unpack_sequence.py	458	3.1 s	0	0
bm_hexiom.py	674	2 m 58 s	0	52

triggered by instantiating a class using non-default arguments. The last benchmark `bm_hexiom.py` has a number of false alarms due to our analysis being unable to distinguish empty lists from non-empty ones.

6   Conclusion

We presented the design of our platform for static analysis by abstract interpretation, based on the idea of a collaboration of loosely coupled, highly reusable abstractions. Compared to existing analysis platforms, it makes a few original choices: using a unified extensible abstract syntax tree to both represent faithfully high-level source languages as well as intermediate languages, unifying iterators and abstract domains, domain collaboration through dynamic expression rewriting, as well as reduced and Cartesian products, possibly sharing abstract state. Currently, our OCaml implementation is not yet able to analyze large programs. Yet, we demonstrated the feasibility of our approach by implementing abstractions of different kinds (numeric as well as pointer, dynamically allocated memory, structured types, objects, strings, etc.) and applying them to the reachability analysis of two widely different languages: Python and C (including a library modeling language). In addition to the implementation of classic abstractions, MOPSA has also been used to implement and test novel abstract domains such as [10–12].

Future work will include improving our implementation to reliably analyze realistic C and Python programs, notably with a better support for libraries. We will also consider incorporating novel abstractions into our framework to improve precision and efficiency, or to prove properties beyond the absence of run-time errors. The framework could also be extended to support backward analysis and incremental analysis. Finally, we will consider supporting new target languages. An interesting aspect is that syntax and abstractions targeting different languages can be included in an analyzer configuration, which opens the possibility of analyzing a program written in several languages. We had some success combining C programs with libraries modeled in a logic-based contract language. It would be an interesting challenge to consider the analysis of programs mixing C and Python.

References

1. Balakrishnan, G., Reps, T.: Recency-abstraction for heap-allocated storage. In: Yi, K. (ed.) SAS 2006. LNCS, vol. 4134, pp. 221–239. Springer, Heidelberg (2006). https://doi.org/10.1007/11823230_15

2. Bertrane, J., et al.: Static analysis and verification of aerospace software by abstract interpretation. In: AIAA Infotech@ Aerospace AIAA, No. 2010–3385, pp. 1–38, April 2010

3. Calcagno, C., Distefano, D., Dubreil, J., Gabi, D., Hooimeijer, P., Luca, M., O'Hearn, P., Papakonstantinou, I., Purbrick, J., Rodriguez, D.: Moving fast with software verification. In: Havelund, K., Holzmann, G., Joshi, R. (eds.) NFM 2015. LNCS, vol. 9058, pp. 3–11. Springer, Cham (2015). https://doi.org/10.1007/978-3-319-17524-9_1

4. Cousot, P., Cousot, R.: Abstract interpretation: A unified lattice model for static analysis of programs by construction or approximation of fixpoints. In: Proceedings of the POPL 1977, pp. 238–252. ACM, January 1977

5. Cousot, P., Cousot, R.: Systematic design of program analysis frameworks. In: Proceedings of the POPL 1979. pp. 269–282. ACM Press (1979)

6. Cousot, P., Cousot, R., Feret, J., Mauborgne, L., Miné, A., Monniaux, D., Rival, X.: Combination of abstractions in the ASTRÉE static analyzer. In: Okada, M., Satoh, I. (eds.) ASIAN 2006. LNCS, vol. 4435, pp. 272–300. Springer, Heidelberg (2007). https://doi.org/10.1007/978-3-540-77505-8_23

7. Cousot, P., Cousot, R., Mauborgne, L.: The Reduced product of abstract domains and the combination of decision procedures. In: Hofmann, M. (ed.) FoSSaCS 2011. LNCS, vol. 6604, pp. 456–472. Springer, Heidelberg (2011). https://doi.org/10.1007/978-3-642-19805-2_31

8. Cousot, P., Halbwachs, N.: Automatic discovery of linear restraints among variables of a program. In: Conference Record of the 5th Annual ACM SIGPLAN/SIGACT Symposium on Principles of Programming Languages POPL 1978, pp. 84–97. ACM (1978)

9. Cuoq, P., Kirchner, F., Kosmatov, N., Prevosto, V., Signoles, J., Yakobowski, B.: Frama-C: a software analysis perspective. Formal Aspects Comput. **27**, 573–609 (2012)

10. Fromherz, A., Ouadjaout, A., Miné, A.: Static value analysis of python programs by abstract interpretation. In: Dutle, A., Muñoz, C., Narkawicz, A. (eds.) NFM 2018. LNCS, vol. 10811, pp. 185–202. Springer, Cham (2018). https://doi.org/10.1007/978-3-319-77935-5_14

11. Journault, M., Miné, A., Ouadjaout, A.: Modular static analysis of string manipulations in C programs. In: Podelski, A. (ed.) SAS 2018. LNCS, vol. 11002, pp. 243–262. Springer, Cham (2018). https://doi.org/10.1007/978-3-319-99725-4_16

12. Journault, M., Miné, A., Ouadjaout, A.: An abstract domain for trees with numeric relations. In: Caires, L. (ed.) ESOP 2019. LNCS, vol. 11423, pp. 724–751. Springer, Cham (2019). https://doi.org/10.1007/978-3-030-17184-1_26

13. Kästner, D., et al.: Astrée: proving the absence of runtime errors. In: Proceedings of the ERTS2 2010, May 2010

14. Lattner, C., Adve, V.: LLVM: a compilation framework for lifelong program analysis & transformation. In: Proceedings of the CGO 2004, March 2004

15. Miné, A.: Field-sensitive value analysis of embedded C programs with union types and pointer arithmetics. In: Proceedings of the LCTES 2006, pp. 54–63. ACM, June 2006

16. Miné, A.: Tutorial on static inference of numeric invariants by abstract interpretation. Found. Trends Programm. Lang. (FnTPL) **4**(3–4), 120–372 (2017)
17. Miné, A., Ouadjaout, A., Journault, M.: Design of a modular platform for static analysis. In: Proceedings of the 9th Workshop on Tools for Automatic Program Analysis (TAPAS 2018), p. 4, 28 August 2018
18. Namjoshi, K.S., Pavlinovic, Z.: The impact of program transformations on static program analysis. In: Podelski, A. (ed.) SAS 2018. LNCS, vol. 11002, pp. 306–325. Springer, Cham (2018). https://doi.org/10.1007/978-3-319-99725-4_19
19. Oh, H., Heo, K., Lee, W., Lee, W., Yi, K.: Design and implementation of sparse global analyses for C-like languages. SIGPLAN Not. **47**(6), 229–238 (2012)
20. Spoto, F.: Julia: a generic static analyser for the Java bytecode. In: Proceedings of FTfJP 2005. p. 17, July 2005

Uncertainty, Modeling and Safety Assurance: Towards a Unified Framework

Marsha Chechik$^{(\boxtimes)}$, Sahar Kokaly, Mona Rahimi, Rick Salay, and Torin Viger

University of Toronto, Toronto, Canada
{chechik,skokaly,mrahimi,rsalay,torinviger}@cs.toronto.edu

Abstract. Uncertainty occurs naturally in software systems, including those that are model-based. When such systems are safety-critical, they need to be assured, e.g., by arguing that the system satisfies its safety goals. But how can we rigorously reason about assurance in the presence of uncertainty? In this paper, we propose a vision for a framework for managing uncertainty in assurance cases for software systems, and in particular, for *model-based* software systems, by systematically *identifying*, *assessing* and *addressing* it. We also discuss a set of challenges that need to be addressed to realize this framework.

1 Motivation and Overview

Uncertainty occurs naturally in software systems. For example, functionality of complex software systems that interact with the open world (e.g., self-driving vehicles) cannot be fully specified due to the uncertain environments they operate in. In model-based software systems, this uncertainty can also come from the models themselves (e.g., representation uncertainty, modeler uncertainty). At the same time, since there is a need to ensure that software meets certain critical properties (e.g., safety, security, privacy) in various domains (e.g., automotive, medical, avionics), the area of software compliance is gaining importance. Compliance claims and arguments are often captured in assurance cases [1], with linked evidence of compliance. Evidence can come from a variety of results, some of which are based on model-based activities, e.g., test cases, verification results, analyses or a combination of these. The uncertainty is then naturally propagated from the system to the assurance case arguing about its safety. Assurance cases can therefore contain uncertainty stemming from the system models (e.g., by adding confidence levels on top of model elements [2]), the evidence used to support the claims, which can be the result of model-based activities) (e.g., model-based testing [3] or validation results), or from the argument used to construct the assurance case (e.g., the decomposition strategies from top level to lower level claims).

In this paper, we propose a framework which separates the process of managing uncertainty into three phases: *identifying*, *assessing* and *addressing* it, as shown in Fig. 1. The goal of the framework is to work towards the following major challenge: construct assurance cases which can be reasoned about in a rigorous way, modulo the uncertainty inherent in them.

S. Chakraborty and J. A. Navas (Eds.): VSTTE 2019, LNCS 12031, pp. 19–29, 2020.
https://doi.org/10.1007/978-3-030-41600-3_2

The *identify* phase deals with explicating the uncertainties and assigning them to their appropriate types from a known taxonomy. This step is essential: anything missed in this step will not be considered in the following two. The *assess* phase assesses the degree of uncertainty (e.g., via confidence levels) and its safety relevance. Some uncertainties could be assigned a high value but could not be relevant to the safety assurance argument. This can be thought of as the risk associated with each uncertainty. Finally, in the *address* phase, the uncertainty is either tolerated or reduced, using such techniques as design changes (adding redundancy, replacing a low-resolution sensor with a higher one).

Fig. 1. A framework for uncertainty management.

Organization. The rest of this paper is structured as follows: Sect. 2 presents an example from the automotive domain; the Lane Management System (LMS), which we use to demonstrate ideas in the rest of the paper. Sects. 3, 4 and 5 discuss how uncertainty can be *identified, assessed* and *addressed*, respectively, in a model-based context. Each step of the framework includes a description of existing related work, an illustration using the LMS model, and an explicit linking to LMS assurance cases. Sect. 6 presents a set of challenges for the modeling community which need to be tackled to realize this framework and concludes the paper.

2   The Lane Management System Example

Consider the Lane Management System (LMS). It is aimed to be placed in automobiles as a safety feature to keep a vehicle in or near the centre of the lane to avoid crashes caused by distracted drivers accidentally leaving their lanes. Its Software Requirements Specification (SRS) document [4] indicates that LMS consists of several subcomponents. A *Lane Departure Warning System* (LDWS) issues warnings to the driver when he/she change the lane unintentionally. A *Lane Centering System* (LCS) works together with a *Lane Keeping System* (LKS) to take control of the vehicle and adjust to a driver-defined centre of the lane. The system uses outputs from several already-developed subsystems including the Vehicle State Estimation System, the Path Prediction Subsystem, the Driver Interface Subsystem and the Supervisory Control System. The LMS is able to take control of the vehicle's braking and steering systems; however, it is unable to accelerate. Finally, the LMS only works at speeds above five miles per hour.

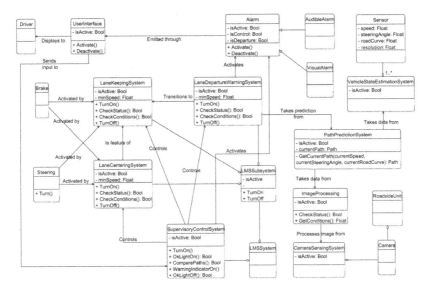

Fig. 2. LMS system class diagram.

LMS is considered to be an Advanced Driver Assistance System (ADAS) which is safety critical and thus subject to the ISO-26262 functional safety standard [5].

A class diagram in Fig. 2 depicts the various LMS subcomponents and relationships between them. Figure 3 shows a corresponding safety case in the Goal Structuring Notation (GSN) [1] for the system. The top high-level safety claim "The LMS system is safe" is decomposed by a strategy **Str1** "Decomposition over all safety goals" into two sub-claims: **G2** and **G3**. There is an assumption **A1** "Assume non-rainy driving conditions" on the environment the system is to operate in, which applies to all the claims below it. We demonstrate how **G2** is further decomposed using a strategy **Str2** "Decomposition over procedure (check failure and then notify)" into the sub-claims **G4** and **G5**. There is a context node linked to **G2**, namely, **C1**, which gives contextual information relevant to this claim. In this case, it is the system hazard that this safety goal was derived from. Finally, **G4** is decomposed into sub-claims **G8-G10** which are considered *leaf* claims that can be supported by solution nodes that point to pieces of evidence (e.g., **S2** points to "expert opinion", **S3** – to "system design models" and **S4-S5** – to test results for each of the audible and visual alarm systems).

3 Identifying Uncertainty

In this section, we discuss various sources of uncertainty which may exist in software systems, focusing on model-based systems. At a high-level of abstraction, sources of uncertainty come from (1) requirements (e.g., missing, changing,

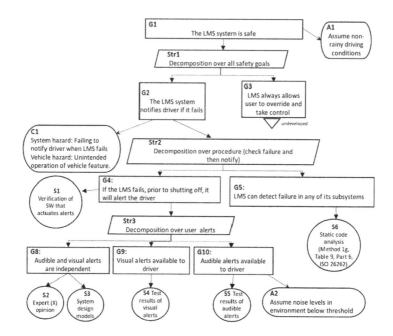

Fig. 3. LMS safety case.

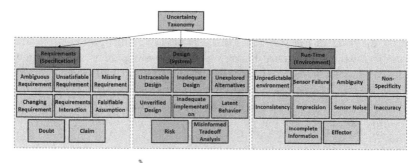

Fig. 4. Conventional uncertainties – a taxonomy (based on [6]).

ambiguous requirements), (2) designs (e.g., inadequate/unverified design and/or implementation), and (3) run-time environments (e.g., sensor failures and/or noise [6]). Figure 4 represents types of uncertainty in Dynamically Adaptive Systems (DAS) [6], but this taxonomy is directly applicable to the broader scope of model-driven systems.

One model-related source of uncertainty missing from the DAS taxonomy is *representational uncertainty*, which refers to whether the model accurately and completely represents what it is supposed to represent. *Measurement uncertainty* is one type of representational uncertainty in models, where the model contains values that measure aspects of the world or subject domain of the model. A large amount of work focuses on managing this type of uncertainty, e.g., [2].

For example, class *Sensor* in Fig. 2 contains an attribute *speed* which can have measurement uncertainty, as can attribute *currentPath* in class in *PathPredictionSystem*. Consider the attribute *isActive* in the *LaneKeepingSystem* class. Presumably, there is a way for the user to turn this system on and off and the *isActive* attribute must be linked to this "switch", but there may be uncertainty in this linkage.

Consider the LMS class diagram, shown in Fig. 2. The LKS component is represented by the *LaneKeepingSystem* class. The SRS document specifies that the system is expected to send commands and steer/adjust the position of the vehicle. This functionality includes taking over control while allowing the driver to override the command if desired [4]. However, this requirement is conditional on there being no other components in the car overriding the LKS-issued command. This is captured by a *requirements interaction* uncertainty in the taxonomy in Fig. 4. Moreover, with this requirements uncertainty, the associations of the class *LaneKeepingSystem* with classes *Brake* and *Steering* in Fig. 2 become uncertain as well. Model uncertainties propagate directly to assurance cases and thus need to be managed. This requirements uncertainty should be propagated to and handled by the current undeveloped extension of **G3** in Fig. 5. We claim that uncertainty taxonomies can and should be used to help identify uncertainties in assurance cases and develop the appropriate claims, as we illustrate in the decomposition of claim **G10** in Fig. 5. Here, requirements-related and design-related uncertainties are coloured in orange and blue, respectively.

4   Assessing Uncertainty

Existing work in the modeling community provides techniques for assessing uncertainty in models. For example, the authors of [2] propose to assess model uncertainty through assigning a confidence value to model elements – both to objects and to relationships. To identify and assess uncertainty in Cyber-Physical Systems, the authors of [7] propose a conceptual model, *U-Model*, where uncertainty is modeled as a *state* of some physical entity, called a *BeliefAgent*, such as a modeler having one or more *beliefs* about a phenomenon/notion. The work in [8] and [9] proposes extensions of the UML/OCL primitive data types to incorporate uncertainty into software models.

To provide an example of existing uncertainties in model elements, consider the class *LaneDepartureWarningSystem (LDWS)* in Fig. 2. LDWS is responsible to warn the driver via sound, warning light and seat vibrations when the vehicle leaves the lane [4]. LDWS generates alarms according to the information provided by the component *PathPredictionSystem* (which, in turn, is based on the input received from the class *Sensor*). Thus the existence of a potential object of class *Alarm*, at each point of time, depends on the measurement uncertainties which may exist in the class *Sensor*. To assess a degree of uncertainty in these model elements using a technique in [2], we can compute a value, C_{alarm}, representing our confidence in the presence of an object of class *Alarm*.

Fig. 5. Uncertainties identified and assessed in the fragment of the LMS assurance case.

The measured model-level confidence value C_{alarm} is directly reflected in the assurance case level when we argue about the goal **G11** in Fig. 5. This *Alarm*-related claim, **G11**, is associated with multiple sources of uncertainties combined and represented as C_{alarm}. In addition to representational uncertainties in Sensor-related evidence **S10**, which was discussed earlier and impacts **G21**, there are modeler uncertainties, associated with **G20**, and requirement-related uncertainties, associated with **G18** and **G19**, shown in Fig. 5. Such uncertainties can be individually identified and similarly assessed with a confidence measure. Once individual uncertainties have been quantified using confidence measures, techniques such as the one suggested in [10] can be used to aggregate and compose individual uncertainty measures in a way that reflects the overall uncertainty in the assurance case.

5   Addressing Uncertainty

By addressing uncertainty coming from various sources (design, argument, evidence), we are looking for ways to accept (i.e., "live with" or tolerate) or mitigate (i.e., reduce) the uncertainty, allowing us to manage it in the assurance case. Hawkins et al. [10] propose different approaches for addressing uncertainty by mitigating the so-called "assurance deficits" in the following ways:

1. Changing the design, e.g., adding a hardware backup when it is impractical to demonstrate with adequate confidence that software has the properties

necessary to ensure system safety. In the LMS example, this could be replacing the sensor feeding information to *VehicleStateEstimationSystem* with the one with a higher resolution, thereby addressing the identified imprecision uncertainty.

2. Changing the system operation. e.g., limiting the conditions under which the system is used, i.e., only when the roads are not covered in snow and thus lane markings are visible.
3. Changing the safety argument, e.g., adding an independent source of evidence.
4. Generating additional evidence to improve confidence, e.g., increasing the coverage of software functional tests.

In addition to these four ways of addressing uncertainty, in this section, we describe two additional ones: argument weakening and evidence composition.

Argument Weakening. Assurance cases are comprised of reasoning steps, each of which decomposes a high-level claim into a set of more refined sub-claims over subsets of the corresponding domain (e.g., **Str1**, **Str2** and **Str3** in Fig. 3). Many of these decompositions are not fully formalizable in practice, which can make it unclear whether the argument steps are sound and give rise to fallacious reasoning.

For example, in the LMS safety case in Fig. 3, have we considered all of the alert combinations for **Str3**? And why do we believe that the safety goals chosen in **Str1** are sufficient to show that the system is safe? Reasoning steps can be made rigorous by explicitly identifying the domain of each claim decomposition and justifying *why* it is sufficient to decompose over this domain, in addition to showing that the set of decomposed claims is *complete* (i.e., that they fully cover the identified domain). It is clear that **Str3** can be made rigorous, as we can identify the set of user alerts and argue that each has been handled. However, the set of safety goals used in **Str1** is typically determined via hazard analysis, and the relationship between these safety goals and total system safety is unclear. A justification (e.g., through the use of GSN justification nodes) must therefore be added expressing why these goals cover all necessary requirements for the system to be safe.

Not only is rigour essential in showing the logical soundness of an assurance argument, the process of creating rigorous arguments enables the identification and explication of uncertainties which exist in the argument implicitly. These uncertainties can be related to the completeness of a decomposition (if it is unclear that the domain of the decomposition has been fully covered by its sub-claims) or to its justification (when no rule of inference can show that the decomposed sub-claims logically imply the parent claim). If the entire domain cannot be covered, explicitly adding the argument that a weakened claim will be used and an assumption or justification why this weakening is acceptable, are then required. For example, for the alert types in LMS, we may want to be explicit that only individual alerts will be reasoned about in **G4** (refer to Fig. 3), under the assumption that our architecture does not allow multiple simultaneous alerts. The above process of uncertainty explication and argument weakening, which we call *rigour modulo uncertainty*, is ultimately aimed at valid assurance for an explicitly weakened claim rather than a fallacious assurance for the original claim.

Evidence Composition. Hawkins et al. [10] suggested techniques for mitigating uncertainty coming from the evidence by either adding a new independent source of evidence or directly improving the confidence of some given evidence by performing a more expensive analysis. We propose to improve the quality of the given evidence by composing it in order to provide evidence with higher confidence (lower uncertainty) levels. There are two ways to do this:

- *Complementary evidence:* Consider the evidence resulting from a verification activity. We say that a verification technique *complements* another if it is able to verify types requirements that the other technique cannot. For example, this was done in the case of the Mars Code presented in [11] by running multiple static analyses to get rid of false positives.
- *Supporting evidence:* We say that a verification technique *supports* another if it is used to detect faults in the other's results, thus providing backing evidence. (e.g., a model checking technique can support a static analysis technique by verifying the faults detected by it), as suggested by Carlan et al. [12]. Since evidence can be the result of model-based activities (e.g., model-based testing and analyses), we propose to use the techniques described above for model-based evidence.

6   Challenges

The modeling community has studied how to address uncertainty in models and model transformations – see a discussion in Sect. 4. In addition, the authors of [13] give a taxonomy which names and organizes model transformation languages/techniques. This taxonomy is intended to assist developers in choosing the most appropriate method of performing any particular model transformation task. Though uncertainty is not explicitly mentioned in this paper, it gives a method of mitigating model uncertainty by allowing developers to make more informed choices about which model transformation language/technique to use for their given purposes.

In [14,15], we developed a formal approach called MAVO for expressing and reasoning with model uncertainty and applied it to design models. In [16], the same approach was applied in the context of managing requirements uncertainties. The work in [17] shows an application of uncertainty modeling for the purpose of reasoning about bidirectional model transformations which are non-bijective. The authors use models with uncertainty to represent the solution space of underspecified non-bijective model transformations, and claim that doing so reduces uncertainty as "the unknown uncertainty at design-time is translated into known uncertainty at run-time".

Finally, the approach in [18] aims at providing a means to manage uncertainty in automatically generated implementation models, specifically, in the automotive domain. This provides the engineer with an expressive representation of model commonalities and differences in order to easily investigate the solution space for making a final decision.

However, there are additional challenges related to uncertainty for assurance of model-based systems. We enumerate some of them below:

1. **Taxonomies of uncertainties.** In the *identify* phase of the framework, we proposed to use complete taxonomies of uncertainty types. Existing taxonomies need to be augmented and new ones developed to consider such issues as model uncertainties as well as uncertainties relevant to individual model types. In this context, one can consider both behavioural and structural uncertainties depending on the model type.
2. **Individual analyses for evidence generation and composition.** As mentioned in the *address* phase, evidence can be generated by model-based techniques, and ways to address uncertainty in the results for each type of evidence are needed. On the other hand, evidence can be composed in order to address uncertainty as discussed in Sect. 5. Here we separate the problems of evidence composition and uncertainty composition in evidence.
3. **Tool support.** A recent study of assurance case tools [19,20] identified work that provided tool support for modeling confidence in assurance cases (e.g., ch1luo2017systematic and the Adelard Safety Case Editor (ASCE) [22]). However, the study did not identify tools for assessing uncertainty in assurance cases.
4. **Addressing systems with machine learned components.** As we move to a world that relies on machine learning, new types of uncertainties are introduced and need to be addressed [23], especially when these systems are safety-critical, such as in self-driving cars.
5. **Model management for uncertainty and assurance.** Some work has considered model management with uncertainty [24], and other work has studied model management for assurance [25,26]. However, there is still a need for work on model management for uncertainty and assurance. For example, we would need model transformation definitions to support model uncertainty [2,27], but in a way that takes assurance into account. Furthermore, we need to understand how to lift model management techniques (e.g., model composition) to systems with uncertainty (e.g., to yield model composition with uncertainty).
6. **Uncertainty at the metamodeling level.** We should separate types of uncertainty that are model-specific and those that can be defined and reasoned about at the metamodel level.

As our world increasingly relies on automation, handling uncertainty is inevitable. We see assurance cases as a unifier for many modeling activities, and addressing uncertainty in assurance cases should be a collective challenge for the modeling community to tackle. By addressing the challenges presented in this section, we can work towards the major challenge presented in the intro: performing rigorous assurance of model-based systems "modulo uncertainty". We believe that through our proposed three-step framework, we can better assure the safety of model-based systems with uncertainty.

References

1. GSN, Goal Structuring Notation Working Group, GSN Community Standard Version 1 (2011). http://www.goalstructuringnotation.info/
2. Burgueño, L., Bertoa, M.F., Moreno, N., Vallecillo, A.: Expressing confidence in models and in model transformation elements. In: Proceedings of MODELS 2018, pp. 57–66 (2018)
3. Dalal, S.R., et al.: Model-based testing in practice. In: Proceedings of the ICSE 1999, pp. 285–294 (1999)
4. Blazy, B., DeLine, A., Frey, B., Miller, M.: Software Requirements Specification (SRS) lane management system. Michigan State University (2014)
5. ISO 26262: Road vehicles - functional safety. International Organization for Standardization, 1st version (2011)
6. Ramirez, A.J., Jensen, A.C., Cheng, B.H.: A taxonomy of uncertainty for dynamically adaptive systems. In: Proceedings of the SEAMS 2012, pp. 99–108 (2012)
7. Zhang, M., Selic, B., Ali, S., Yue, T., Okariz, O., Norgren, R.: Understanding uncertainty in cyber-physical systems: a conceptual model. In: Wąsowski, A., Lönn, H. (eds.) ECMFA 2016. LNCS, vol. 9764, pp. 247–264. Springer, Cham (2016). https://doi.org/10.1007/978-3-319-42061-5_16
8. Mayerhofer, T., Wimmer, M., Vallecillo, A.: Adding uncertainty and units to quantity types in software models. In: Proceedings of the SLE 2016, pp. 118–131 (2016)
9. Bertoa, M.F., Moreno, N., Barquero, G., Burgueño, L., Troya, J., Vallecillo, A.: Expressing measurement uncertainty in OCL/UML datatypes. In: Pierantonio, A., Trujillo, S. (eds.) ECMFA 2018. LNCS, vol. 10890, pp. 46–62. Springer, Cham (2018). https://doi.org/10.1007/978-3-319-92997-2_4
10. Hawkins, R., Kelly, T., Knight, J., Graydon, P.: A new approach to creating clear safety arguments. In: Dale, C., Anderson, T. (eds.) Advances in Systems Safety, pp. 3–23. Springer, London (2011). https://doi.org/10.1007/978-0-85729-133-2_1
11. Holzmann, G.J.: Mars code. Commun. ACM **57**(2), 64–73 (2014)
12. Cârlan, C., Ratiu, D., Schätz, B.: On using results of code-level bounded model checking in assurance cases. In: Skavhaug, A., Guiochet, J., Schoitsch, E., Bitsch, F. (eds.) SAFECOMP 2016. LNCS, vol. 9923, pp. 30–42. Springer, Cham (2016). https://doi.org/10.1007/978-3-319-45480-1_3
13. Mens, T., Van Gorp, P.: A taxonomy of model transformation. Electron. Notes Theoret. Comput. Sci. **152**, 125–142 (2006)
14. Salay, R., Famelis, M., Chechik, M.: Language independent refinement using partial modeling. In: de Lara, J., Zisman, A. (eds.) FASE 2012. LNCS, vol. 7212, pp. 224–239. Springer, Heidelberg (2012). https://doi.org/10.1007/978-3-642-28872-2_16
15. Famelis, M., Salay, R., Chechik, M.: Partial models: towards modeling and reasoning with uncertainty. In: Proceedings of the ICSE 2012, pp. 573–583 (2012)
16. Salay, R., Chechik, M., Horkoff, J., Di Sandro, A.: Managing requirements uncertainty with partial models. J. Requirements Eng. **18**(2), 107–128 (2013)
17. Eramo, R., Pierantonio, A., Rosa, G.: Managing uncertainty in bidirectional model transformations. In: Proceedings of the SLE 2015, pp. 49–58 (2015)
18. Bucaioni, A., Cicchetti, A., Ciccozzi, F., Mubeen, S., Pierantonio, A., Sjödin, M.: Handling uncertainty in automatically generated implementation models in the automotive domain. In: Proceedings of the SEAA 2016, pp. 173–180 (2016)

19. Maksimov, M., Fung, N.L.S., Kokaly, S., Chechik, M.: Two decades of assurance case tools: a survey. In: Gallina, B., Skavhaug, A., Schoitsch, E., Bitsch, F. (eds.) SAFECOMP 2018. LNCS, vol. 11094, pp. 49–59. Springer, Cham (2018). https://doi.org/10.1007/978-3-319-99229-7_6
20. Maksimov, M., Kokaly, S., Chechik, M.: A survey of tool-supported assurance case assessment techniques. ACM Comput. Surv. **52**, 1–34 (2019)
21. Luo, Y., van den Brand, M., Li, Z., Saberi, A.K.: A Systematic approach and tool support for GSN-based safety case assessment. J. Syst. Archit. **76**, 1–16 (2017)
22. Bloomfield, R., Bishop, P.: Safety and assurance cases: past, present and possible future-an adelard perspective. In: Dale, C., Anderson, T. (eds.) Making Systems Safer, pp. 51–67. Springer, London (2010). https://doi.org/10.1007/978-1-84996-086-1_4
23. Czarnecki, K., Salay, R.: Towards a framework to manage perceptual uncertainty for safe automated driving. In: Gallina, B., Skavhaug, A., Schoitsch, E., Bitsch, F. (eds.) SAFECOMP 2018. LNCS, vol. 11094, pp. 439–445. Springer, Cham (2018). https://doi.org/10.1007/978-3-319-99229-7_37
24. Famelis, M., Chechik, M.: Managing design-time uncertainty. Softw. Syst. **18**(2), 1249–1284 (2019)
25. Kokaly, S., Salay, R., Sabetzadeh, M., Chechik, M., Maibaum, T.: Model management for regulatory compliance: a position paper. In: Proceedings of the MiSE 2016, pp. 74–80 (2016)
26. Kokaly, S., Salay, R., Cassano, V., Maibaum, T., Chechik, M.: A model management approach for assurance case reuse due to system evolution. In: Proceedings of the MODELS 2016, pp. 196–206 (2016)
27. Famelis, M., Salay, R., Di Sandro, A., Chechik, M.: Transformation of models containing uncertainty. In: Moreira, A., Schätz, B., Gray, J., Vallecillo, A., Clarke, P. (eds.) MODELS 2013. LNCS, vol. 8107, pp. 673–689. Springer, Heidelberg (2013). https://doi.org/10.1007/978-3-642-41533-3_41

Quantifying Information Leakage Using Model Counting Constraint Solvers

Tevfik Bultan$^{(\boxtimes)}$

University of California, Santa Barbara, USA
bultan@cs.ucsb.edu

Abstract. This paper provides a brief overview of recent results in quantitative information flow analysis, model counting constraints solvers, side-channel analysis and attack synthesis. By combining model counting constraints solvers with symbolic execution it is possible to quantify the amount of information that a program leaks about a secret input. As discussed below, this type of analysis is crucial for detection and analysis of side channel vulnerabilities.

Keywords: Quantitative program analysis · Model counting · Quantitative information flow · Side channels

1 Quantitative Program Analysis

Quantitative program analysis is an emerging area with applications to software reliability, quantitative information flow, side-channel detection and attack synthesis [5,7–9,16,17,20–22]. The goal in quantitative program analysis is to provide a quantitative answer to a query about the program's behavior instead of a "yes" or "no" answer. For example, rather than answering if there is information leakage in a program with a "yes" or "no" answer, quantitative analysis techniques can compute the amount of information leaked. This type of analysis is crucial for many domains since "yes" or "no" answers may not sufficient, and may lead to too many false alarms.

For example, every password checker leaks some information about the password (even saying a password does not match a guess leaks information), but a faulty password checker may leak more information than necessary. A quantitative vulnerability detection tool can quantify the amount of information leakage in a program using a model counting constraint solver. As another example,

This material is based on research supported by an Amazon Research Award, by NSF under Grant CCF-1817242, and by DARPA under the agreement number FA8750-15-2-0087. The U.S. Government is authorized to reproduce and distribute reprints for Governmental purposes notwithstanding any copyright notation thereon. The views and conclusions contained herein are those of the authors and should not be interpreted as necessarily representing the official policies or endorsements, either expressed or implied, of DARPA or the U.S. Government.

© Springer Nature Switzerland AG 2020
S. Chakraborty and J. A. Navas (Eds.): VSTTE 2019, LNCS 12031, pp. 30–35, 2020.
https://doi.org/10.1007/978-3-030-41600-3_3

most symbolic execution tools cannot guarantee absence of an assertion failure in general since they search the state space up to a certain execution depth. When combined with a model counting constraint solver, a symbolic execution tool can quantify the likelihood of reaching an unexplored part of the state space, hence providing a probabilistic upper bound on observing an assertion violation.

One recent approach to quantitative program analysis is to extend symbolic execution using model counting constraint solvers [5,7–9,16,17,20–22]. The basic idea is to first generate path conditions using symbolic execution that capture the constraints on program inputs for each execution path. Then, using a model counting constraint solver the number of input values that satisfy the path condition for a given execution path can be computed. Assuming a uniform distribution for inputs, this count can be used to compute the probability of execution for a given path. By building on this basic approach, symbolic execution and model counting constraint solvers have been used in probabilistic analysis [9,17], reliability analysis [16], quantitative information flow [5,7,21,22], and attack synthesis [8,20].

2 Automata-Based Model Counting

Static quantitative program analysis techniques we briefly discussed above rely on model counting constraint solvers. A model counting constraint solver computes the number of solutions for a given constraint within a given bound [3,6,10,13,14,19].

A powerful approach to model counting is the automata-based approach implemented in the model counting constraint solver Automata-Based model Counter (ABC) [3]. ABC counts the number of models (solutions) for a constraint by first constructing an automaton that recognizes (accepts) the solutions to the given constraint. Then, the number of models for a given constraint within a given bound can be computed by counting the number of accepting paths in the corresponding automaton within a length that corresponds to the given bound. A dynamic programming algorithm that computes the kth power of the adjacency matrix that corresponds to the transitions of the automaton can be used to count the number of accepting paths in the automaton of length k or less than or equal to k [3]. This approach has been implemented in ABC for string constraints [3], string and numeric constraints [7] and combinations of string and numeric constraints [4].

Model counting problem is at least as difficult as the satisfiability problem, hence, in the worst case model counting problem is also intractable like satisfiability. However, as recent results demonstrate, like satisfiability checkers such as SAT and SMT solvers, model counting constraint solvers can also be effective in realistic software verification, analysis and security tasks. As with the satisfiability checkers, improving the efficiency of model counting constraint solvers can have a significant impact on automated program analysis. Recent work on model counting constraint solvers shows that formula caching can significantly improve the performance of model counting constraint solvers and improve its scalability [11,15].

3 Side-Channel Analysis

Software systems that access secret data can have measurable non-functional characteristics that can reveal information about the secret data. For example, execution time, memory usage or network communication behavior of a software system can reveal information about the secret data it accesses. This can allow a malicious user to infer information about the secret data by measuring these non-functional characteristics. This type of unintended leakage of information about secret data due to non-functional behavior of a program is called a side-channel vulnerability.

Side channel vulnerabilities in software can have significant consequences. Exploitable timing channel information flows were discovered for Google's Keyczar Library [18], the Xbox 360 [1], implementations of RSA encryption [12], and the open authorization protocol OAuth [2]. These vulnerabilities highlight the need for preemptive discovery and removal of side-channel vulnerabilities in software.

One recent approach to side-channel analysis and detection is quantitative information flow analysis via symbolic execution and model counting constraint solvers. Symbolic execution can be extended to keep track of non-functional characteristics of program behavior such as number of instructions executed or the amount of memory allocated. This type of extended symbolic execution generates path conditions with constraints on both input values and the observable side-channel values. When combined with a model counting constraint solver, these extended path conditions can be used to determine the probability of each observable event (for example probability of observing a particular execution time or memory usage value) and the number of secret values that are consistent with that observable event. Assuming a uniform distribution of input values, probability of each observable event can then be computed. Finally, using information theoretic measures such as Shannon entropy, it is possible to compute and quantify the amount of information leakage about the secret using this approach. Symbolic Path (SPF) is a symbolic execution tool for Java [23] and the approach outlined above has been implemented as an extension to SPF by integrating SPF with the model counting constraint solver ABC [7].

Using this approach, in addition to detecting side channels, we can also quantify the amount of information leaked by side channels. This is important because for many applications (such as password checking as discussed above) some information leakage is unavoidable. So, it is important to quantify how much information is being leaked in order to separate vulnerable programs that leak a lot of information from programs with benign information leakage.

4 Attack Synthesis

The approach outlined above can be extended to attack synthesis, i.e., automatically generating attacks that reveal the secret information. In this framework, an attack is a sequence of public inputs fed to a program that has a side-channel vulnerability in order to gather information about the secret data accessed by the program. The goal is to find the smallest sequence of inputs that an attacker can provide in order to discover the secret. For example, even for a perfectly implemented password checker, there is an attack that reveals the secret. It is the brute-force attack that tries all possible input values. Knowing that such an attack requires many tries, as a remedy, we can set a small bound on the number of different inputs a user can enter to a password checker.

Automated attack synthesis techniques can be used to discover the shortest input sequences that reveal a secret, which in turn can be used to defend against such attacks by either limiting the number of public interactions with the software system or by eliminating the information leakage that is discovered by the analysis.

Attack synthesis techniques generate inputs in an iterative manner which, when fed to code that accesses the secret, reveal information about the secret based on the side-channel observations. There has been recent work on attack synthesis which follow the approach outline above: symbolic execution is used to extract path conditions and automata-based model counting is used to estimate probabilities of execution paths. In order to generate the shortest attacks, optimization techniques are used to maximize information gain based on entropy [20]. Different meta-heuristics such as simulated annealing or genetic algorithms can be used to search for input values that maximize the information gain [25]. In order to obtain more accurate results, it is necessary to combine symbolic execution based static analysis with runtime profiling for modeling the noisy side channels [8]. Finally, due to the high cost of model counting, use of an incremental attack synthesis strategy that reuses model counting results from prior iterations in each attack step can significantly improve the performance of attack synthesis [24].

5   Conclusions and Future Directions

Model counting constraint solvers are the enabling technology for quantitative program analyses. Automata-based approach provides an elegant solution to model counting however it has its limitations. For example, non-linear numeric and string constraints are not easy to handle with the automata-based approach. Developing efficient model counting techniques for such constraints is an important direction for future research. Future improvements in efficiency and expressiveness of model counting constraint solvers can lead to dramatic improvements in quantitative program analyses, similar to the impact SAT and SMT solvers had on program verification and testing.

Combination of symbolic execution with model counting constraint solvers is a powerful approach that can lead to many novel quantitative program analyses. It would be worthwhile to investigate approximate quantitative analysis techniques in order to improve scalability. Finally, detection and prevention of information leakage in software systems is likely to become an increasingly important topic. Combining symbolic and static approaches with dynamic and enumerative approaches for quantitative program analysis could be a promising direction for scalable information leakage detection.

References

1. Xbox 360 timing attack (2007). http://beta.ivc.no/wiki/index.php/Xbox_360_Timing_Attack
2. OAuth protocol HMAC byte value calculation timing disclosure weakness (2013). https://osvdb.info/OSVDB-97562
3. Aydin, A., Bang, L., Bultan, T.: Automata-based model counting for string constraints. In: Kroening, D., Păsăreanu, C.S. (eds.) CAV 2015, Part I. LNCS, vol. 9206, pp. 255–272. Springer, Cham (2015). https://doi.org/10.1007/978-3-319-21690-4_15
4. Aydin, A., et al.: Parameterized model counting for string and numeric constraints. In: Proceedings of the 2018 ACM Joint Meeting on European Software Engineering Conference and Symposium on the Foundations of Software Engineering, ESEC/SIGSOFT FSE 2018, Lake Buena Vista, FL, USA, 04–09 November 2018, pp. 400–410 (2018)
5. Backes, M., Köpf, B., Rybalchenko, A.: Automatic discovery and quantification of information leaks. In: 30th IEEE Symposium on Security and Privacy (S&P 2009), Oakland, California, USA, 17–20 May 2009, pp. 141–153 (2009)
6. Baldoni, V., et al.: LattE Integrale v1.7.2 (2004)
7. Bang, L., Aydin, A., Phan, Q.S., Păsăreanu, C.S., Bultan, T.: String analysis for side channels with segmented oracles. In: Proceedings of the 24th ACM SIGSOFT International Symposium on the Foundations of Software Engineering (2016)
8. Bang, L., Rosner, N., Bultan, T.: Online synthesis of adaptive side-channel attacks based on noisy observations. In: 2018 IEEE European Symposium on Security and Privacy, EuroS&P 2018, London, United Kingdom, 24–26 April 2018, pp. 307–322 (2018)
9. Borges, M., Filieri, A., d'Amorim, M., Păsăreanu, C.S.: Iterative distribution-aware sampling for probabilistic symbolic execution. In: Proceedings of the 2015 10th Joint Meeting on Foundations of Software Engineering, ESEC/FSE 2015, Bergamo, Italy, 30 August–4 September 2015, pp. 866–877 (2015)
10. Borges, M., Phan, Q.-S., Filieri, A., Păsăreanu, C.S.: Model-counting approaches for nonlinear numerical constraints. In: Barrett, C., Davies, M., Kahsai, T. (eds.) NFM 2017. LNCS, vol. 10227, pp. 131–138. Springer, Cham (2017). https://doi.org/10.1007/978-3-319-57288-8_9
11. Brennan, T., Tsiskaridze, N., Rosner, N., Aydin, A., Bultan, T.: Constraint normalization and parameterized caching for quantitative program analysis. In: Proceedings of the 2017 11th Joint Meeting on Foundations of Software Engineering, pp. 535–546. ACM (2017)
12. Brumley, D., Boneh, D.: Remote timing attacks are practical. In: Proceedings of the 12th Conference on USENIX Security Symposium, SSYM 2003, vol. 12, p. 1. USENIX Association, Berkeley (2003)
13. Chakraborty, S., Fremont, D.J., Meel, K.S., Seshia, S.A., Vardi, M.Y.: Distribution-aware sampling and weighted model counting for SAT. In: Proceedings of the Twenty-Eighth AAAI Conference on Artificial Intelligence, pp. 1722–1730 (2014)
14. Chakraborty, S., Meel, K.S., Mistry, R., Vardi, M.Y.: Approximate probabilistic inference via word-level counting. In: Proceedings of the Thirtieth AAAI Conference on Artificial Intelligence, pp. 3218–3224 (2016)

15. Eiers, W., Saha, S., Brennan, T., Bultan, T.: Subformula caching for model counting and quantitative program analysis. In: 34th IEEE/ACM International Conference on Automated Software Engineering, ASE 2019, San Diego, CA, USA, 11–15 November 2019, pp. 453–464. IEEE (2019)
16. Filieri, A., Păsăreanu, C.S., Visser, W.: Reliability analysis in symbolic pathfinder. In: 35th International Conference on Software Engineering, ICSE 2013, San Francisco, CA, USA, 18–26 May 2013, pp. 622–631 (2013)
17. Geldenhuys, J., Dwyer, M.B., Visser, W.: Probabilistic symbolic execution. In: International Symposium on Software Testing and Analysis, ISSTA 2012, Minneapolis, MN, USA, 15–20 July 2012, pp. 166–176 (2012)
18. Lawson, N.: Timing attack in Google Keyczar library (2009). https://rdist.root.org/2009/05/28/timing-attack-in-google-keyczar-library/
19. Luu, L., Shinde, S., Saxena, P., Demsky, B.: A model counter for constraints over unbounded strings. In: Proceedings of the ACM SIGPLAN Conference on Programming Language Design and Implementation (PLDI), p. 57 (2014)
20. Phan, Q.S., Bang, L., Păsăreanu, C.S., Malacaria, P., Bultan, T.: Synthesis of adaptive side-channel attacks. In: 30th IEEE Computer Security Foundations Symposium, CSF 2017, Santa Barbara, CA, USA, 21–25 August 2017, pp. 328–342 (2017)
21. Phan, Q.S., Malacaria, P., Păsăreanu, C.S., d'Amorim, M.: Quantifying information leaks using reliability analysis. In: Proceedings of the International Symposium on Model Checking of Software, SPIN 2014, San Jose, CA, USA, pp. 105–108 (2014)
22. Phan, Q.S., Malacaria, P., Tkachuk, O., Păsăreanu, C.S.: Symbolic quantitative information flow. ACM SIGSOFT Softw. Eng. Notes **37**(6), 1–5 (2012)
23. Păsăreanu, C.S., Visser, W., Bushnell, D., Geldenhuys, J., Mehlitz, P., Rungta, N.: Symbolic PathFinder: integrating symbolic execution with model checking for Java bytecode analysis. Autom. Softw. Eng. **20**, 1–35 (2013)
24. Saha, S., Eiers, W., Kadron, I.B., Bultan, T.: Incremental attack synthesis (2019)
25. Saha, S., Kadron, I.B., Eiers, W., Bang, L., Bultan, T.: Attack synthesis for strings using meta-heuristics (2018)

Verifiable Homomorphic Tallying
for the Schulze Vote Counting Scheme

Thomas Haines[1], Dirk Pattinson[2], and Mukesh Tiwari[2(✉)]

[1] NTNU, Trondheim, Norway
[2] Research School of Computer Science, ANU, Canberra, Australia
mukesh.tiwari@anu.edu.au

Abstract. The encryption of ballots is crucial to maintaining integrity and anonymity in electronic voting schemes. It enables, amongst other things, each voter to verify that their encrypted ballot has been recorded as cast, by checking their ballot against a bulletin board.

We present a verifiable homomorphic tallying scheme for the Schulze method that allows verification of the correctness of the count—on the basis of encrypted ballots—that only reveals the final tally. We achieve verifiability by using zero knowledge proofs for ballot validity and honest decryption of the final tally. Our formalisation takes places inside the Coq theorem prover and is based on an axiomatisation of cryptogtaphic primitives, and our main result is the correctness of homomorphic tallying. We then instantiate these primitives using an external library and show the feasibility of our approach by means of case studies.

1 Introduction

Secure elections are a balancing act between integrity and privacy: achieving either is trivial but their combination is notoriously hard. One of the key challenges faced by both paper based and electronic elections is that results must substantiated with verifiable evidence of their correctness while retaining the secrecy of the individual ballot [5]. Technically, the notion of "verifiable evidence" is captured by the term *end-to-end (E2E) verifiability*, that is

- every voter can verify that their ballot was cast as intended
- every voter can verify that their ballot was collected as cast
- everyone can verify final result on the basis of the collected ballots.

While end-to-end verifiability addresses the basic assumption that no entity (software, hardware and participants) are inherently trustworthy, ballot secrecy addresses the privacy problem. Unfortunately, it appears as if coercion resistance is not achievable in the remote setting without relying on overly optimistic—to say the least—assumptions. A weaker property called receipt-freeness captures the idea that an honest voter—while able to verify that their ballot was counted—is required to keep no information that a possible coercer could use to verify how that voter had voted.

© Springer Nature Switzerland AG 2020
S. Chakraborty and J. A. Navas (Eds.): VSTTE 2019, LNCS 12031, pp. 36–53, 2020.
https://doi.org/10.1007/978-3-030-41600-3_4

End to end verifiability and the related notation of software independence [22] have been claimed properties for many voting schemes. Küsters, Truderung and Vogt [14] gave a cryptographic formulation whose value is highlighted by the attacks it revealed against established voting schemes [15].

The combination of privacy and integrity can be realised using cryptographic techniques, where encrypted ballots (that the voters themselves cannot decrypt) are published on a bulletin board, and the votes are then processed, and the correctness of the final tally is substantiated, using homomorphic encryption [12] and verifiable shuffling [2]. (Separate techniques exist to prevent ballot box stuffing and to guarantee cast-as-intended.) Integrity can then be guaranteed by means of Zero Knowledge Proofs (ZKP), first studied by Goldwasser, Micali, and Rackoff [11]. Informally, a ZKP is a probabilistic and interactive proof where one entity interacts with another such that the interaction provides no information other than that the statement being proved is true with overwhelming probability. Later results [3,10] showed that all problems for which solutions can be efficiently verified have zero knowledge proofs.

This paper addresses the problem of verifiable homomorphic tallying for a preferential voting scheme, the Schulze Method. We show how it can be implemented in a theorem prover to guarantee both provably correct and verifiable counting on the basis of encrypted ballots, relative to an axiomatisation of the cryptographic primitives. We then obtain, via program extraction, a provably correct implementation of vote counting, that we turn into executable code by providing implementations of the primitives based on a standard cryptographic library. We conclude by presenting experimental results, and discuss trust the trust base, security and privacy as well as the applicability of our work to real-world scenarios.

The Schulze Method. The Schulze Method [24] is a preferential, single-winner vote counting scheme that is gaining popularity due to its relative simplicity while retaining near optimal fairness [23]. A *ballot* is a rank-ordered list of candidates where different candidates may be given the same rank. The protocol proceeds in two steps, and first computes the *margin matrix* m, where $m(x, y)$ is the relative margin of x over y, that is, the number of voters that prefer x over y, minus the number of voters that prefer y over x. In symbols, given a collection B of ballots,

$$m(x, y) = \sharp\{b \in B \mid x <_b y\} - \sharp\{b \in B \mid y <_b x\}$$

where $\sharp$ denotes cardinality, and $<_b$ is the preference relation encoded by ballot b. We note that $m(x, y) = -m(y, x)$, i.e. the margin matrix is symmetric. In a second step, a *generalised margin* g is computed as the strongest path between two candidates

$$g(x, y) = \max\{\mathsf{str}(p) \mid p \text{ path from } x \text{ to } y\}$$

where a path from x to y is simply a sequence $x = x_0, \ldots, x_n = y$ of candidates, and the strength

$$\mathsf{str}(x_0, \ldots, x_n) = \min\{m(x_i, x_{i+1}) \mid 0 \leq i < n\}$$

is the lowest margin encountered on a path. Informally, one may think of the generalised margin $g(x, y)$ as transitive accumulated support for x over y. We say that x beats y if $g(x, y) \geq g(y, x)$ and a winner is a candidate that cannot be beaten by anyone. That is, w is a *winner* if $g(w, x) \geq g(x, w)$ for all other candidates x. Note that winners may not be uniquely determined (e.g. in the case where no ballots have been cast).

In previous work [20] we have demonstrated how to achieve verifiability of counting plaintext ballots by producing a verifiable *certificate* of the count, where ballot privacy and receipt freeness are not addressed. The certificate has two parts: The first part witnesses the computation of the margin matrix where each line of the certificate amounts to updating the margin matrix by a single ballot. The second part witnesses the determination of winners based on the margin matrix. In the first phase, i.e. the computation of the margin matrix, we perform the following operations for every ballot:

1. if the ballot is informal it will be discarded
2. if the ballot is formal, the margin matrix will be updated

The certificate then contains one line for each ballot and thus allows to independently verify the computation of the margin matrix. Based on the final margin matrix, the second part of the certificate presents verifiable evidence for the computation of winners. Specifically, if a candidate w is a winner, it includes:

1. an integer k and a path of strength k from w to any other candidate
2. evidence, in the form of a co-closed set, of the fact that there cannot be a path of strength $> k$ from any other candidate to w.

Crucially, the evidence of w winning the election *only* depends on the margin matrix. We refer to [20] for details of the second part of the certificate as this will remain unchanged in the work we are reporting here.

Related Work. The paper that is closest to our work is an algorithm for homomorphic counting for Single Transferable Vote [4]. While single transferable vote is arguably more complex that the Schulze Method, we have demonstrated the viability of our approach by implementing it in a theorem prover, and have extracted, and evaluated, an executable based on the formal proof development. The idea of formalising evidence for winning elections has been put forward (for plaintext ballots) in [19]. For non-preferential (plurality) voting, homomorphic tallying is now standard, and implemented e.g. in the Helios electronic voting system [8] from Version 2.0 onwards, and is used e.g. in public elections in Estonia [18].

2   Verifiable Homomorphic Tallying

The realisation of verifiable homomorphic tallying that we are about to describe follows the same two phases as the protocol: We first homomorphically compute the margin matrix, and then compute winners on the basis of the (decrypted) margin. The computation also produces a verifiable certificate that leaks no information about individual ballots other than the (final) margin matrix, which in turn leaks no information about individual ballots if the number of voters is large enough. As for counting of plaintext ballots, we disregard informal ballots in the computation of the margin. In accord with the two phases of computation, the certificate consists of two parts: the first part evidences the correct (homomorphic) computation of the margin, and the second part the correct determination of winners. We describe both in detail.

Format of Ballots. In preferential voting schemes, ballots are rank-ordered lists of candidates. For the Schulze Method, we require that all candidates are ranked, and two candidates may be given the same rank. That is, a ballot is most naturally represented as a function $b : C \to \mathbb{N}$ that assigns a numerical rank to each candidate, and the computation of the margin amounts to computing the sum

$$m(x, y) = \sum_{b \in B} \begin{cases} +1 & b(x) > b(y) \\ 0 & b(x) = b(y) \\ -1 & b(x) < b(y) \end{cases}$$

where B is the multi-set of ballots, and each $b \in B$ is a ranking function $b : C \to \mathbb{N}$ over a (finite) set C of candidates.

We note that this representation of ballots is not well suited for homomorphic computation of the margin matrix as practically feasible homomorphic encryption schemes do not support comparison operators and case distinctions as used in the formula above.

We instead represent ballots as matrices $b(x, y)$ where $b(x, y) = +1$ if x is preferred over y, $b(x, y) = -1$ if y is preferred over x and $b(x, y) = 0$ if x and y are equally preferred.

While the advantage of the first representation is that each ranking function is necessarily a valid ranking, the advantage of the matrix representation is that the computation of the margin matrix is simple, that is

$$m(c, d) = \sum_{b \in B} b(x, y)$$

where B is the multi-set of ballots (in matrix form), and can moreover be transferred to the encrypted setting in a straight forward way: if ballots are matrices $e(x, y)$ where $e(x, y)$ is the encryption of an integer in $\{-1, 0, 1\}$, then

$$em = \bigoplus_{eb \in EB} eb(x, y) \tag{1}$$

where $\oplus$ denotes homomorphic addition, eb is an encrypted ballot in matrix form (i.e. decrypting $eb(x, y)$ indicates whether x is preferred over y), and EB is the multi-set of encrypted ballots. The disadvantage is that we need to verify that a matrix ballot is indeed valid, that is

- that the decryption of $eb(x, y)$ is indeed one of $1, 0$ or -1
- that eb indeed corresponds to a ranking function.

Indeed, to achieve verifiability, we not only need *verify* that a ballot is valid, we also need to *evidence* its validity (or otherwise) in the certificate.

Validity of Ballots. By a plaintext (matrix) ballot we simply mean a function $b : C \times C \to \mathbb{Z}$, where C is the (finite) set of candidates. A plaintext ballot $b(x, y)$ is *valid* if it is induced by a ranking function, i.e. there exists a function $f : C \to \mathbb{N}$ such that $b(x, y) = 1$ if $f(x) < f(y)$, $b(x, y) = 0$ if $f(x) = f(y)$ and $b(x, y) = -1$ if $f(x) > f(y)$. A *ciphertext (matrix) ballot* is a function $eb : C \times C \to \mathbb{CT}$ (where $\mathbb{CT}$ is a chosen set of ciphertexts), and it is valid if its decryption, i.e. the plaintext ballot $b(x, y) = \mathsf{dec}(eb(x, y))$ is valid (where dec denotes decryption).

For a plaintext ballot, it is easy to decide whether it is valid (and should be counted) or not (and should be discarded). We use shuffles (ballot permutations) to evidence the validity of encrypted ballots. One observes that a matrix ballot is valid if and only if it is valid after permuting both rows and columns with the same permutation. That is, $b(x, y)$ is valid if and only if $b'(x, y)$ is valid, where

$$b'(x, y) = b(\pi(x), \pi(y))$$

and $\pi : C \to C$ is a permutation of candidates. (Indeed, if f is a ranking function for b, then $f \circ \pi$ is a ranking function for b'). As a consequence, we can evidence the validity of a ciphertext ballot eb by

- publishing a shuffled version eb' of eb, that is shuffled by a secret permutation, together with evidence that eb' is indeed a shuffle of eb
- publishing the decryption b' of eb' together with evidence that b' is indeed the decryption of eb'.

We use zero-knowledge proofs in the style of [25] to evidence the correctness of the shuffle, and zero-knowledge proofs of honest decryption [7] to evidence correctness of decryption. This achieves ballot secrecy as the (secret) permutation is never revealed.

In summary, the evidence of correct (homomorphic) counting starts with an encryption of the zero margin em, and for each ciphertext ballot eb contains

1. a shuffle of eb together with a ZKP of correctness
2. decryption of the shuffle, together with a ZKP of correctness
3. the updated margin matrix, if the decrypted ballot was valid, and
4. the unchanged margin matrix, if the decrypted ballot is not valid.

Once all ballots have been processed in this way, the certificate determines winners and contains winners by

5. the fully constructed margin, together with its decryption and ZKP of honest decryption after counting all the ballots
6. publishes the winner(s), together with evidence to substantiate the claim

Cryptographic Primitives. We require an additively homomorphic cryptosystem to compute the (encrypted) margin matrix according to Eq. 1 (this implements

Item 3 above). All other primitives fall into one of three categories. *Verification primitives* are used to syntactically define the type of valid certificates. For example, when publishing the decrypted margin matrix in Item 5 above, we require that the zero knowledge proof in fact evidences correct decryption. To guarantee this, we need a verification primitive that – given ciphertext, plaintext and zero knowledge proof – verifies whether the supplied proof indeed evidences that the given ciphertext corresponds to the given plaintext. In particular, verification primitives are always boolean valued functions. While verification primitives *define* valid certificates, *generation primitives* are used to *produce* valid certificates. In the example above, we need a decryption primitive (to decrypt the homomorphically computed margin) and a primitive to generate a zero knowledge proof (that witnesses correct decryption). Clearly verification and generation primitives have a close correlation, and we need to require, for example, that zero knowledge proofs obtained via a generation primitive has to pass muster using the corresponding verification primitive.

The three primitives described above (decryption, generation of a zero knowledge proof, and verification of this proof) already allow us to implement the entire protocol with exception of ballot shuffling (Item 1 above). Here, the situation is more complex. While existing mixing schemes (e.g. [2]) permute an array of ciphertexts and produce a zero knowledge proof that evidences the correctness of the shuffle, our requirement dictates that every row and column of the (matrix) ballot is shuffled with the *same* (secret) permutation. In other words, we need to retain the identity of the permutation to guarantee that each row and column of a ballot have been shuffled by the same permutation. We achieve this by committing to a permutation using Pedersen's commitment scheme [21]. In a nutshell, the Pedersen commitment scheme has the following properties.

- Hiding: the commitment reveals no information about the permutation
- Binding: no party can open the commitment in more than one way, i.e. the commitment is to one permutation only.

A combination of Pedersen's commitment scheme with a zero knowledge proof leads to a similar two step protocol, also known as commitment-consistent proof of shuffle [26].

- Commit to a secret permutation and publish the commitment (hiding).
- Use a zero knowledge proof to show that shuffling has used the same permutation which we committed to in previous step (binding).

This allows us to witness the validity (or otherwise) of a ballot by generating a permutation π which is used to shuffle every row and column of the ballot. We hide π by committing it using Pedersen's commitment scheme and record the commitment c_π in the certificate. However, for the binding step, rather than opening π we generate a zero knowledge proof, zkp_π, using π and c_π, which can be used to prove that c_π is indeed the commitment to some permutation used in the (commitment consistent) shuffling without being opened [26]. We can now use the permutation that we have committed to for shuffling each row and column of a ballot, and evidence the correctness of the shuffle via a zero knowledge proof. To evidence validity (or otherwise) of a (single) ballot, we therefore:

1. generate a (secret) permutation and publish a commitment to this permutation, together with a zero knowledge proof that evidences commitment to a permutation
2. for each row of the ballot, publish a shuffle of the row with the permutation committed to, together with a zero knowledge proof that witnesses shuffle correctness
3. for each column of the row shuffled ballot, publish a shuffle of the column, also together with a zero knowledge proof of correctness
4. publish the decryption the ballot shuffled in this way, together with a zero knowledge proof that witnesses honest decryption
5. decide the validity of the ballot based on the decrypted shuffle.

The cryptographic primitives needed to implement this again fall into the same classes. To define validity of certificates, we need verification primitives

– to decide whether a zero knowledge proof evidences that a given commitment indeed commits to a permutation
– to decide whether a zero knowledge proof evidences the correctness of a shuffle relative to a given permutation commitment.

Dual to the above, to generate (valid) certificates, we need the ability to

– generate permutation commitments and accompanying zero knowledge proofs that evidence commitment to a permutation
– generate shuffles relative to a commitment, and zero knowledge proofs that evidence the correctness of shuffles.

Again, both need to be coherent in the sense that the zero knowledge proofs produced by the generation primitives need to pass validation. In summary, we require an additively homomorphic cryptosystem that implements the following:

Decryption Primitives. decryption of a ciphertext, creation and verification of honest decryption zero knowledge proofs.
Commitment Primitives. generating permutations, creation and verification of commitment zero knowledge proofs.
Shuffling Primitives. commitment consistent shuffling, creation and verification of commitment consistent zero knowledge shuffle proofs.

Witnessing of Winners. Once all ballots are counted, the computed margin is decrypted, and winners (together with evidence of winning) are computed using plaintext counting. We discuss this part only briefly, for completeness, as it is identical to the existing work on plaintext counting [20]. For each of the winners w and each candidate x we publish

- a natural number $k(w, x)$ and a path $w = x_0, \ldots, x_n = x$ of strength k
- a set $C(w, x)$ of pairs of candidates that is k-coclosed and contains (x, w)

where a set S is k-coclosed if for all $(x, z) \in C$ we have that $m(x, z) < k$ and either $m(x, y) < k$ or $(y, z) \in S$ for all candidates y. Informally, the first requirement ensures that there is no direct path (of length one) between a pair $(x, z) \in S$, and the second requirement ensures that for an element $(x, z) \in S$, there cannot be a path that connects x to an intermediate node y and then (transitively) to z that is of strength $\geq k$. We refer to $op. cit.$ for the (formal) proofs of the fact that existence of co-closed sets witnesses the winning conditions.

3   Realisation in a Theorem Prover

We formalise homomorphic tallying for the Schulze Method inside the Coq theorem prover [6]. Apart from supporting an expressive logic and (crucial for us) dependent inductive types, Coq has a well developed extraction facility that we use to extract proofs into OCaml programs. Indeed, our basic approach is to first formally define the notion of a valid certificate, and then prove that a valid certificate can be obtained from any set of (encrypted) ballots. Extracting this proof as a programme, we obtain an executable that is correct by construction.

The purpose of this paper is not to verify cryptographic primitives, but use them as a tool to construct evidence which can be used to audit and verify the outcome during different phase of election. Here, we treat them as abstract entities and assume axioms about them inside Coq. In particular, we assume the existence of functions that implement each of the primitives described in the previous section, and postulate natural axioms that describe how the different primitives interact. As a by-product, we obtain an axiomatisation of a cryptographic library that we could, in a later step, verify the implementation of a cryptosystem against. In particular, this allows us to not commit to any particular cryptosystem in particular (although our development, and later instantiation, is geared towards El Gamal [9]).

The first part of our formalisation concerns the cryptographic primitives that we collect in a separate module. Below is an example of the generation/verification primitives for decryption, together with coherence axioms.

```
Variable decrypt_message:
   Group -> Prikey -> ciphertext ->  plaintext.

Variable construct_zero_knowledge_decryption_proof:
   Group -> Prikey -> ciphertext -> DecZkp.

Axiom verify_zero_knowledge_decryption_proof:
   Group -> plaintext -> ciphertext -> DecZkp -> bool.

Axiom honest_decryption_from_zkp_proof: forall group c d zkp,
   verify_zero_knowledge_decryption_proof group d c zkp = true
   -> d = decrypt_message grp privatekey c.
```

```
Axiom verify_honest_decryption_zkp (group: Group):
   forall (pt : plaintext) (ct : ciphertext) (pk : Prikey),
   (pt = decrypt_message group pk ct) ->
   verify_zero_knowledge_decryption_proof group pt ct
   (construct_zero_knowledge_decryption_proof group pk ct)
   = true.
```

The difference between the keyword Variable and Axiom is purely syntactic, and in our case, used as a convenience for extraction. In the above, the first two functions, decrypt_message and construct_zero_knowledge_decryption_proof are *generation* primitives, whereas verify_zero_knowledge_decryption_proof is a *verification* primitive. We have two coherence axioms. The first says that if the verification of a zero knowledge proof of honest decryption succeeds, then the ciphertext indeed decrypts to the given plaintext. The second stipulates that generated zero knowledge proofs indeed verify.

For ballots, we assume a type cand of candidates, and represent plaintext and encrypted ballots as two-argument functions that take plaintext, and ciphertexts, as values.

```
Definition pballot := cand -> cand -> plaintext.
Definition eballot := cand -> cand -> ciphertext.
```

We now turn to the representation of certificates, and indeed to the definition of what it means to (a) count encrypted votes correctly according to the Schulze Method, and (b) produce a verifiable certificate of this fact. At a high level, we split the counting (and accordingly the certificate) into *states*. This gives rise to a (dependent, inductive) type ECount, parameterised by the ballots being counted.

```
Inductive ECount (group : Group) (bs : list eballot) :
   EState -> Type
```

Given a list bs of ballots, ECount bs is a dependent inductive type. In this case, given a state of counting (i.e. an inhabitant estate of EState), the type level application ECount bs estate is the *type of evidence that proves that estate is a state of counting that has been reached according to the method*. The states itself are represented by the type EState where

- epartial represents a partial state of counting, consisting of the homomorphically computed margin so far, the list of uncounted ballots and the list of invalid ballots encountered so far
- edecrypt represents the final decrypted margin matrix, and
- ewinners is the final determination of winners.

This is readily translated to the following Coq code:

```
Inductive EState : Type :=
 | epartial : (list eballot * list eballot) ->
              (cand -> cand -> ciphertext) -> EState
 | edecrypt : (cand -> cand -> plaintext) -> EState
 | ewinners : (cand -> bool) -> EState.
```

The constructors of `EState` then allow us to move from one state to the next, under appropriate conditions that guarantee correctness of the count.

The first constructor, `Ecax` kick-starts the count, and ensures that

– all ballots are initially uncounted
– margin matrix is an encryption of the zero matrix

The first constructor, as well as all the others, require

state data here, the list of uncounted and invalid ballots, and the encrypted homomorphic margin
verification data a zero knowledge proof that the encrypted homomorphic margin is indeed an encryption of the zero margin
correctness constraints here, the constuctor may only be applied if the list of uncounted ballots is equal to the list of ballots cast, and the fact that the zero knowledge proofs indeed verify that the intitial margin matrix is identically zero.

The main difference between the correctness condition, and the verification data is that the former can be simply be inspected (here by comparing lists) whereas the latter requires additional data (here in the form of a zero knowledge proof).

The translation of high level representation into Coq representation is now easy, and we arrive at the following Coq code.

```
ecax (us : list eballot) (encm : cand -> cand -> ciphertext)
(decm : cand -> cand -> plaintext)
(zkpdec : cand -> cand -> DecZkp) :
us = bs -> (forall c d : cand, decm c d = 0) ->
(forall c d, verify_zero_knowledge_decryption_proof
  group (decm c d) (encm c d) (zkpdec c d) = true) ->
ECount group bs (epartial (us, []) encm)
```

The constructor `ecvalid` represents the effect of counting a valid ballot. Here the crucial aspect is that validity needs to be evidenced. As before, we have:

state data as before, the list of uncounted and invalid ballots, the homomorphic margin, but additionally evidence that the previous state has been obtained correctly
verification data a commitment to a (secret) permutation, a row permutation of the ballot being counted, and a column permutation of this, and a decryption of the row- and column permuted ballot (all with accompanying zero knowledge proofs)

correctness constraints all the zero knowledge proofs verify, the new margin is the homomorphic addition of the previous margin and the counted ballot, and the decrypted (shuffled) ballot is indeed valid.

We elide the description of the third constructor that is applied when an invalid ballot is being encountered (the only difference is that the margin matrix is not being updated). Counting finishes when there are no more uncounted ballots, in which case the next step is to publish the decrypted margin matrix. Also here, we have

state data the decrypted margin matrix, plus evidence that a state with no more uncounted ballots has been obtained correctly

verification data a zero knowledge proof that demonstrates honest decryption of the final margin matrix

correctness constraints the given zero knowledge proof verifies, i.e. the given decrypted margin is indeed the decryption of the (last) homomorphically computed margin matrix.

The last constructor finally declares the winners of the election, and we have:

state data a function `cand -> bool` that determines winners, plus evidence of the fact that the decrypted final margin matrix has been obtained correctly

verification data paths and co-closed sets that evidence the correctness of the function above

correctness constraints that ensure that the verification data verifies the winners given by the state data.

This last part is identical to our previous formalisation of the Schulze Method (for plaintext ballots), and we refer to [20] for more details.

4   Correctness by Construction and Verification

In the previous section, we have presented a data type that *defines* the notion of a verifiably correct count of the Schulze Method, on the basis of encrypted ballots. To obtain an executable that in fact *produces* a verifiable (and provably correct) count, we can proceed in either of two ways:

1. implement a function that – give a list `bs` of ballots – produces a boolean function w (for winners) and an element of the type `ECount bs` (`winners w`). This gives both the election winners (w) as well as evidence (the element of the `ECount` data type).
2. to prove that for every set `bs` of encrypted ballots, we have a boolean function w and an inhabitant of the type `ECount bs` (`winners w`).

Under the proofs-as-programs interpretation of constructive type theory, both amount to the same. We chose the latter approach, and our first main theorem formally states that all elections can be counted according to the Schulze Method (with encrypted ballots), i.e. a winner can always be found. Formally, our main theorem takes the following form:

```
Lemma encryption_schulze_winners (group : Group)
 (bs : list eballot) : existsT (f : cand -> bool),
 ECount group bs (ewinners f ).
```

The proof proceeds by successively building an inhabitant of EState by homomorphically computing the margin matrix, then decrypting and determining the winners. Within the proof, we use both generation primitives (e.g. to construct zero knowledge proofs) and coherence axioms (to ensure that the zero knowledge proofs indeed verify).

The correctness of our entire approach stands or falls with the correct formalisation of the inductive data type ECount that is used to determine the winners of an election counted according to the Schulze Method. While one can argue that the data type itself is transparent enough to be its own specification, the cryptographic aspect makes things slightly more complex. For example, it appears to be credible that our mechanism for determining validity of a ballot is correct – however we have not given proof of this. Rather than scrutinising the details of the construction of this data type, we follow a different approach: we demonstrate that homomorphic counting always yields the same results as plaintext counting, where plaintext counting is already verified against its specification. Plaintext counting has been formalised, and verified, in the precursor paper [20]. This correspondence has two directions, and both assume that we are given two lists of ballots that are the encryption (resp. decryption) of one another.

The first theorem, plaintext_schulze_to_homomorphic, reproduced below shows that every winner that can be determined using plaintext counting can also be evidenced on the basis of encrypted ballots. The converse of this is established by Theorem homomorphic_schulze_to_plaintext.

```
Lemma plaintext_schulze_to_homomorphic
 (group : Group) (bs : list ballot):
 forall (pbs : list pballot) (ebs : list eballot)
 (w : cand -> bool), (pbs = map (fun x => (fun c d =>
 decrypt_message group privatekey (x c d))) ebs) ->
 (mapping_ballot_pballot bs pbs) ->
 Count bs (winners w) -> ECount group ebs (ewinners w).

Lemma homomorphic_schulze_to_plaintext
 (group : Group) (bs : list ballot):
 forall (pbs : list pballot) (ebs : list eballot)
 (w : cand -> bool) (pbs = map (fun x => (fun c d =>
 decrypt_message group privatekey (x c d))) ebs) ->
 (mapping_ballot_pballot bs pbs) ->
 ECount grp ebs (ewinners w) -> Count bs (winners w).
```

The theorems above feature a third type of ballot that is the basis of plaintext counting, and is a simple ranking function of type cand -> Nat, and the two hypotheses on the three types of ballots ensure that the encrypted ballots (ebs) are in fact in alignment with the rank-ordered ballots (bs) that are used in plaintext counting. The proof, and indeed the formulation, relies on an inductive data type Count that can best be thought of as a plaintext version of the inductive type ECount given here. Crucially, Count is verified against a formal specification of the Schulze Method. Both theorems are proven by induction on the definition of the respective data types, where the key step is to show that the (decrypted) final margins agree. The key ingredient here are the coherence axioms that stipulate that zero knowledge proofs that verify indeed evidence shuffle and/or honest decryption.

5   Extraction and Experiments

As already mentioned, we are using the Coq extraction mechanism [16] to extract programs from existence proofs[1]. In particular, we extract the proof of the Theorem pschulze_winners, given in Sect. 4 to a program that delivers not only provably correct counts, but also verifiable evidence. Give a set of encrypted ballots and a Group that forms the basis of cryptographic operations, we obtain a program that delivers not only a set of winners, but additionally independently verifiable evidence of the correctness of the count.

Indeed, the entire formulation of our data type, and the split into state data, verification data, and correctness constraints, has been geared towards extraction as a goal. Technically, the verification conditions are *propositions*, i.e. inhabitants of Type *Prop* in the terminology of Coq, and hence erased at extraction time. This corresponds to the fact that the assertions embodied in the correctness constraints can be verified with minimal computational overhead, given the state and the verification data. For example, it can simply be verified whether or not a zero knowledge proof indeed verifies honest decryption by running it through a verifier. On the other hand, the zero knowledge proof itself (which is part of the verification data) is crucially needed to be able to verify that a plaintext is the honest decryption of a ciphertext, and hence cannot be erased during extraction. Technically, this is realised by formulating both state and verification data at type level (rather than as propositions).

As we have explained in Sect. 3, the formal development does not pre-suppose any specific implementation of the cryptographic primitives, and we assume the existence of cryptographic infrastructure. From the perspective of extraction, this produces an executable with "holes", i.e. the cryptographic primitives need to be supplied to fill the holes and indeed be able to compile and execute the extracted program.

To fill this hole, we implement the cryptoraphic primitives with help of the UniCrypt library [17]. UniCrypt is a freely available library, written in Java, that provides nearly all of the required functionality, with the exception of honest decryption zero knowledge proofs. We extract our proof development into OCaml and use Java/OCaml bindings [1] to make the UniCrypt functionality available to our OCaml program. Due to differences in the type structure between

---

[1] https://github.com/mukeshtiwari/EncryptionSchulze/tree/master/code/Working code.

Java and OCaml, mainly in the context of sub-typing, this was done in the form of an OCaml wrapper around Java data structures. After instantiating the cryptographic primitives in the extracted OCaml code with wrapper code that calls UniCrypt we tested the executable on a three candidate elections between candidates A, B and C. The computation produces a tally sheet that is schematically given below: it is trace of computation which can be used as a checkable record to verify the outcome of election. We elide the cryptographic detail, e.g. the concrete representation of zero knowledge proofs. A certificate is be obtained from the type ECount where the head of the certificate corresponds to the base case of the inductive type, here ecax. Below, M is encrypted margin matrix, D is its decrypted equivalent, required to be identically zero, and Z represents a matrix of zero knwoledge proofs, each establishing that the XY-component of M is in fact an encryption of zero. All these matrices are indexed by candidates and we display these matrices by listing their entries prefixed by a pair of candidates, e.g. the ellipsis in AB(...) denotes the matrix entry at row A and column B.

```
M: AB(rel-marg-of-A-over-B-enc), AC(rel-marg-of-A-over-C-enc), ...
D: AB(0)                        , AC(0)                        , ...
Z: AB(zkp-for-rel-marg-A-B)     , AC(zkp-for-rel-marg-A-C)     , ...
```

Note that one can verify the fact that the initial encrypted margin is in fact the zero margin by just verifying the zero knowledge proofs. Successive entries in the certificate will generally be obtained by counting valid, and discarding invalid ballots. If a valid ballot is counted after the counting commences, the certificate would continue by exhibiting the state and verification data contained in the ecvalid constructor which can be displayed schematically as follows:

```
V:  AB(ballot-entry-A-B) , AC(ballot-entry-A-C), ...
C:  permutation-commitment
P:  zkp-of-valid-permutation-commitment
R:  AB(row-perm-A-B)      , AC(row-perm-A-C)      , ...
RP: A(zkp-of-perm-row-A), B(zkp-of-perm-row-B), ...
C:  AB(col-perm-A-B),       AC(col-perm-A-C)      , ...
CP: A(zkp-of-perm-col-A), B(zkp-of-perm-col-B), ...
D:  AB(dec-perm-bal-A-B) , AC(dec-perm-bal-A-C), ...
Z:  AB(zkp-for-dec-A-B)  , AC(zkp-for-dec-A-C) , ...
M:  AB(new-marg-A-B)     , AC(new-marg-A-C)      , ...
```

Here V is the list of ballots to be counted, where we only display the first element. We commit to a permutation and validate this commitment with a zero knowledge proof, here given in the second and third line, prefixed with C and P. The following two lines are a row permutation of the ballot V, together with a zero knowledge proof of correctness of shuffling (of each row) with respect to the permutation committed to by C above. The following two lines achieve the same for subsequently permuting the columns of the (row permuted) ballot. Finally, D is the decrypted permuted ballot, and Z a zero knowledge proof of honest decryption. We end with an updated homomorphic margin matrix M. Again, we note that the validity of the decrypted ballot can be checked easily, and validating zero knowledge proofs substantiate that the decrypted ballot is indeed a shuffle of the original one. Homomorphic addition can simply be re-computed.

The steps where invalid ballots are being detected is similar, with the exception of not updating the margin matrix. Once all ballots are counted, the only applicable constructor is `ecdecrypt`, the data content of which would continue a certificate schematically as follows:

```
V: []
M: AB(fin-marg-A-B), AC(fin-marg-A-C), ...
D: AB(dec-marg-A-B), AC(dec-marg-A-C), ...
Z: AB(zkp-dec-A-B) , AC(zkp-dec-A-C) , ...
```

Here the first line indicates that there are no more ballots to be counted, M is the final encrypted margin matrix, D is its decryption and Z is a matrix of zero knowledge proofs verifying the correctness of decryption.

The certificate would end with the determination of winners based on the encrypted margin, and would end with the content of the `ecfin` constructor

```
winning: A, <evidence that A wins against B and C>
losing:  B, <evidence that B loses against A and C>
losing:  C, <evidence that C loses against A and B>
```

where the notion of evidence for winning and losing is as in the plaintext version of the protocol [20].

We note that the schematic presentation of the certificate above is nothing but a representation of the data contained in the extracted type ECount that we have chosen to present schematically. Concrete certificates can be inspected with the accompanying proof development, and are obtained by simply implementing datatype to string conversion on the type ECount.

To demonstrate proof of concept, we have run our experiment on an Intel i7 2.6 GHz Linux desktop computer with 8 GB of RAM for three candidates and randomly generated ballots. The largest amount of ballot we counted was 10,000

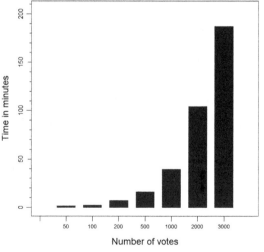

(not included in graph), with a runtime of 25 h. A more detailed analysis reveals that the bottleneck are the bindings between OCaml and Java. More specifically, producing the cryptographic evidence using the UniCrypt Library for 10,000 ballots takes about 10 min, and the subsequent computation (which is the same as for the plaintext count) takes negligible time. This is consistent with the mechanism employed by the bindings: each function call from OCaml to Java is inherently memory bounded and creates an instance of the Java runtime, the conversion of OCaml data structures into Java data structures, computation by respective Java function producing result, converting the result back into OCaml data structure, and finally destroying the Java runtime instance when the function returns. While the proof of concept using OCaml/Java bindings falls short of being practically feasible, our timing analysis substantiates that feasibility can be achieved by eliminating the overhead of the bindings.

6   Analysis

Summary. The main contribution of our formalisation is that of independently verifiable *evidence* for a set of candidates to be the winners of an election counted according to the Schulze method. Our main claim is that our notion of evidence is both safeguarding the privacy of the individual ballot (as the count is based on encrypted ballots) and is verifiable at the same time (by means of zero knowledge proofs). To do this, we have axiomatised a set of cryptographic primitives to deal with encryption, decryption, correctness of shuffles and correctness of decryption. From formal and constructive proof of the fact that such evidence can always be obtained, we have then extracted executable code that is provably correct by construction and produces election winners together with evidence once implementations for the cryptographic primitives are supplied.

In a second step, we have supplied an implementation of these primitives, largely based on the UniCrypt Library. Our expertiments have demonstrated that this approach is feasible, but quite clearly much work is still needed to improve efficiency.

Assumptions for Provable Correctness. While we claim that the end product embodies a high level of reliability, our approach necessarily leaves some gaps between the executable and the formal proofs. First and foremost, this is of course the implementation of the cryptographic primitives in an external (and unverified) library. We have minimised this gap by basing our implementation on a purpose-specific existing library (UniCrypt) to which we relegate most of the functionality. Another gap is the extraction mechanism of the Coq theorem prover which does not come with formal correctness guarantees that reach down to the machine code level such as for example CakeML [13].

Modelling Assumptions. In our modelling of the cryptographic primitives, in particular the zero knowledge proofs, we assumed properties which in reality only hold with very high probability. As a consequence our correctness assertions only hold to the level of probability that is guaranteed by zero knowledge proofs.

Scalability. We have analysed the feasibility of the extracted code by counting an increasing number of ballots. While this demonstrates a proof of concept, our results show that the bindings used to couple the cryptographic layer with our code adds significant overhead compared to plaintext tallying [20]. Given that both parts are practically efficient by themselves, scalability is merely the question of engineering a more efficient coupling.

Future Work. Our axiomatisation of the needed cryptographic primitives lays the foundation of creating a verified library. For scalability, a more detailed analysis (and profiling) of the software artefact are necessary. Orthogonal to what we have presented here, it would also be of interest to develop a provably correct verifier for the notion of certificate presented here.

References

1. Aguillon, J.: OCaml ↔ Java Interface. https://github.com/Julow/ocaml-java. Accessed 29 April 2019
2. Bayer, S., Groth, J.: Efficient zero-knowledge argument for correctness of a shuffle. In: Pointcheval, D., Johansson, T. (eds.) EUROCRYPT 2012. LNCS, vol. 7237, pp. 263–280. Springer, Heidelberg (2012). https://doi.org/10.1007/978-3-642-29011-4_17
3. Ben-Or, M., et al.: Everything provable is provable in zero-knowledge. In: Goldwasser, S. (ed.) CRYPTO 1988. LNCS, vol. 403, pp. 37–56. Springer, New York (1990). https://doi.org/10.1007/0-387-34799-2_4
4. Benaloh, J., Moran, T., Naish, L., Ramchen, K., Teague, V.: Shuffle-sum: coercion-resistant verifiable tallying for STV voting. IEEE Trans. Inf. Forensics Secur. **4**(4), 685–698 (2009)
5. Bernhard, M., et al.: Public evidence from secret ballots. In: Krimmer, R., Volkamer, M., Braun Binder, N., Kersting, N., Pereira, O., Schürmann, C. (eds.) E-Vote-ID 2017. LNCS, vol. 10615, pp. 84–109. Springer, Cham (2017). https://doi.org/10.1007/978-3-319-68687-5_6
6. Bertot, Y., Castéran, P., Huet, G., Paulin-Mohring, C.: Interactive theorem proving and program development: Coq'Art : the calculus of inductive constructions. Texts in theoretical computer science. Springer, Heidelberg (2004). https://doi.org/10.1007/978-3-662-07964-5
7. Chaum, D., Pedersen, T.P.: Wallet databases with observers. In: Brickell, E.F. (ed.) CRYPTO 1992. LNCS, vol. 740, pp. 89–105. Springer, Heidelberg (1993). https://doi.org/10.1007/3-540-48071-4_7
8. de Marneffe, O., Pereira, O., Quisquater, J.-J.: Electing a university president using open-audit voting: analysis of real-world use of Helios. In: Jefferson, D., Hall, J.L., Moran, T., (ed.) Proceedings of the EVT/WOTE 2009. USENIX Association (2009)
9. ElGamal, T.: A public key cryptosystem and a signature scheme based on discrete logarithms. In: Blakley, G.R., Chaum, D. (eds.) CRYPTO 1984. LNCS, vol. 196, pp. 10–18. Springer, Heidelberg (1985). https://doi.org/10.1007/3-540-39568-7_2
10. Goldreich, O., Micali, S., Wigderson, A.: Proofs that yield nothing but their validity for all languages in NP have zero-knowledge proof systems. J. ACM **38**(3), 691–729 (1991)

11. Goldwasser, S., Micali, S., Rackoff, C.: The knowledge complexity of interactive proof-systems (extended abstract). In: STOC, pp. 291–304. ACM (1985)
12. Hirt, M., Sako, K.: Efficient receipt-free voting based on homomorphic encryption. In: Preneel, B. (ed.) EUROCRYPT 2000. LNCS, vol. 1807, pp. 539–556. Springer, Heidelberg (2000). https://doi.org/10.1007/3-540-45539-6_38
13. Kumar, R., Myreen, M.O., Norrish, M., Owens, S.: CakeML: a verified implementation of ML. In: Jagannathan, S., Sewell, P., (eds.) Proceedings of the POPL 2014, pp. 179–192. ACM (2014)
14. Küsters, R., Truderung, T., Vogt, A.: Accountability: definition and relationship to verifiability. In: ACM Conference on Computer and Communications Security, pp. 526–535. ACM (2010)
15. Küsters, R., Truderung, T., Vogt, A.: Clash attacks on the verifiability of e-voting systems. In: IEEE Symposium on Security and Privacy, pp. 395–409. IEEE Computer Society (2012)
16. Letouzey, P.: A new extraction for Coq. In: Geuvers, H., Wiedijk, F. (eds.) TYPES 2002. LNCS, vol. 2646, pp. 200–219. Springer, Heidelberg (2003). https://doi.org/10.1007/3-540-39185-1_12
17. Locher, P., Haenni, R.: A lightweight implementation of a shuffle proof for electronic voting systems. In: Jahrestagung der Gesellschaft für Informatik, Informatik 2014, Big Data - Komplexität meistern, 22–26 September 2014, vol. 44, pp. 1391–1400, Stuttgart (2014)
18. Parsovs, A.: Homomorphic tallying for the estonian internet voting system. IACR Cryptology ePrint Archive 2016, 776 (2016)
19. Pattinson, D., Schürmann, C.: Vote counting as mathematical proof. In: Pfahringer, B., Renz, J. (eds.) AI 2015. LNCS (LNAI), vol. 9457, pp. 464–475. Springer, Cham (2015). https://doi.org/10.1007/978-3-319-26350-2_41
20. Pattinson, D., Tiwari, M.: Schulze voting as evidence carrying computation. In: Ayala-Rincón, M., Muñoz, C.A. (eds.) ITP 2017. LNCS, vol. 10499, pp. 410–426. Springer, Cham (2017). https://doi.org/10.1007/978-3-319-66107-0_26
21. Pedersen, T.P.: Non-interactive and information-theoretic secure verifiable secret sharing. In: Feigenbaum, J. (ed.) CRYPTO 1991. LNCS, vol. 576, pp. 129–140. Springer, Heidelberg (1992). https://doi.org/10.1007/3-540-46766-1_9
22. Rivest, R.L.: On the notion of software independence' in voting systems. Philos. Trans. R. Soc. A: Math. Phys. Eng. Sci. 366(1881), 3759–3767 (2008)
23. Rivest, R.L., Shen, E.: An optimal single-winner preferential voting system based on game theory. In: Conitzer, V., Rothe, J., (eds.) Proceedings of the COMSOC 2010. Duesseldorf University Press (2010)
24. Schulze, M.: A new monotonic, clone-independent, reversal symmetric, and condorcet-consistent single-winner election method. Soc. Choice Welfare 36(2), 267–303 (2011)
25. Terelius, B., Wikström, D.: Proofs of restricted shuffles. In: Bernstein, D.J., Lange, T. (eds.) AFRICACRYPT 2010. LNCS, vol. 6055, pp. 100–113. Springer, Heidelberg (2010). https://doi.org/10.1007/978-3-642-12678-9_7
26. Wikström, D.: A commitment-consistent proof of a shuffle. In: Boyd, C., González Nieto, J. (eds.) ACISP 2009. LNCS, vol. 5594, pp. 407–421. Springer, Heidelberg (2009). https://doi.org/10.1007/978-3-642-02620-1_28

Incremental Minimization of Symbolic Automata

Jonathan Homburg[1] and Parasara Sridhar Duggirala[2(⊠)]

[1] Department of Computer Science and Engineering, University of Connecticut,
Storrs, USA
jonhom1996@gmail.com
[2] Department of Computer Science, University of North Carolina Chapel Hill,
Chapel Hill, USA
psd@cs.unc.edu

Abstract. Symbolic automata are generalizations of finite automata that have symbolic predicates over the alphabet as transitions instead of symbols. Recently, traditional automata minimization techniques have been generalized to symbolic automata. In this paper, we generalize the incremental minimization algorithm to symbolic automata such that the algorithm can be halted at any point for obtaining a partially minimized automaton. Instead of computing the sets of equivalence classes, the incremental algorithm checks for equivalence between pairs of states and if they are equivalent, merges them into a single state. We evaluate our algorithm on SFAs corresponding to Unicode regular expressions and compare them to the state-of-the-art symbolic automata minimization implementations.

1 Introduction

As opposed to classical automata where the alphabet is given as a finite set, symbolic automata have an alphabet given by a Boolean algebra that may have an infinite domain. The transitions between states in symbolic automata are labeled with predicates in a Boolean algebra. Symbolic automata are used in regular expressions over large alphabets such as Unicode, program analysis, and satisfiability modulo theories. In [5], the notion of minimality of a symbolic automaton has been studied and extensions of classical automata minimization algorithms to symbolic setting were presented.

In this paper, we investigate a new class of minimization algorithms called incremental minimization. An incremental minimization algorithm can be interrupted at any point of time to obtain a partially minimized automaton that recognizes the same language as the input automaton. The algorithm can later be resumed with the partially minimized automaton. Upon termination, the algorithm returns the automaton with minimal number of states recognizing the same language. Hence, such an algorithm is suitable for deployment in web-services, such as spam-detection, and pattern matching in DNA sequences where server downtime for minimization is not acceptable.

S. Chakraborty and J. A. Navas (Eds.): VSTTE 2019, LNCS 12031, pp. 54–67, 2020.
https://doi.org/10.1007/978-3-030-41600-3_5

This paper generalizes the incremental minimization algorithm for DFAs presented in [3] to the symbolic setting. Unlike the traditional minimization algorithms [11–13], which compute equivalence classes over states by repeated partitioning, the algorithm in [3] merges equivalent states to create a partially minimized automata. For checking equivalence between pairs of states, the algorithm makes recursive calls and maintains a set of dependencies that need to be resolved. The primary principle in checking equivalence of two states is:

> States p and q are not distinguishable if and only if for all states p' and q' such that $p \xrightarrow{a} p'$ and $q \xrightarrow{a} q'$, p' and q' are not distinguishable.

The corresponding statement for symbolic automata is:

> States p and q are not distinguishable if and only if for all states p' and q' such that such that $p \xrightarrow{\phi} p'$ and $q \xrightarrow{\psi} q'$ where $\phi \wedge \psi$ is satisfiable, p' and q' are not distinguishable.

The primary difference between the above statements and their counterpart in [5] is that the former are useful in iteratively building equivalence classes whereas the latter are useful in partitioning a set of states to arrive at equivalence classes.

In this paper, we present an incremental minimization algorithm for symbolic automata which takes advantage of the symbolic representation of the transitions. Similar to [5], our generalization of algorithm in [3] relies on the observation that a relevant set of predicates can be computed locally rather than computing all the minterms of an automaton's predicate set.

Instead of checking equivalence for every pair of states, we use a heuristic to decrease the number of checks. We observe that two states cannot be equivalent if they have different *minimum distance to an accepting state*. Therefore, we initialize the *non-equivalence* relation between states with all pairs of states that have different minimum distance to accepting states.

This paper is organized as follows. The preliminaries are presented in Sect. 2. We present the incremental minimization algorithm in Sect. 3. The evaluation of our algorithm and its comparison with other symbolic automata minimization techniques in presented in Sect. 4. We discuss related work in Sect. 5 and present our conclusions and future work in Sect. 6.

2 Preliminaries

Symbolic automata have the domain of a Boolean algebra as input alphabet. An effective Boolean algebra $\mathcal{A}$ has components $(\mathcal{D}, \Psi, [\![\_]\!], \bot, \top, \vee, \wedge, \neg)$. $\mathcal{D}$ is a recursively enumerable (r.e.) set of domain elements. Ψ is an r.e. set of predicates closed under Boolean operations and $\bot, \top \in \Psi$. $[\![\_]\!]$ is a denotation function (which is recursively enumerable) $[\![\_]\!] : \Psi \to 2^{\mathcal{D}}$ is such that $[\![\bot]\!] = \emptyset$, $[\![\top]\!] = \mathcal{D}$, for all $\phi, \psi \in \Psi$, $[\![\phi \vee \psi]\!] = [\![\phi]\!] \cup [\![\psi]\!]$, $[\![\phi \wedge \psi]\!] = [\![\phi]\!] \cap [\![\psi]\!]$, and $[\![\neg\phi]\!] = \mathcal{D} \setminus [\![\psi]\!]$. For $\phi \in \Psi$, we say $IsSat(\phi)$ if and only if $[\![\phi]\!] \neq \emptyset$ and say that ϕ is satisfiable. $\mathcal{A}$ is said to be decidable if $IsSat$ is decidable.

In our experiments, we only deal with Boolean algebra whose domain is a bit vector of length k ($k = 16$). Each bit vector corresponds to a unique symbol in the unicode alphabet. Predicates over this domain can be represented as BDDs (or boolean formulas) with the boolean operations corresponding to operations on BDDs (or calls to a SAT solver). Another Boolean algebra discussed in [5] is a theory over some domain σ with the various operations implemented using calls to an SMT solver.

A symbolic automaton, informally, is a finite automaton where the transitions are labeled with predicates over the domain of a Boolean algebra instead of symbols in the domain. We require these predicates originate from a Boolean algebra to ensure closure under set operations such as complement, intersection, union, etc.

Definition 1. *A symbolic finite automaton (SFA) M is a tuple $(\mathcal{A}, Q, q_0, F, \Delta)$ where $\mathcal{A}$ is an effective Boolean algebra, called the* alphabet, *Q is a finite set of states, $q_0 \in Q$ is the* initial *state, $F \subseteq Q$ is the set of* accepting *states or* final *states, and $\Delta \subseteq Q \times \Psi_\mathcal{A} \times Q$ is a finite set of transitions.*

Elements of $\mathcal{D}_\mathcal{A}$ are called symbols or characters and finite sequence of characters are called *strings* (elements in $\mathcal{D}_\mathcal{A}^*$). ϵ denotes the empty string. A transition $\rho = (q, \phi, q') \in \Delta$ is also denoted as $q \xrightarrow{\phi} q'$ (when M is clear from the context). ρ is said to be *feasible* if ϕ is satisfiable. Given a character $a \in \mathcal{D}_\mathcal{A}$, an a-transition is $q \xrightarrow{\phi} q'$ such that $a \in \llbracket \phi \rrbracket$, also denoted as $q \xrightarrow{a} q'$.

Definition 2. *A string $w = a_1 a_2 \ldots a_k \in \mathcal{D}_\mathcal{A}^*$, is accepted at state q of $M = (\mathcal{A}, Q, q_0, F, \Delta)$, denoted as $w \in L_M(q)$, if there exist states $q_1, q_2, \ldots, q_{k+1}$, such that $q_1 = q$, $\forall 1 \leq i \leq k, q_i \xrightarrow{a_i} q_{i+1}$, and $q_{k+1} \in F$. The language recognized by M is $L(M) = L_M(q_0)$.*

We adopt the terminology used in [5] for symbolic automata M and present the definitions for completeness.

- M is *deterministic* if for all $p \xrightarrow{\phi} q$, $p \xrightarrow{\psi} q' \in \Delta$, if $IsSat(\phi \wedge \psi)$ then $q = q'$.
- A state q of M is said to be *partial* if there exists a symbol a such that there is no a-transition for the state q. M is said to be complete if it has no partial states.
- M is clean if for all $p \xrightarrow{\phi} q \in \Delta$, p is reachable from q_0 and $IsSat(\phi)$.
- M is normalized if for all $q, q' \in Q$, there is at most one transition from q to q'.
- Given a deterministic, complete, clean, and normalized M, it is said to be minimal if for all $q, q' \in Q$, $q = q'$ if $L_M(q) = L_M(q')$.

For a deterministic and complete symbolic automaton, we denote the transition function as $\delta_M \colon Q \times \mathcal{D}_\mathcal{A} \to Q$ such that for all $a \in \mathcal{D}_\mathcal{A}$ and $q \in Q$, $\delta_M(q, a) \triangleq q'$, where $q \xrightarrow{a} q'$. We drop the subscript when the automaton is clear from the context. In the rest of the paper, we assume that all the automata that we consider are deterministic, complete, clean, and normalized. Steps for obtaining such an automaton have been discussed in [5].

Definition 3. *Given M and $q \in Q$, we define the distance of the state from the accepting set of states as $dist(q) = min\{ |w| \mid w \in L_M(q)\}$ if $L_M(q) \neq \emptyset$ and $|w|$ represents the length of string w. $dist(q) = \infty$ otherwise.*

We now present an equivalence relation on states of an automaton M and define the minimal automaton using the equivalence relation described in [5].

Definition 4. *Given SFA M, two states q and q' are said to be equivalent, $q \equiv_M q'$ if and only if $L_M(q) = L_M(q')$.*

A couple of trivial observations about $\equiv_M$:

1. $\equiv_M$ is an equivalence relation.
2. q and q' are not equivalent if $dist(q) \neq dist(q')$.

Given any equivalence relation $\equiv$ over the states Q, for any $q \in Q$, $q_\equiv$ is the equivalence class containing q, for $X \subseteq Q$, $X_\equiv = \{ q_\equiv \mid q \in X\}$, and the corresponding SFA is $M_\equiv \triangleq (\mathcal{A}, Q_\equiv, q_{0_\equiv}, F_\equiv, \Delta_\equiv)$ where

$$\Delta_\equiv \triangleq \{(q_\equiv, \bigvee_{(q,\psi,q')\in\Delta} \psi, q'_\equiv) \mid q, q' \in Q, \exists \psi, (q, \psi, q') \in \Delta\}$$

Theorem 1 (Theorem 2 from [5]). *Given a clean, complete, normal, and deterministic SFA M, $M_{\equiv_M}$ is minimal and $L(M) = L(M_{\equiv_M})$.*

3   Incremental Minimization of Symbolic Automata

Typical algorithms for automata minimization attempt to construct the largest possible equivalences classes of states and iteratively refine them. These algorithms initially partition the states into one of two classes, first is the set of accepting states, and second is the set of non-accepting states. Each of these classes are partitioned further if the states in one partition can be *differentiated* from the states in the other. This partitioning continues until no two states in the same class can be differentiated and hence are equivalent. Halting the algorithm abruptly would not yield any partially minimized automaton.

In contrast, incremental minimization attempts to merge states that are provably equivalent and construct new equivalence classes. Checking the equivalence of states p and q would require proving the equivalence of all pairs of states p' and q' that are reached after every a-transition from p and q respectively. If the equivalence of p and q is established, then these two states are merged to form a new equivalent state. Hence, as only equivalent states are merged, halting the algorithm abruptly would yield a partially minimized automaton that accepts the same language as the input automaton.

Informally, the algorithm proceeds as follows. First, a pair of states u and v are chosen from the set of states. Then, for a given input symbol a (chosen from the alphabet), the states reached after a-transition u' and v' are identified. Next, the algorithm performs a recursive call to prove the equivalence of u' and v'.

In addition, it keeps a set *path* of all the pairs of states that are waiting to be proved equivalent. If the recursive calls returns *true*, then a different symbol a' is chosen from the alphabet and the equivalence of next states on a'-transition is checked by another recursive call. In a symbolic automata, the number of symbols can possibly be infinite, and hence, we decrease the number of recursive calls by leveraging the symbolic predicates.

```
1 Function IncrementalMinimize(M = (A, Q, q₀, F, Δ)):
2       for q ∈ Q do
3           Make(q)
4       neq = {Normalize(p,q) | p ∈ Q, q ∈ Q, Dist(p) ≠ Dist(q)};
5       for p ∈ Q do
6           for q ∈ {x ∈ Q | x > p} do
7               if (p, q) ∈ neq then
8                   continue;
9               if Find(p) = Find(q) then
10                  continue;
11              equiv, path = ∅
12              if Equiv-p (p,q) then
13                  for ((p', q') ∈ equiv) do
14                      Union(p',q');
15              else
16                  for (p', q') ∈ path do
17                      neq = neq ∪ {(p',q')};
18      return JoinStates(M)
```

Algorithm 1. Algorithm for incremental minimization of symbolic automata.

The incremental minimization algorithm for a complete, deterministic, clean, normalized SFA is provided in Algorithm 1. This algorithm makes a call to a recursive procedure `Equiv-p()` that is given in Algorithm 2.

We first define a few data structures that are used in the minimization algorithm. A disjoint set data structure will be used to represent equivalence classes of states. Specifically, for n disjoint sets, the following operations will be defined:

1. `Make(i)`, a set containing only i will be created
2. `Find(i)`, returns a (consistent) identifying element for S_i, the set containing i.
3. `Union(i, j)`, creates a new set S_k such that $S_k = S_i \cup S_j$ and sets S_i, S_j are destroyed

This algorithm for SFA minimization was adapted from [3]. There are two primary modifications. First, the *neq* relation is initialized to contain all pairs

```
1  Function Equiv-p(p, q):
2  |    if (p, q) ∈ neq then
3  |    |    return False
4  |    if (p, q) ∈ path then
5  |    |    return True
6  |    path = path ∪ {(p, q)}
7  |    Out_p = {φ ∈ Ψ_A | ∃p', (p, φ, p') ∈ Δ}
8  |    Out_q = {ψ ∈ Ψ_A | ∃q', (q, ψ, q') ∈ Δ}
9  |    while Out_p ∪ Out_q ≠ ∅ do
10 |    |    Let a ∈ [[(⋁_{φ∈Out_p} φ) ∧ (⋁_{ψ∈Out_q} ψ)]]
   |    |    (p', q') = Normalize(Find(δ(p, a)), Find(δ(q, a)))
11 |    |    if p' ≠ q' and (p', q') ∉ equiv then
12 |    |    |    equiv = equiv ∪ {(p', q')}
13 |    |    |    if not Equiv-p(p', q') then
14 |    |    |    |    return False
15 |    |    |    else
16 |    |    |    |    path = path \ {(p', q')}
17 |    |    Let φ ∈ Out_p with a ∈ [[φ]]
18 |    |    Let ψ ∈ Out_q with a ∈ [[ψ]]
19 |    |    Out_p = Out_p \ {φ} ∪ {φ ∧ ¬ψ}
20 |    |    Out_q = Out_q \ {ψ} ∪ {ψ ∧ ¬φ}
21 |    equiv = equiv ∪ {(p, q)}
22 |    return True
```

Algorithm 2. Algorithm that checks equivalence of states p and q.

of states that have different minimal distance from accepting states, instead of just the pairs of states that contain one accepting and one non-accepting state. Second, the Equiv-p function (which returns true on (p, q) if and only if p, q are equivalent) given in Algorithm 2 leverages the symbolic nature of the predicates over the transitions. The usage of data structures $equiv$ and $path$ – $equiv$ tracking the pairs of equivalent states discovered and $path$ tracking the path through the sets of pairs of states – is similar to the algorithm presented in [3].

Note that we assume there exists an ordering on Q (i.e. $p < q$ makes sense for all $p, q \in Q$). This can be done easily by labeling each state with a unique positive integer. Normalize takes a pair (p, q) as input and reorders it so that the first element is less than the second. JoinStates merges the states that share the same equivalence class (i.e. share the same disjoint set). Dist measures the minimum distance from a given state to an accepting state.

We will now prove the correctness of the above incremental algorithm for symbolic automata minimization.

Lemma 1. Equiv-p *terminates.*

Proof. First, note that there are a finite number of recursive calls to Equiv-p. This is because there are a finite number of pairs of states that Equiv-p can be called on and `Equiv-p` immediately returns if it recognizes that it has already been called on a given pair of states. So, to prove `Equiv-p` terminates, it needs only be shown that the loop over $Out_p \cup Out_q$ beginning on line 9 is finite.

During each iteration over $Out_p \cup Out_q$, we find some $\varphi \in Out_p$ and $\psi \in Out_q$ such that there exists an $a \in \mathcal{D}_\mathcal{A}$ with $a \in [\![\varphi \wedge \psi]\!]$. Later, during the same iteration, we replace φ in Out_p with $\varphi \wedge \neg\psi$ and ψ in Out_q with $\psi \wedge \neg\varphi$. These new predicates denote strictly smaller subsets of $\mathcal{D}_\mathcal{A}$ (because a does not satisfy either predicate). If $\mathcal{D}_\mathcal{A}$ is finite, this is enough to ensure the loop terminates. Otherwise, if $\mathcal{D}_\mathcal{A}$ is infinite, it needs to be proven that for all $\varphi \in Out_p$, there exist some finite set $S \subseteq Out_q$ such that $[\![\varphi \wedge \neg(\bigvee_{\psi \in S} \psi)]\!] = \varnothing$. Because Out_p is always finite, this is sufficient to prove that the loop terminates.

Fix $\varphi \in Out_p$. Define $S = \{\psi \in Out_q \mid IsSat(\varphi \wedge \psi)\}$. Assume that $\varphi \wedge \neg(\bigvee_{\psi \in S} \psi)$ is satisfiable. Therefore, there exists some $a \in [\![\varphi]\!]$ such that $a \notin \bigvee_{\psi \in S} \psi$. We will inductively prove that this is a contradiction on every iteration of this loop such that $\varphi \in Out_p$.

During the first loop iteration, Out_q is equivalent to the predicates of the outgoing transitions of q. Because M is complete, there exists some $\psi \in Out_q$ such that $a \in [\![\psi]\!]$. So, $\varphi \wedge \psi$ is satisfiable and ψ is an element of S which is a contradiction because $a \notin [\![\bigvee_{\psi \in S} \psi]\!]$. Beyond the first iteration, assume that there exists some $\psi \in Out_q$ at the start of the iteration such that $a \in [\![\psi]\!]$. There are two cases which we must consider:

1. If ψ is not removed from Out_q during this iteration of the loop, then $\psi \wedge \varphi$ is satisfiable and $a \in [\![\psi]\!]$ which is a contradiction.
2. If ψ is removed from Out_q during this iteration, then there exists some $\varphi' \neq \varphi$ in Out_p with $IsSat(\psi \wedge \varphi')$. At the end of this iteration, $\psi \wedge \neg\varphi'$ replaces ψ in Out_q. However, because M is deterministic and $\varphi \neq \varphi'$, $a \notin [\![\varphi']\!]$. Therefore, $a \in [\![\psi \setminus \varphi']\!]$ and $\varphi \wedge (\psi \wedge \varphi')$ is satisfiable. Because $\psi \wedge \varphi' \in Out_q$, this is a contradiction.

So, for any given point in the iteration of this loop, $\varphi \in Out_p$ implies that there exists a finite set $S \subseteq Out_q$ such that $[\![\varphi \wedge \neg(\bigvee_{\psi \in S} \psi)]\!] = \varnothing$. This ensures that the loop over $Out_p \cup Out_q$ is finite. Therefore, `Equiv-p` terminates.

Lemma 2. *A call to* `Equiv-p` *from the body of* `IncrementalMinimize` *returns true if and only if the states p and q of SFA M initially passed to it are equivalent.*

Proof. `Equiv-p` returns false on (p, q) only if the pair (p, q) is contained in *neq*, which only contains pairs of states known to be distinguishable, or if a recursive call to `Equiv-p` returns false. In the later case, we know that p, q can not be equivalent because we have found a string $w \in \mathcal{D}_\mathcal{A}^*$ such that $\delta(p, w)$ and $\delta(q, w)$ are known to be distinguishable.

A recursive call to `Equiv-p` returns true only if (p, q) is contained in *path*, which only occurs if a cycle of indistinguishable states is found, or if all of its recursive calls to `Equiv-p` return true. Therefore, when called from the body of `IncrementalMinimize`, `Equiv-p` returns true only if for all $w \in \mathcal{D}_\mathcal{A}^*$, $\delta(p, w)$ is either known to be equivalent or is indistinguishable from $\delta(q, w)$. Therefore, p, q are equivalent.

Lemma 3. *If a call to* `Equiv-p` *from the body of* `IncrementalMinimize` *returns true, equiv contains only pairs of states* (p, q) *such that p and q are equivalent. If a call to* `Equiv-p` *from the body of* `IncrementalMinimize` *returns false, then path contains only pairs of states* (p, q) *such that p and q are distinguishable.*

Proof. *equiv* is a set of pairs of states such that for all $(p', q') \in equiv$ there exists some $w \in \mathcal{D}_{\mathcal{A}}^*$ with $p' = \delta(p, w)$ and $q' = \delta(q, w)$. If `Equiv-p` returns true on (p, q) then p and q are equivalent by the previous lemma. So, for all $w \in \mathcal{D}_{\mathcal{A}}^*$, $\delta(p, w)$ is equivalent to $\delta(q, w)$. Therefore, each pair of states in *equiv* contains equivalent states.

path is a set of pairs of states that initially contains (p_0, q_0), the initial arguments passed to `Equiv-p`. From that it tracks the path of `Equiv-p` in the depth first traversal of the automata's set of states. That is, for all $(p_i, q_i) \in path$, either $i = 0$ or there exists $(p_{i-1}, q_{i-1}) \in path$ with $p_i = \delta(p_{i-1}, a)$ and $q_i = \delta(q_{i-1}, a)$ for some $a \in \mathcal{D}_A$. If `Equiv-p` returns false on (p_0, q_0), then, every recursive call to $(p_i, q_i) \in path$ has returned false. Since the contents of *path* are not changed if `Equiv-p` returns false, every pair of states in *path* is distinguishable. Hence, these are added to *neq*.

Theorem 2. *Running* `IncrementalMinimize` *on M until termination returns an SFA M' such that M' is minimal and $L(M) = L(M')$.*

Proof. Consider the loop starting in line 5 in `IncrementalMinimize`. This loop checks for all normalized pairs of states p, q for equivalence (if the states have same minimum distance to accepting set of states). Each equivalence check is performed by a call to `Equiv-p`. If `Equiv-p` returns true then, from Lemma 3, every pair of states in *equiv* (including the initial arguments) are equivalent.

Hence, when the loop terminates, the equivalence check on all pairs of states is performed and all possible pairs of equivalent states would be identified. Since `IncrementalMinimize` only merges states that are proved to be equivalent (line 14), all equivalent states would be merged into the same equivalence class. Since all the states that are not merged are not-equivalent, `IncrementalMinimize` returns the minimal symbolic automata.

Our algorithm is incremental because each disjoint set only ever contains states that are known to be equivalent. So, the option to halt computation and return a partially minimized SFA comprised of the merged sets is always available.

`IncrementalMinimize` makes several calls to `Equiv-p`. From the proof of Lemma 1, it follows that at most n^2 recursive calls are made to `Equiv-p`. Each of these recursive calls would take at most k iterations where k is the number of local minterms computed in the loop starting at line 9. Further, each call to the theory solver to generate a in line 10 would take worst-case $f(k)$ time. Finally, the operations for performing `Union` and `Find` can be performed in worst case $\alpha(n)$ where α is the inverse Ackermann's function. Hence, the worst case complexity is $O(n^2 k f(k) \alpha(n))$. Notice that this is comparable to the time complexity of $O(n^2 log n \cdot f(nl))$ of the Hopcroft minimization without minterm generation in [5].

4 Evaluation

We have implemented our symbolic incremental algorithm[1] using the *Symbolic Automata Library*[2] in Java. To evaluate the performance of our algorithm and understand its properties, we have used the automata generated by parsing regular expressions acquired from [7] and initially obtained from the regular expressions library RegExLib [1] as the test suite. Our test suite consists of a nearly two thousand symbolic automata with under 400 states.

Our evaluation consists of 4 parts. First, we compare the performance of incremental symbolic minimization with the symbolic adaptations of the Moore's and Hopcroft's minimization algorithms in [5]. Second, we compare the performance of "naïve" incremental minimization with symbolic incremental minimization. Third, we provide a computational budget that is equal to the running time of the most efficient minimization algorithm and observe the minimization achieved by incremental algorithm. Lastly, we observe the fraction of time spent and compare it with the fraction of minimization achieved.

Comparison with Other Minimization Techniques: In [5], the authors extend Moore's and Hopcroft's algorithm to symbolic domain using minterm generation and present a modified Hopcroft algorithm (i.e., without minterm generation). While Hopcroft's algorithm with minterm generation works better than Moore's for larger state spaces, Moore's algorithm outperforms in the case of larger predicates. For this purpose, we choose Moore's minterm generation and modified Hopcroft algorithm (without minterms) to serve as baseline for our comparison.

Figure 1 compares the average running time of symbolic incremental minimization algorithm to Moore's minterm algorithm and modified Hopcroft's algorithm. In comparison to Moore's algorithm, the incremental algorithm is generally quicker for automata of small size (under about 150 states). However, the minimization time for incremental algorithm grows at almost the same rate (if not more, as seen in some cases) as Moore's algorithm. Additionally, the modified Hopcroft algorithm *almost* always outperforms incremental minimization.

However, there are a few instances, where incremental minimization outperforms modified Hopcroft. These are instances where the automata is already minimized (such as automata with less number of states) or are nearly minimal (e.g. automata with 129 states has 122 equivalence classes). We believe that there are two primary reasons for this behavior. First, the number of partitions created by modified Hopcroft algorithm increases when the automata is near minimal. Second, the worst case time complexity of incremental minimization and modified Hopcroft are close.

---

[1] https://github.uconn.edu/jah12014/symbolic-automata-research.
[2] https://github.com/lorisdanto/symbolicautomata.

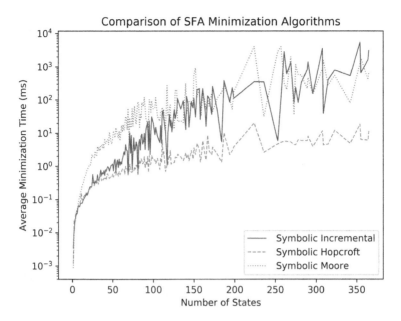

Fig. 1. Plot of the time taken by incremental minimization, Moore's algorithm with minterm generation and modified Hopcroft without minterm generation.

Comparison Between Naïve and Symbolic Incremental Minimization: Figure 2 compares our symbolic incremental algorithm to a "naïve" incremental algorithm. This naive algorithm consists of computing the minterms, i.e., the maximal set of satisfiable Boolean combinations of the predicate set in Boolean algebra. It then treats the symbolic automata as if it were a classical DFA with the minterm set as its alphabet, and runs the incremental DFA minimization algorithm on it. In general, any classical algorithm can be modified to run symbolic automata in this way [8]. However, because of this upfront computational cost of minterm computation, the naïve algorithm runs noticeably slower than our symbolic algorithm for small automata. Interestingly though, as the number of states in the automata increases, both algorithms appear to converge to the same running time. This is a surprising but not unreasonable result. Intuitively, our symbolic algorithm computes the local minterms between the predicates of outgoing states while minimization is in progress. On the other hand, the naive algorithm performs all of this computation upfront.

Incremental Minimization Under Time Budget: We run the incremental minimization (both with and without minterm generation) under a time budget. The time budget corresponds to the minimization time taken by the modified Hopcroft algorithm. When the time budget expires, the minimization algorithms are halted and the fraction of minimization achieved is reported. Figure 3 presents the fraction of minimization achieved with the budget.

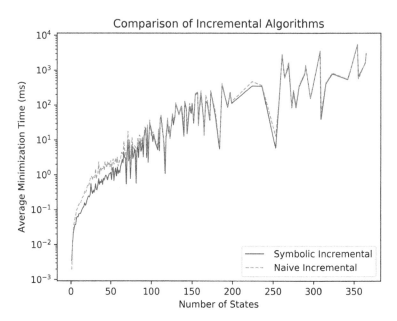

Fig. 2. Time taken by incremental minimization with minterm generation vs without minterm generation.

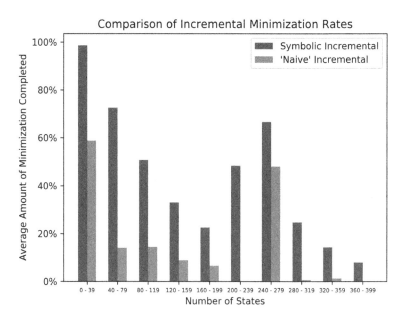

Fig. 3. Incremental minimization achieved under computational budget.

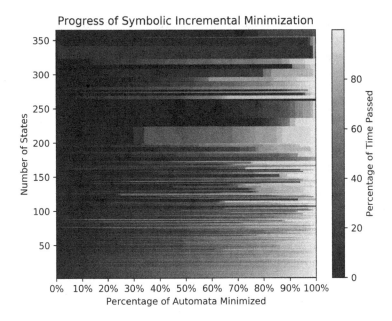

Fig. 4. Heatmap of the time taken over number of states and minimization achieved.

The symbolic incremental minimization always outperforms the naïve incremental minimization with minterms. Although both incremental algorithms take about the same time to fully complete minimization, Fig. 3 reveals that the symbolic incremental algorithm reduces the state size of the given automata significantly quicker than the naive algorithm during its early runtime. Furthermore, the number of minterms might be exponential in the number of predicates. Hence, using an incremental minimization algorithm that takes exponential time pre-processing does not capture the spirit of incremental minimization.

Time Taken vs Minimization Achieved: To understand the nature of incremental minimization, we present a heat map of the average time (as a fraction of the total minimization time) that the algorithm took to reach a certain amount of minization in Fig. 4. Blue regions correspond to less amount of time taken (0–50%) and Yellow corresponds to the more time (50–100%). Observe that for automata with less number of states (<100), the time taken for minimization is fairly proportional to the minimization achieved. However, as the number of states increases (>200), it takes less than 20% of time to achieve 80% minimization for majority of the automata.

5   Related Work

Minimization of automata has been a very well studied topic with classical results from Huffman [12], Moore [13], Hopcroft [11], and Brzozowski [4]. The concept of automata with transitions labeled by predicates was first conceived in [17] and first studied in [15]. Moore's algorithm for DFA minimization was first extended to symbolic automata in [16]. The non-incremental algorithms that we compare our algorithm against in Fig. 1 were adapted from the symbolic minimization algorithms presented in [5]. These algorithms were generalized to the computation of forward bisimulations for nondeterministic symbolic finite automata in [6]. The minimization of symbolic transducers is also studied in [14]. A good overview of the theory and applications of symbolic automata and symbolic transducers is included in [8].

An incremental algorithm for DFA minimization was first proposed by Watson [18]. However, the worst case performance of this algorithm was exponential. An efficient incremental algorithm was presented by Almeida et al. in [3] and tended to outperform Hopcroft's algorithm in empirical evaluation [2]. Our symbolic incremental algorithm was an adaptation of algorithm in [3]. An incremental hybrid of the algorithms by Hopcroft and Almeida et al. was given in [9]. To the best of our knowledge, this paper is the first in presenting an incremental algorithm for minimization of symbolic automata.

In a seminal work on algebraic properties of sequential machines [10], the authors present a notion of partitions (subsets of states) over set of states and prove that they form a lattice. The minimization algorithms are essentially various lattice traversal mechanisms that eventually reach the partition corresponding to automata with minimal number of state. Incremental minimization is a strictly upward lattice traversal mechanism, whereas traditional minimization algorithms are strictly downward lattice traversal mechanisms.

6   Conclusion and Future Work

We have extended an incremental DFA minimization algorithm to symbolic automata. For large automata, this incremental algorithm does not perform as well as the most efficient algorithms for symbolic minimization. However, unlike the other symbolic minimization algorithms, the incremental algorithm can be halted at any time to return a partially minimized automata. Additionally, our algorithm is preferable to the naïve adaptation of incremental minimization via minterm generation. Our experimental results show that, unlike the naive algorithm, the symbolic algorithm achieves the majority of minimization during its early runtime. This makes the symbolic algorithm superior as an incremental algorithm.

As a part of the future work, we would like to improve the efficiency of symbolic incremental minimization by performing memoization. We would also like to extend the incremental minimization to non-deterministic symbolic automata.

Acknowledgements. The authors would like to thank anonymous reviews for their feedback. The work done in this paper is based upon work supported by the National Science Foundation (NSF) under grant numbers CNS 1739936, 1935724. Any opinions, findings, and conclusions or recommendations expressed in this publication are those of the authors and do not necessarily reflect the views of NSF.

References

1. Regexlib. http://www.regexlib.com/
2. Almeida, M., Moreira, N., Reis, R.: On the performance of automata minimization algorithms. In: Proceedings of the 4th Conference on Computation in Europe: Logic and Theory of Algorithms, pp. 3–14 (2007)
3. Almeida, M., Moreira, N., Reis, R.: Incremental DFA minimisation. In: Domaratzki, M., Salomaa, K. (eds.) CIAA 2010. LNCS, vol. 6482, pp. 39–48. Springer, Heidelberg (2011). https://doi.org/10.1007/978-3-642-18098-9_5
4. Brzozowski, J.A.: Canonical regular expressions and minimal state graphs for definite events. Math. Theory Automata 12(6), 529–561 (1962)
5. D'Antoni, L., Veanes, M.: Minimization of symbolic automata. In: ACM SIGPLAN Notices, vol. 49, pp. 541–553. ACM (2014)
6. D'Antoni, L., Veanes, M.: Forward bisimulations for nondeterministic symbolic finite automata. In: Legay, A., Margaria, T. (eds.) TACAS 2017. LNCS, vol. 10205, pp. 518–534. Springer, Heidelberg (2017). https://doi.org/10.1007/978-3-662-54577-5_30
7. D'Antoni, L.: Symbolicautomata. https://github.com/lorisdanto/symbolicautomata/. Accessed 30 Oct 2017
8. D'Antoni, L., Veanes, M.: The power of symbolic automata and transducers. In: Majumdar, R., Kunčak, V. (eds.) CAV 2017. LNCS, vol. 10426, pp. 47–67. Springer, Cham (2017). https://doi.org/10.1007/978-3-319-63387-9_3
9. García, P., de Parga, M., Velasco, J.A., López, D.: A split-based incremental deterministic automata minimization algorithm. Theory Comput. Syst. 57(2), 319–336 (2015)
10. Hartmanis, J.: Algebraic structure theory of sequential machines (prentice-hall international series in applied mathematics) (1966)
11. Hopcroft, J.: An n log n algorithm for minimizing states in a finite automaton. In: Theory of Machines and Computations, pp. 189–196, Elsevier (1971)
12. Huffman, D.A.: The synthesis of sequential switching circuits. J. Franklin Inst. 257(3), 161–190 (1954)
13. Moore, E.F.: Gedanken-experiments on sequential machines. Automata stud. 34, 129–153 (1956)
14. Saarikivi, O., Veanes, M.: Minimization of symbolic transducers. In: Majumdar, R., Kunčak, V. (eds.) CAV 2017. LNCS, vol. 10427, pp. 176–196. Springer, Cham (2017). https://doi.org/10.1007/978-3-319-63390-9_10
15. van Noord, G., Gerdemann, D.: Finite state transducers with predicates and identities. Grammars 4(3), 263–286 (2001)
16. Veanes, M., De Halleux, P., Tillmann, N.: Rex: symbolic regular expression explorer. In: International Conference on Software Testing, Verification and Validation, pp. 498–507. IEEE (2010)
17. Watson, B.W.: Implementing and using finite automata toolkits. Nat. Lang. Eng. 2(4), 295–302 (1996)
18. Watson, B.W.: An incremental DFA minimization algorithm. In: International Workshop on Finite-State Methods in Natural Language Processing, Helsinki, Finland (2001)

Seamless Interactive Program Verification

Sarah Grebing[1]([✉]), Jonas Klamroth[2], and Mattias Ulbrich[1]([✉])

[1] Karlsruhe Institute of Technology, Karlsruhe, Germany
grebing@ira.uka.de, ulbrich@kit.edu
[2] FZI Research Center for Information Technology, Karlsruhe, Germany

Abstract. Deductive program verification has made considerable progress in recent years. Automation is the goal, but it is apparent that there will always be challenges that cannot be verified fully automatically, but require some form of user input. We present a novel user interaction concept that allows the user to interact with the verification system on different abstraction levels and on different verification/proof artifacts. The elements of the concept are based on the findings of qualitative user studies we conducted amongst users of interactive deductive program verification systems. Moreover, the concept implements state-of-the-art user interaction principles. We prototypically implemented our concept as an interactive verification tool for Dafny programs.

Deductive program verification tasks lead to challenging logical reasoning tasks. Recent and ongoing progress of satisfiability modulo theories (SMT) solvers allow these tasks to be more and more automated. As program verification is an undecidable problem, one can always find verification tasks which cannot be verified automatically – in practice, many real-world verification tasks require user guidance such that automatic reasoning engines can find a proof. With rising success of automatic verification engines, programs that require inspection become more and more sophisticated. They are likely to operate on complex data structures or make use of advanced features like concurrency.

This complexity contributes to the fact that guiding the verification tool is a non-trivial, iterative process which, in addition, requires knowledge about internals of the verification tool. First proof attempts for a verification task are likely to result in an unfinished proof either because the code does not satisfy its specification or because the given guidance is not sufficient to allow automation to close the proof. To proceed in the verification process, it is crucial for the user to be able to understand the reason for a failed proof attempt to either remedy the flaw or to provide the right guidance.

The main contribution of this paper is an interaction concept for interactive verification that supports users in understanding unfinished program verification situations and allows them to provide the right guidance to the underlying automatic reasoning engines. It allows users (a) to choose from different representations of the proof state and the kind of interaction style for proof construction according to the user's preferences and the current proof situation, (b) to seamlessly switch between proof state representations when another one seems more

S. Chakraborty and J. A. Navas (Eds.): VSTTE 2019, LNCS 12031, pp. 68–86, 2020.
https://doi.org/10.1007/978-3-030-41600-3_6

informative, (c) to easily recognize relations between information artifacts shown to the user in the different representations, and (d) to focus on challenging proof subtasks, leaving trivial subtasks to the (automatic) prover.

In state-of-the-art verification systems, the user can interact on different *scopes* of the verification problem: the formal specification, the program code, and the logical representation of the proof state. Depending on which scope a verification system focuses on, different advantages arise: Systems that allow conducting proofs by annotating the source code have the advantage that the user can operate on the same abstraction level as the original source code and needs not understand the logical encoding. Comprehending why a proof attempt failed can be difficult in these verification systems because of the high degree of abstraction. In contrast, systems that allow users to directly manipulate on the logical encoding level may lack the possibility to understand how the encoding relates to the source code. Either way the user is faced with the problem that most state-of-the-art verification systems either offer only one possible representation or do no support the user in understanding the relations between different representations.

Our hypothesis is that one major bottleneck for finding proofs with verification tools is the difficulty of comprehending and exploring unfinished proofs. Without providing methods to support these tasks, advancing proofs gets extremely challenging. Users need means to be able to understand and explore the proof state in order to make an informed decision for the next goal-oriented action.

The remainder of this paper is structured as follows. In Sect. 1, we present preliminaries, followed by a brief summary of the results of our user studies in Sect. 2. Based on these results we present our interaction concept in Sect. 3 and its realization in a prototype in Sect. 4. We present related work in Sect. 5 and conclude the paper with future work in Sect. 6.

1 Setting the Stage: Interactive Program Verification

1.1 Verification Task

To prove properties of programs with a verification system, different proof artifacts interact during the verification process. First the user has to express the desired properties of a software system, the *requirement specification*, using a specification formalism understood by the verification system. Moreover, the user may provide additional specification elements for prover guidance, called *auxiliary specification* [1].

We refer to the program to be verified, together with its specification as *proof input artifacts*. In our case the specification is given in form of annotations of the program. We consider a software system to be composed of different modules and each module may in turn contain different methods and functions. The most basic components of a software system we consider here for verification are thus single methods. We will call a pair of a requirement specification and a software system currently under verification a *concern* [2]. Depending on the context, a requirement specification of a concern may in turn be an auxiliary specification in the larger picture.

Listing 1.1. Running Example Linked List

```
1   class List {
2     ghost var seqq: seq<int>
3     ghost var nodeseqq: seq<Node>
4     var head: Node
5     method getAt(pos: int) returns (v: int)
6       requires 0 ≤ pos < |seqq| ∧ Valid()
7       ensures v == seqq[pos]
8     {
9       var idx := 0;
10      var node := head;
11      while(idx < pos)
12        decreases |seqq| - idx
13        invariant 0 ≤ idx ≤ pos
14        invariant node == nodeseqq[idx]
15      {
16        node := node.next;
17        idx := idx + 1;
18      }
19      v := node.value;
20    } ...
21  }
```

As running example we use the Dafny implementation of a singly-linked list in Listing 1.1 The program contains two classes Node and List. A node has a value field and a pointer to the next node. A list object points to the first node (the head) of the list (line 4). The class List contains the method getAt() (in lines 5–20) and a function Valid() (not shown in the Listing 1.1). For verification purposes we added two *ghost fields* seqq and nodeseqq (lines 2 and 3) which have no effect on the program execution. They shadow the list's content. The sequence seqq is the sequence of values, and nodeseqq is the sequence of the list nodes. The function Valid() is a predicate which is true if these sequences correspond to the list's content and serves as the *object invariant* of the list. We will focus on the method getAt() returning the value at a given index. In the implementation we iterate until the given index is reached and then return the value of that node. The requirement specification of the method getAt() is its pre- and postcondition pair in lines 6–7.

The proof task for a concern (e.g., the correctness of a method) can be divided into smaller individual and located proofs units which we will call *verification conditions (VC)*. We distinguish two levels of the proof process: the *global level*, i.e., finding the right formalization for a concern, and the *local level*, i.e., proving single VCs. One example for VCs is to generate a proof obligation for each conjunct in the postcondition when considering a method contract. If all VCs can be proven valid, the system is correct w.r.t. its requirement specification. In our running example, one VC would be to prove that the second part of the loop invariant (line 14) is preserved in each loop iteration. The proof obligation then encodes this VC logically, as shown in the screenshot in Fig. 4.

1.2   Interaction Styles

Program verification systems can be categorized by their type of user interaction from purely automatic systems, over auto-active systems up to interactive program verification systems (see Fig. 1).

While user interaction in automatic systems is limited to starting the proof system, in auto-active systems user interaction is limited to adding guiding annotations to the program to be verified. Interactive systems allow users to interact and guide the proof search on the logical representation of the proof problem. Mainly two interaction styles are supported for proof construction: direct manipulation (e.g., in KeY [3]) and text-based interaction (e.g., in Coq [4] or Isabelle/HOL [5]). Text-based interaction can furthermore be divided into script-based and command-language-based styles. In the following, we will briefly introduce these different styles.

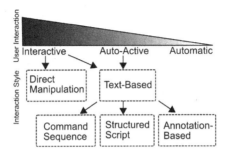

Fig. 1. Categorization of program verification systems and their user interaction

Direct Manipulation. According to Schneiderman [6], the central ideas for *direct manipulation* are that the objects the users are interacting with have a visual representation on the screen and the actions applied to these objects are "rapid, reversible and incremental". Users use a pointing device to select objects on the screen which they then can perform actions on. It is crucial that the representation of the elements of the task domain is chosen thoughtfully – otherwise, the representation may be more confusing than helpful. In interactive program verification the objects are the proof obligations, the program with its specification and the proof. Actions on these objects include changing parts of the program or its specification, applying rules to parts of a proof obligation and modifying parts of the proof.

Text-Based Interaction. The *command-language* or *command line interaction* forms the basic principle for text-based interaction. Users formulate actions as commands followed by a textual representation of the objects that are being manipulated. The action is only executed when users complete their commands and explicitly execute them. For more complex actions *command sequences* can be provided, where the commands are executed in a sequential order.

The *structured script-based interaction* is a more sophisticated form of the textual interaction style. In addition to the commands in the CLI interaction the user may use control flow structures to combine commands to more complex actions. Script-based interaction can be found in different theorem provers, e.g., Isabelle/HOL [5] or the Coq [4] verification system. The kind of proof language differs between the systems. While Isabelle's proof language Isar [7] follows a more textbook style of proof construction, Coq's proof language together with its tactic language LTac [8] is closer to a programming language. Feedback is given by presenting the goal states after executing a proof script. If the proof attempt was not successful, the user needs to inspect the proof to find the cause for any remaining open goal. Advantages of this interaction style is that experienced users are able to formulate proofs efficiently as long as the interface supports the user in text editing and programming (e.g., with auto-completion or syntax highlighting). A disadvantage of this interaction style is that the principle *recognition rather than recall* [9–11] for applying the appropriate tactic can be missing, even if auto completion exists. Also, insight into the application of tactics is often missing in these systems.

Auto-active systems, such as OpenJML [12] or Dafny [13] also allow for a kind of text-based interaction purely on *annotation-level*. In this textual interaction style, users interact with the proof system by providing the program and its specification together with further assertions in the source code. These assertions serve as hints for the proof system for the proof search. Feedback is only given in terms of the program and its specification by using visual highlights on program statements alongside with textual messages. Compared to programming the auto-active style is similar to the idea of literate programming [14], where the documentation and the source code are interweaved. One idea behind this interaction style is to hide the proof object and the verification system from the user. Hence, the user does not need to change between different proof artifacts (and thus contexts) when constructing the program and its specification. However, when trying to find the cause for a failed proof attempt detailed insight into the logical representation of the proof problem may be needed [15].

2   User Activities Revealed in User Studies

To gain insights into which actions users perform in the program verification process and to identify factors for time-consuming interactions, we conducted qualitative, explorative user studies with intermediate and expert users of interactive verification systems. In particular, we were interested in the proof step granularities, the time-consuming actions and the feedback mechanisms the verification systems offer. We conducted two focus group discussions [16–18]: one for Isabelle/HOL as a representative for a verification system with script-based interaction and one for the interactive program verification system for Java programs KeY [3], as representative for the direct manipulation interaction style.

Subsequently, we conducted semi-structured interviews together with practical tasks where the participants were asked to perform a proof for a small program with the help of KeY. In this study we have also shown different proof states to the participants and asked for a description of the states [18].[1]

The actions of the participants in the practical tasks have been recorded, and in the analysis phase we have extracted consolidated sequence models [19, 20]. The answers to the interview questions and the voices of the focus group discussions have been evaluated using qualitative content analysis methods [21].

The following are the key results of our user studies influencing our concept.

Different Domain Elements have to be Combined. The evaluation of the user interactions in the practical tasks revealed that one common interaction was that users switched between the different representations of the proof state and the annotated program to relate parts of the specification, respectively program to the formulas in the proof state. One participant in the KeY user study even placed the text editor containing the annotated program next to the proof state with its open goals to find the relation between the artifacts. Switching between contexts can be costly for users: firstly, users needs to (re)gain the orientation in each representation, and, secondly, users need to relate artifacts to each other that refer to the same state but are represented in a different formalism.

Many Degrees of Freedom. Our evaluation also revealed that there is not *one single* proof process that is followed, rather users take advantage of the many degrees of freedom in user interaction for proof construction and proof comprehension provided by the systems. One example is that some participants used KeY in a first attempt to gain feedback on an initial specification they provided to be able to step-wise adjust it, while others started by using a lot of time to come up with the right specification before using the KeY system for proof construction. For proof construction participants used the full range from performing single proof steps, combinations with sequences of proof steps that were performed automatically by the prover up to fully automatic proof search. For creative tasks like proof construction the degrees of freedom in the interaction are advantageous, however, when developing an interaction concept these degrees of freedom need to be taken into account to not limit expert users.

Alternation of Abstraction and Focusing. As users tried to gain orientation in the proof, we were able to observe an alternation between abstracting from and focusing on specific details of the proof state: users tried to gain an overview over the proof by adjusting the view onto the proof tree, e.g., with hiding features that remove intermediate proof steps from the displayed tree such that only branching nodes are visible. After gaining an overview, users then focused on specific open goals by navigating to them to see in which cases the proof stays open and then focused on sequents and single formulas in the goal. In a subsequent step, users related the inspected elements to the input artifacts.

From our observations in the user studies, we derived the hypothesis that users of interactive program verification systems need both an overview over the system and the bigger picture of the proof task and a way to focus on specific

---

[1] Further details can also be found https://formal.iti.kit.edu/~grebing/SWC.

parts of the proof problem. At the same time users need different ways to interact with the proof system for proof comprehension and proof construction.

3   Seamless Interaction Concept

Our interaction concept presented in the following is based on observations from our user studies, on established design principles, on existing interaction functionalities of state-of-the-art verification systems, and on the usability principles for theorem provers by Easthaughffe [22]. Our concept follows the assumption that users must have the ability to interact on a high level of abstraction, the programming language level like in the auto-active approach, but at the same time must be able to learn about and work on the level of the logical proof encoding, like in the interactive approach.

In our concept, we support users (a) in accessing and combining information from different domains during proof state inspection and proof construction by structuring the proof state into views, (b) in gaining both an overview over the proof state and focusing on details, by providing a view containing proof and system information, together with a mechanism to seamlessly switch between the views. At the same time, our concept retains the idea of many degrees of freedom, e.g., by allowing proof construction in each view and by providing mechanisms to inspect dependencies between the views.

We have seen in our user studies that users need different context information both to comprehend the proof situation and to advance the proof. Which information is needed depends both on the concern the user is focused on and also on whether the user is working on the global or local level.

One challenge of providing the user with the right amount of information are existing dependencies between the different constituents of the system and between the requirement specification and auxiliary specification currently in focus. To support users in proof construction and proof comprehension, we provide multiple *projections* of the proof problem and proof state (shown in Fig. 2), each with their own set of available interactions. The complexity of the proof problem is reduced by concentrating on a subset of dependencies at a time and by providing the required information (resp. hiding unnecessary information) whenever possible during the verification process.

Our concept also supports verification by means for *abstraction* of, as well as *focusing* on details of the proof problem and by breaking down the proof task into smaller *subtasks*. This step-wise focusing should help the user in keeping the overview and dependency information gained from one representation and transferring this knowledge between representations.

One key feature of our concept is that users can choose their preferred way of interacting with the proof system and use the different interaction styles interchangeably. For this we integrate direct manipulation with structured scripts. Actions performed using the direct manipulation style are textually encoded and added to the proof script, adhering to the usability principle of *substituitivity* [23]. The script also serves as a mean to advance the proof by allowing users to textually add proof commands to the script and executing it.

3.1 Projections: Multiple Views onto the Proof Problem

To support users in the verification task we propose multiple projections on the proof problem to be presented to users in different views. These views support users on the level they are currently working on but also take into account that users shift their focus during the proof process. Presenting multiple views of the proof state and allowing meaningful operations on those views are considered as two usability principles for theorem provers. The different views should support users in forming models of the proof task to be able to choose the most appropriate representation for the next goal-directed action [22].

To allow for a seamless change from the global to the local level, users have to be able to inspect dependencies between the components of the verification target, as well as the relations between levels. As a prerequisite, these dependencies need to be made visible to the user.

We assume that the user has a different *focus* on the components on each level and thus different context information may have to be shown to the user. This idea adheres to the usability principle of *anticipation*, which makes the claim that "all information and tools needed for each step in the process" [24] should be provided to the user.

We consider the following views (see Fig. 2) as essential for program verification: ① a view showing the system and proof structure as well as the proof progress overview, ② a view showing the proof input artifacts, i.e, the source code and its annotations,

③ a view that focuses on the logical representation of a single VC with the possibility to construct a deductive proof for this VC(④).

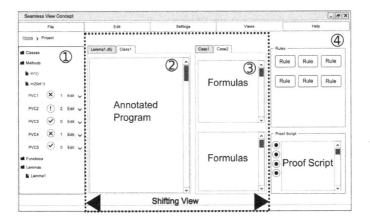

Fig. 2. Abstract concept of our user interface. From left to right: the *System and Proof Overview* (①), the *Source Code View* (②), the *Logical View* (③) and the *Proof Manipulation View* (④). The user can access two adjacent views at the same time (indicated by the dotted rectangle).

Source Code View

In our user study (described in Sect. 2), participants accessed the annotated program in different phases of the process and with different intents and actions: to formulate the requirement and auxiliary annotations at the beginning of the process, as well as for inspection and modification of the annotated program during the proof.

There are different possibilities to display the program and its annotations to the user: both artifacts can be either shown in a combined view or shown separately, but also the amount of annotations that are shown can vary (e.g., showing all annotations as provided by the user, or only certain parts).

Showing both artifacts in a combined view allows users to access information that is closely related and allows for an easy navigation of dependencies between the annotations and the source code locations for inspection. A further advantage is that the maintenance of annotations is simplified such that when changing the source code, the annotations can be directly adjusted as well.

Using two separate views for the program and the annotations would provide more *visual clarity* compared to the sometimes cluttered source code shown in a combined view. Furthermore, a multi-formalism document is avoided, allowing users to stay in one formalism for each view, reducing the user's cognitive load.

The source code view needs to provide actions to capture the following user intents: the comprehension of the proof problem or the proof state, the search for mistakes in the proof input artifacts, the construction of the program and adding (auxiliary) annotations.

As support for inspection, mechanisms have to be provided to inspect the relation between elements of the proof state and the proof input artifacts to support the comprehension tasks. Support to proceed in the verification process should include functionalities similar to common text editing features found in IDEs (e.g., program refactoring) and features for navigation through the source code. Furthermore, to provide immediate feedback to the user, support for writing the annotated program in the form of auto-completion and checking for syntax errors should be provided.

System and Proof Overview

Similarly to the systems to be verified, also concerns have an internal (hierarchical) structure. This structure helps to divide the large task into smaller sub-tasks. It is crucial for the user to gain an overview over the system and its dependencies to build up a mental model about the problem and the proof progress to facilitate decisions about the next actions to take. Providing dependency information also supports the user in keeping track of parts of specifications that influence each other during the proof process.

We devise a view to support the user in gaining a *global* overview over the concern and the proof task. This view allows for activities to progress in the proof process on a more global level, as well as provide means for navigation to the individual proofs for a concern. Typical activities we consider for this view are the *selection* of proof artifacts for inspection, *selection* of proof tasks to work on and *browsing activities* to build a mental model about the problem structure.

The system and verification task structure in this view is shown as a collapsible tree. A further possibility to show call dependencies and dependencies between different specifications needs to be available in this view to support the user in comprehending impacts of modifications to one of involved elements.

In addition to the browsing activities, the user is able to apply general proof search strategies to all or a part of the VCs in this view without the need to know the internal details of the proof. If the proof search is able to prove the concern there is no need for the user to look into the proof, allowing the user to focus on VCs that need further attention. We observed such activities during the user study, where some participants used the automatic proof search strategies of KeY to determine which parts need detailed inspection or interaction.

Logical and Proof Construction View

In auto-active verification systems, users need to come up with auxiliary annotations for which often insight into the logical encoding is needed [1,15]. We propose a view that enables users to gain insight into the logical encoding (VC) and the deduction steps performed, if they are not able to solve the problem on the program level. Users should be able to focus on one verification task in isolation.

The notation of the logical encoding should be as close as possible to the input artifacts, e.g., names of identifiers such as fields in the program should not be renamed by deduction steps. This would adhere to the principle of *consistency* [23,25]. In cases where renaming cannot be avoided, a possibility to trace back to the original version of an entity should be provided. In the user study the renaming issue and the retracing of the origin of symbols was criticized by participants.

On the logical view, proof construction takes place on the most detailed level. Here, the user focuses on the individual propositions that are either assumed or need to be proven for the corresponding program state. We argue that formulas with similar origins should be displayed close to each other, e.g., by grouping formulas resulting from the precondition of a program together.

To deal with large logical representations, the user should have possibilities to freely customize the logical view. It should be possible to abstract from formula sets by hiding them or by abbreviating them by names. Furthermore, formulas should be arbitrarily arrangeable (by grouping and sorting).

A natural choice to allow proof construction in this view is via direct manipulation: by pointing and clicking onto terms and formulas the user retrieves possible rule applications for the selected position and is able to apply them. As users should be prevented from performing actions by mistake, it is essential to be able to observe the result of a rule application before actually applying it. This information should be given both on a more abstract level, to give a rough estimate about the rule's effect (e.g., by showing how many branches result from the rule application) and on a more detailed level, to provide an insight into how the proof would evolve if the rule would be applied.

Additionally, to be able to persist the interaction we devise that also a sub view of the logical view should contain the possibility to perform the proof using textual interaction. We will call this sub view *script-view*.

Both interaction styles should be usable interchangeably and in alternation, to allow for different user preferences. Interactions performed using direct manipulation have to automatically extend the proof script. This also allows that the actions performed using direct manipulation are reversible, as users just have to delete the corresponding statement in the script.

Besides the single VCs, also the current overall proof state needs to be presented to the user to allow for navigation through the proof performed so far.

3.2   Relations Between Proof Artifacts

Up to now, we have addressed the difficulties that arise with the system's and problem's structure and dependencies on each view individually. However, dependency relations also exist between the different proof artifacts across the different proposed views. These dependencies are often implicit and users need to keep them in mind while proving or invest resources to search for these dependencies, as was also observable in our user study. One building block of our concept is thus to make these *hidden dependencies* [26] visible to the user.

Concerning the verification target, each implementation in the *source code view* has a representation in the *system overview* that shows its location in the system hierarchy. This information about call contexts of subsystems can be used by the user when formulating requirement specifications of the subsystems.

For an overview over the proof task, not only the proof progress is important but also the information about dependencies between the proof obligations, the proof input artifacts, the VCs, as well as lemmas. This dependency information is necessary to get an overview about what can be (re)used during the proofs.

The VCs in the *system and proof overview* have a relation to the properties of a subsystem, i.e., a VC has a relation to a path through the program and the annotations along this path. A VC also has a direct relation to the *logical view* where the logical representation is a formalization of the VC. The two relations together induce the relation between the individual formulas in the logical representation and the annotated program. Formulas in the *logical view* can have their origin from statements in the program or the annotations or from specific rule applications, such as the cut-rule.

Between the Script View and the Logical View relations exist as well. Each statement in the script corresponds to a proof state of a VC, which evolves by applying rules. Altogether, there exists a relation between a rule application, a statement in the proof script and the logical representation of the proof state, e.g., a node in a proof tree. It is crucial for user support to make these relations visible. As the number of relations may become large, it is advisable to display this information on user request.

Furthermore, we devise to support "zooming-in" from the abstract overview to the detailed representation, which was also observable in the user study. This especially means to support the user in switching between the different views and keeping track of the dependencies that exist in one view but also the dependencies between the views. This can be supported by positioning views sequentially, i.e., starting with the most abstract view (proof and project overview) down to the detailed logical view, and thus restricting the work-flow to the "zooming-in" process. This restriction ensures that important relations are always visible and can be inspected. The proposed arrangement of views supports users in carrying over relevant information from one view to another in two ways: firstly by placing contextually close views next to each other and secondly by always keeping the last view present when switching to a new one. Further support could be to allow the user to trace the origin of element across the different views.

4 Realization of the Concept

The presented concept is prototypically implemented as a tool called DIVE (Dafny Interactive Verification Environment)[2] for programs written in Dafny.

The main window of DIVE is split up into 4 different views (as shown in Fig. 2): the *System and Proof Overview*, the *Source Code View*, *Logical View* and the *Proof Manipulation View*. Each view corresponds to a different projection of the same proof state. In the course of this section we will first present each view and their relations in more detail and then give an exemplary walk-through to depict a common series of user interactions. The reader might choose to read the walk-through first depending on their preferences.

The Source Code View. (② in Fig. 3) shows the proof input artifacts. In DIVE this view is a tabbed window with standard text editor features. We included

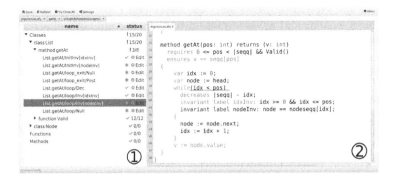

Fig. 3. The *Project and Proof Overview* (①) and the *Source Code View* (②) of DIVE adjacent to each other. This view is the first view users see when loading a project.

---

[2] Available at https://github.com/mattulbrich/dive.

syntax highlighting for the annotated source code as a visual user guidance, as well as syntax checking with a visual highlighting of the location containing a syntax error.

As soon as users edit any proof input artifact in the source code view, the contents of *all* other views are disabled as the information presented in these views is outdated. This decision has been made to maintain a consistent state of all proof artifacts. These views are re-enabled as soon as the user saves the changes. We chose to refresh the project state only if the user explicitly requests this refresh to avoid unnecessary reload attempts during typing.

The System and Proof Overview. (see ① in Fig. 3) enables users to quickly get an overview of the overall progress made so far. It allows users to see how many VCs are still open/closed, as well as the structure of the overall proof and the navigation to the logical representation of a VC.

We show the hierarchical structure of the components of the verification target in a tree view. Besides these (sub)systems of the verification target, we also include lemmas written by the user in this tree view. The tree structure is collapsible and expandable to allow the user to either gain a more abstract overview or to be able to focus on single components of the system.

To support the user in relating a VC to the annotated program the VC identifiers encode the symbolic execution path, followed by the VC's purpose. Also, users can add labels that are used in the VC's name.

To allow for an overview over the proof progress, for proof inspection and proof construction on the system level, we included means for interacting with the VCs in the tree structure. For each VC, an indicator of its proof status is shown, the number of proof branches in a proof and a possibility to select the VC for proof construction on the local level. Users can start proof construction in this view by selecting a (sub)system or VC and applying a general SMT solver or script. When selecting a system, the corresponding implementation is shown in the *Source Code View*. Expanding a system results in displaying the hierarchical structure of the system down to all VCs. Users can retrieve a presentation of the VCs for a system and a VC's relation to the program control structure by selecting a single VC. Upon selection, in the *Source Code View* the relevant part of the source code is put into focus together with a highlight of those statements that correspond to the symbolic execution path for the selected VC.

The Logical View. (see ③ in Fig. 4) shows the logical representation of a VC. We decided to use a sequent calculus as underlying logic so VCs are shown as sequents. This view consists of two list views which represent the antecedent and succedent of a sequent. Formulas in the antecedent may be assumed for the selected VC (e.g., preconditions) whereas to discharge the VC at least one of the formulas of the succedent has to be shown (e.g., assertions or post-conditions).

During proof construction branching rules may be applied to a sequent such that the VC has more than one branch. In this case the logic view is tabbed to allow the user to navigate between different branches. When applying rules the effect of the last rule application is also shown as graphical hints in the logic view so that users are able to see the consequences of actions.

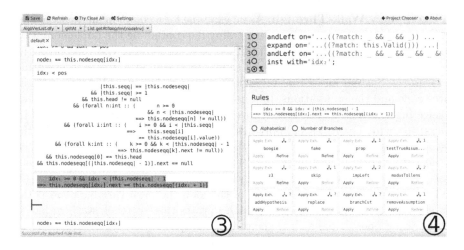

Fig. 4. The *Logical View* (③) and the *Proof Manipulation View* (④) of DIVE. These views adjoin to the right of the views in Fig. 3

Additionally users are able to request the origin of (sub-)formulas displayed in the logic view. These origins may stem from the source code (e.g. a pre- or postcondition) in which case the responsible part in the source code is highlighted or may have resulted from rule applications in which case the relevant part of the script in the *Proof Manipulation View* is highlighted. This allows users to relate the elements in the projections to each other and build up as well as keep a mental model consistent with the proof state.

The Proof Manipulation View. (see ④ in Fig. 4) allows proof construction using the two interaction styles direct manipulation and text-based interchangeably. Each manipulation technique is modeled in DIVE with one subview which supports users in manipulating the proof in their desired way.

The *Script View* is a text field where the user can manually extend the proof script. This view also allows users to navigate through different proof states of one VC by placing the cursor in the script on a proof command or clicking on *checkpoint markers* next to the script. The script is only executed on request to prevent repeated executions when no full command has been provided.

The *Rule View* allows users to apply rules using direct manipulation. Users select formulas (or sub-formulas) in the *Logical View* and a list of applicable rules appear in the rule view. Each rule is displayed as panel with the name of the rule, the number of branches that would be opened if this rule is applied and the possibility to apply this rule to the selected formula. Additionally if a panel is selected the effects of applying this rule are shown in the *Logical View*. All these features support users in gaining information about the effect of applying a certain rule and thus allows users to make an informed decision which rule to apply in which situation. Applying a rule automatically updates the script and the *Logical View* to represent the new proof state.

An Exemplary Walk-Through. As an example for a common interaction with DIVE, consider that the user loads the Dafny file containing the implementation of our running example. This results in the system showing the content of the file in the Source Code View, at the same time, the VCs are generated and shown in the System and Proof Overview. The user is now able to modify the source code and the annotations. In a next step the proof process can be started by selecting the VCs in the system overview and applying solvers (e.g., SMT solvers) to them. The result of applying these solvers to all generated VCs of the class `List` is depicted in Fig. 3. In our example, some VCs stay open (indicated by the red symbol). The user may now focus on those VCs in the subsequent steps. For example, the second invariant remains open. The proof obligation (③ in Fig. 4) states that at each iteration of the loop the local variable `node` is the `i`-th element of the ghost sequence which mirrors the list (thus stating that at each iteration `node` is the `i`-th element of the list).

To close the proof the correct instantiation of a quantifier in the antecedent is missing. The user can select this quantified formula in the logical view and apply the rule "forall-instantiation" in the proof manipulation view. Now the SMT solver is able to close this part of the proof and the user can focus on the next VC. Alternatively, the user could have provided a script to close the proof.

Another scenario is to inspect the sequent and recognize a contradiction due to which the proof could not be closed. In this case the user would like to determine the origin of the contradiction. To do so it is possible to request the origins of the involved formulas. Thus, users are able to see whether the contradiction is due to an error in the source code or is introduced by a rule application (e.g., a cut).

5   Related Work

One of the key features of our concept is to present different projections of the proof state in adjacent views and allowing a seamless switch between these views. Systems such as KIV [27,28], Why3 [29], KeY, KeYmaeraX [30–32], SED [33], Coq [4] or Isabelle [5] provide views with different purposes to the user. These systems show the current proof state in a view that is different from the view containing the whole proof structure. Each view should support users in specific tasks, thus each view contains actions and features that are necessary for the task. For example, in KIV or KeY the current goal view allows to retrieve the applicable rules and context-sensitive support for rule application, or the script view in Isabelle or Coq allows to extend the proof script with support for text-editing.

In KeYmaeraX, the actions accessible in the view containing *deduction paths* allow for a step-wise focusing on the different steps of a proof branch, by expanding details of the path in a tab, starting at the open goal. With progressing proof, this view may become cluttered as a deduction path may contain a large number of proof steps. Structuring of proof goals is also possible in KeYmaeraX: users can change the sequent view by hiding formulas.

The hierarchical structuring of concerns, and the color-coded highlighting of relevant parts of the source code in DIVE have been inspired by the presentation in the Why3 platform. Recently, Why3 has been amended with a scripting language for text-based interaction [34]. Its design allows the language connect higher-level proof scripting languages for the target programming language in case Why3 acts as intermediate verification language. A connection to the IDE of SPARK that allows script-based verification for SPARK programs has been presented.

Also KeY offers support for inspecting relations between proof artifacts. In response to our user study, KeY was improved to show the relation between the annotated program and the proof state in a new window, where all symbolically executed statements are highlighted. However, changing the annotated program requires an external editor and a restart of the verification process.

In our concept we integrate interactive with auto-active verification as found in tools like VCC [35] and Dafny [36]. These tools give feedback on the program level, and provide integration into an IDE. Users may retrieve information about violated assertions at specific program locations and inspect the values of variables for a program path. Concerning the direct manipulation style, mainly KeY, KeYmaeraX and KIV were role-models for our concept.

Similarly to the concept presented here, in previous work we integrated direct manipulation and script-based interaction for KeY [37,38]. Other systems that allow for different combinations of interaction styles include KeYmaeraX which also allows for both direct manipulation and text-based interaction interchangeably.

6   Conclusion and Future Work

We have presented a concept for a user interface for a seamless interactive program verification process, which is based on results from user studies, general usability principles, and principles for theorem provers. One of the goals of the concept is to support users in step-wise focusing on the different parts of the proof artifacts for inspection and proof construction, as well as the possibility to seamlessly switch to more abstract presentations if necessary. At the same time users are supported in the inspection of relations between the proof artifacts. The concept integrates auto-active and interactive program verification and allows for an alternating use of text-based interaction and direct manipulation.

We also presented DIVE as an implementation of our concept. Different views structure the proof artifacts and are arranged in a way to support step-wise focusing on more detailed parts. Only adjacent views are shown to the user at the same time. The goal of the arrangement is to support the users in carrying over information about relations and dependencies between different proof artifacts from one view to the other, by trying to keep the cognitive load low. Additionally, users may invoke mechanisms for inspecting relations and dependencies.

Future work includes integrating missing features like a view showing the call or usage dependencies, or proof exploration techniques for the logical view.

Existing techniques to support users in coming up with annotations and means for debugging failed verification attempts remain to be added. This includes, in particular, displaying possible counterexamples from SMT solvers for invalid VCs in the source code view. Examples for such an integration for the Dafny system is presented in [39] and for the Ivy system in [40].

Following the user-centered design process, case studies, as well as user studies have to be performed in a next step to evaluate the effectiveness of the interaction concepts and the user experience. The user studies should also evaluate whether our proposed work-flow may need to be adapted for expert users.

To evaluate whether the integration of the interactions styles is improving user support, we suggest performing a comparative evaluation using the prototype. Groups of participants should perform comparable verification tasks with either using only a single interaction style or with a combination of styles. Both task completion time should be measured, as well as the user experience using standardized questionnaires, such as UEQ [41] or SUMI [42].

References

1. Beckert, B., Bormer, T., Klebanov, V.: Improving the usability of specification languages and methods for annotation-based verification. In: Aichernig, B.K., de Boer, F.S., Bonsangue, M.M. (eds.) FMCO 2010. LNCS, vol. 6957, pp. 61–79. Springer, Heidelberg (2011). https://doi.org/10.1007/978-3-642-25271-6_4

2. Beckert, B., Bormer, T., Grahl, D.: Deductive verification of legacy code. In: Margaria, T., Steffen, B. (eds.) ISoLA 2016. LNCS, vol. 9952, pp. 749–765. Springer, Cham (2016). https://doi.org/10.1007/978-3-319-47166-2_53

3. Ahrendt, W., Beckert, B., Bubel, R., Hähnle, R., Schmitt, P.H., Ulbrich, M. (eds.): Deductive Software Verification – The KeY Book: From Theory to Practice. LNCS, vol. 10001. Springer, Heidelberg (2016)

4. Bertot, Y., Castran, P.: Interactive Theorem Proving and Program Development: Coq'Art The Calculus of Inductive Constructions. Texts in Theoretical Computer Science an EATCS Series, 1st edn. Springer, Heidelberg (2004). https://doi.org/10.1007/978-3-662-07964-5

5. Nipkow, T., Paulson, L.C., Wenzel, M.: Isabelle/HOL: A Proof Assistant for Higher-Order Logic. LNCS, vol. 2283. Springer, Heidelberg (2002). https://doi.org/10.1007/3-540-45949-9

6. Schneiderman, B.: Direct manipulation. A step beyond programming languages. IEEE Trans. Comput. **16**(8), 57–69 (1983)

7. Wenzel, M.: Isar—a generic interpretative approach to readable formal proof documents. In: Bertot, Y., Dowek, G., Théry, L., Hirschowitz, A., Paulin, C. (eds.) TPHOLs 1999. LNCS, vol. 1690, pp. 167–183. Springer, Heidelberg (1999). https://doi.org/10.1007/3-540-48256-3_12

8. Paulin-Mohring, C.: Introduction to the Coq proof-assistant for practical software verification. In: Meyer, B., Nordio, M. (eds.) LASER 2011. LNCS, vol. 7682, pp. 45–95. Springer, Heidelberg (2012). https://doi.org/10.1007/978-3-642-35746-6_3

9. Nielsen, J.: Enhancing the explanatory power of usability heuristics. In: SIGCHI Conference on Human Factors in Computing Systems, CHI 1994, ACM, pp. 152–158 (1994)

10. Molich, R., Nielsen, J.: Improving a human-computer dialogue. Commun. ACM **33**(3), 338–348 (1990)
11. Nielsen, J.: 10 usability heuristics for user interface design (1995)
12. Cok, D.R.: OpenJML: JML for Java 7 by extending OpenJDK. In: Bobaru, M., Havelund, K., Holzmann, G.J., Joshi, R. (eds.) NFM 2011. LNCS, vol. 6617, pp. 472–479. Springer, Heidelberg (2011). https://doi.org/10.1007/978-3-642-20398-5_35
13. Leino, K.R.M.: Dafny: an automatic program verifier for functional correctness. In: Clarke, E.M., Voronkov, A. (eds.) LPAR 2010. LNCS (LNAI), vol. 6355, pp. 348–370. Springer, Heidelberg (2010). https://doi.org/10.1007/978-3-642-17511-4_20
14. Knuth, D.E.: Literate programming. Comput. J. **27**(2), 97–111 (1984)
15. Bormer, T.: Advancing deductive program-level verification for real-world application: lessons learned from an industrial case study. Ph.D. thesis, Karlsruhe Institute of Technology (2014)
16. Beckert, B., Grebing, S., Böhl, F.: A usability evaluation of interactive theorem provers using focus groups. In: Canal, C., Idani, A. (eds.) SEFM 2014. LNCS, vol. 8938, pp. 3–19. Springer, Cham (2015). https://doi.org/10.1007/978-3-319-15201-1_1
17. Beckert, B., Grebing, S., Böhl, F.: How to put usability into focus: using focus groups to evaluate the usability of interactive theorem provers. In: UITP 2014. EPTCS, vol. 167, pp. 4–13 (2014)
18. Grebing, S.: User interaction in interactive deductive program verification. Ph.D. thesis, Karlsruhe Institute of Technology (2019, to appear)
19. Beyer, H., Holtzblatt, K.: Contextual Design: Defining Customer-Centered Systems. Morgan Kaufmann Publishers Inc., San Francisco (1998)
20. Benyon, D.: Designing Interactive Systems: A Comprehensive Guide to HCI and Interaction Design. Addison Wesley (2010)
21. Kuckartz, U.: Qualitative Inhaltsanalyse. Computerunterstützung. Grundlagentexte Methoden. Beltz Juventa, Methoden, Praxis (2014)
22. Easthaughffe, K.A.: Support for interactive theorem proving: some design principles and their application. In: UITP 1998 (1998)
23. Dix, A., Finlay, J., Abowd, G., Beale, R.: Human-Computer Interaction. Prentice-Hall, Inc. (2004)
24. Tognazzini, B.: First Principles of Interaction Design (rev. and exp.) (1987–2014)
25. Ben Shneiderman, C.P.: Designing the User Interface: Strategies for Effective Human-Computer Interaction. Pearson (2005)
26. Blackwell, A., Green, T.R.: A cognitive dimensions questionnaire (v. 5.1.1), February 2007. www.cl.cam.ac.uk/~afb21/CognitiveDimensions/CDquestionnaire.pdf
27. Haneberg, D., et al.: The user interface of the KIV verification system - a system description. In: UITP 2005 (2005)
28. Balser, M., Reif, W., Schellhorn, G., Stenzel, K., Thums, A.: Formal system development with KIV. In: Maibaum, T. (ed.) FASE 2000. LNCS, vol. 1783, pp. 363–366. Springer, Heidelberg (2000). https://doi.org/10.1007/3-540-46428-X_25
29. Filliâtre, J.-C., Paskevich, A.: Why3 — where programs meet provers. In: Felleisen, M., Gardner, P. (eds.) ESOP 2013. LNCS, vol. 7792, pp. 125–128. Springer, Heidelberg (2013). https://doi.org/10.1007/978-3-642-37036-6_8
30. Mitsch, S., Platzer, A.: The KeYmaera X proof IDE - concepts on usability in hybrid systems theorem proving. In: F-IDE 2016. EPTCS, vol. 240, pp. 67–81. Open Publishing Association (2017)

31. Platzer, A.: Logical Foundations of Cyber-Physical Systems. Springer, Cham (2018). https://doi.org/10.1007/978-3-319-63588-0

32. Fulton, N., Mitsch, S., Quesel, J.-D., Völp, M., Platzer, A.: KeYmaera X: an axiomatic tactical theorem prover for hybrid systems. In: Felty, A.P., Middeldorp, A. (eds.) CADE 2015. LNCS (LNAI), vol. 9195, pp. 527–538. Springer, Cham (2015). https://doi.org/10.1007/978-3-319-21401-6_36

33. Hentschel, M., Bubel, R., Hähnle, R.: The symbolic execution debugger (SED): a platform for interactive symbolic execution, debugging, verification and more. Int. J. Softw. Tools Technol. Transf. **21**, 485–513 (2018)

34. Dailler, S., Marché, C., Moy, Y.: Lightweight interactive proving inside an automatic program verifier. F-IDE **2018**, 1–15 (2018)

35. Dahlweid, M., Moskal, M., Santen, T., Tobies, S., Schulte, W.: VCC: contract-based modular verification of concurrent C. In: International Conference on Software Engineering - Companion Volume, pp. 429–430 (2009)

36. Leino, K.R.M., Wüstholz, V.: The Dafny integrated development environment. In: F-IDE 2014. EPTCS, vol. 149, pp. 3–15 (2014)

37. Beckert, B., Grebing, S., Ulbrich, M.: An interaction concept for program verification systems with explicit proof object. Hardware and Software: Verification and Testing. LNCS, vol. 10629, pp. 163–178. Springer, Cham (2017). https://doi.org/10.1007/978-3-319-70389-3_11

38. Grebing, S., Luong, A.T.T., Weigl, A.: Adding text-based interaction to a direct-manipulation interface for program verification - lessons learned. In: UITP 2018 (2018, to appear)

39. Christakis, M., Leino, K.R.M., Müller, P., Wüstholz, V.: Integrated environment for diagnosing verification errors. In: Chechik, M., Raskin, J.-F. (eds.) TACAS 2016. LNCS, vol. 9636, pp. 424–441. Springer, Heidelberg (2016). https://doi.org/10.1007/978-3-662-49674-9_25

40. McMillan, K.L., Padon, O.: Deductive verification in decidable fragments with Ivy. In: Podelski, A. (ed.) SAS 2018. LNCS, vol. 11002, pp. 43–55. Springer, Cham (2018). https://doi.org/10.1007/978-3-319-99725-4_4

41. Laugwitz, B., Held, T., Schrepp, M.: Construction and evaluation of a user experience questionnaire. In: Holzinger, A. (ed.) USAB 2008. LNCS, vol. 5298, pp. 63–76. Springer, Heidelberg (2008). https://doi.org/10.1007/978-3-540-89350-9_6

42. Kirakowski, J.: The use of questionnaire methods for usability assessment (1994)

Formal Verification of Workflow Policies for Smart Contracts in Azure Blockchain

Yuepeng Wang[1]([✉]), Shuvendu K. Lahiri[2], Shuo Chen[2], Rong Pan[1], Isil Dillig[1],
Cody Born[3], Immad Naseer[3], and Kostas Ferles[1]

[1] University of Texas at Austin, Austin, USA
{ypwang,rpan,isil,kferles}@cs.utexas.edu
[2] Microsoft Research, Redmond, USA
{Shuvendu.Lahiri,shuochen}@microsoft.com
[3] Microsoft Azure, Redmond, USA
{Cody.Born,imnaseer}@microsoft.com

Abstract. Ensuring correctness of smart contracts is paramount to ensuring trust in blockchain-based systems. This paper studies the safety and security of smart contracts in the *Azure Blockchain Workbench*, an enterprise Blockchain-as-a-Service offering from Microsoft. In particular, we formalize *semantic conformance* of smart contracts against a state machine workflow with access-control policy and propose an approach to reducing semantic conformance checking to safety verification using program instrumentation. We develop a new Solidity program verifier VERISOL that is based on translation to Boogie, and have applied it to analyze *all* application contracts shipped with the Azure Blockchain Workbench and found previously unknown bugs in these published smart contracts. After fixing these bugs, VERISOL was able to successfully perform full verification for all of these contracts.

1 Introduction

As a decentralized and distributed consensus protocol to maintain and secure a shared ledger, the blockchain is seen as a disruptive technology with far-reaching impact on diverse areas. As a result, major cloud platform companies, including Microsoft, IBM, Amazon, SAP, and Oracle, are offering Blockchain-as-a-Service (BaaS) solutions, primarily targeting enterprise scenarios, such as financial services, supply chains, escrow, and consortium governance. A recent study by Gartner predicts that the business value-add of the blockchain has the potential to exceed $3.1 trillion by 2030 [3].

Programs running on the blockchain are known as *smart contracts*. High-level languages such as Solidity and Serpent have been developed to enable traditional application developers to author smart contracts. However, since blockchain transactions are immutable, bugs in smart contract code have devastating consequences, and vulnerabilities in smart contracts have resulted in several high-profile exploits that undermine trust in the underlying blockchain technology. For example, the infamous TheDAO exploit [1] resulted in the loss

© Springer Nature Switzerland AG 2020
S. Chakraborty and J. A. Navas (Eds.): VSTTE 2019, LNCS 12031, pp. 87–106, 2020.
https://doi.org/10.1007/978-3-030-41600-3_7

of almost \$60 million worth of Ether, and the `Parity Wallet` bug caused 169 million USD worth of ether to be locked forever [5]. The only remedy for these incidents was to hard-fork the blockchain and revert one of the forks back to the state before the incident. However, this remedy itself is devastating as it defeats the core values of blockchain, such as immutability and decentralized trust.

Motivated by the serious consequences of bugs in smart contract code, recent work has studied many types of security bugs such as reentrancy, integer underflow/overflow, and issues related to delegatecalls on Ethereum. While these low-level bugs have drawn much attention due to high-visibility incidents on public blockchains, we believe that the BaaS infrastructure and enterprise scenarios bring a set of interesting, yet less well-studied security problems.

In this paper, we present our research on smart contract correctness in the context of Azure Blockchain, a BaaS solution offered by Microsoft [4]. Specifically, we focus on a cloud service named *Azure Blockchain Workbench* (or Workbench for short) [8,9]. The Workbench allows an enterprise customer to easily build and deploy a smart contract application integrating active directory, database, web UI, blob storage, etc. A customer implements the smart contract application (that meets the requirements specified in an application policy) and uploads it onto the Workbench. The code is then deployed to the underlying blockchain ledger to function as an end-to-end application.

Customer contracts in the Workbench architecture implement complex business logic, starting with a high-level finite-state-machine (FSM) *workflow* policy. Intuitively, the workflow describes (a) a set of categories of users called *roles*, (b) the different states of a contract, and (c) the set of enabled actions (or functions) at each state restricted to each role. The high-level policy is useful to design contracts around state machine abstractions as well as specify the required *access-control* for the actions. While these state machines offer powerful abstraction patterns during smart contract design, it is non-trivial to decide whether a given smart contract faithfully implements the intended FSM. In this paper, we define *semantic conformance checking* as the problem of deciding whether a customer contract correctly implements the underlying workflow policy expressed as an FSM. Given a Workbench policy π that describes the workflow and a contract $\mathcal{C}$, our approach first constructs a new contract $\mathcal{C}'$ such that $\mathcal{C}$ semantically conforms to π if and only if $\mathcal{C}'$ does not fail any assertions.

In order to automatically check the correctness of the assertions in a smart contract, we develop a new verifier called VERISOL for smart contracts written in Solidity. VERISOL is a general-purpose Solidity verifier and is not tied to Workbench. The verifier encodes the semantics of Solidity programs into a low-level intermediate verification language Boogie and leverages the well-engineered Boogie verification pipeline [15] for both verification and counter-example generation. In particular, VERISOL takes advantage of existing bounded model checking tool CORRAL [24] for Boogie to generate witnesses to assertion violations, and it leverages practical verification condition generators for Boogie to automate correctness proofs. In addition, VERISOL uses monomial predicate abstraction [17,22] to automatically infer so-called *contract invariants*, which we have found to be crucial for automatic verification of semantic conformance.

To evaluate the effectiveness and efficiency of our approach, we have performed an experiment on all 11 sample applications that are shipped with the Workbench. In the experiment, we find 4 previously unknown defects in these published smart contracts, all of which have been confirmed as true bugs by the developers. The experimental results also demonstrate the practicality of VERISOL in that it can perform full verification of all the fixed contracts with modest effort; most notably, VERISOL can automatically verify 10 out of 11 of the fixed versions of sample smart contracts within 1.7 s on average.

Contributions. This paper makes the following contributions:

- We study the safety and security of smart contracts present in Azure Blockchain Workbench, a BaaS offering.
- We formalize the Workbench application policy language and define the *semantic conformance* checking problem between a contract and a policy.
- We propose an approach to reducing semantic conformance checking to safety property verification using program instrumentation.
- We describe a new formal verifier called VERISOL for verifying smart contracts written in Solidity based on translation to Boogie [13,30].
- We evaluate our approach by verifying semantic conformance on all the sample application contracts shipped with Workbench, and report previously unknown bugs that have been confirmed by developers.

2 Overview

In this section, we give an example of a Workbench application policy for a sample contract and describe our approach for semantic conformance verification.

2.1 Workbench Application Policy

Workbench requires every application to provide a *policy* (or *model*) representing the high-level workflow of the application[1]. The policy consists of several attributes such as the application name, a set of *roles*, as well as a set of *workflows*.

For example, Fig. 1 provides an informal pictorial representation of the policy for a simple application called `HelloBlockchain`[2]. The application consists of two *global* roles (see "Application Roles"), namely REQUESTOR and RESPONDER. Informally, each role represents a set of user addresses and provides access control or permissions for various actions exposed by the application. We distinguish a global role from an *instance role* in that the latter applies to a specific instance of the workflow. It is expected that the instance roles are always a subset of the user addresses associated with the global role.

---

[1] https://docs.microsoft.com/en-us/azure/blockchain/workbench/configuration.

[2] The details can be found on the associated web page: https://github.com/Azure-Samples/blockchain/tree/master/blockchain-workbench/application-and-smart-contract-samples/hello-blockchain.

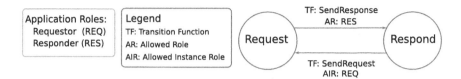

Fig. 1. Workflow policy diagram for HelloBlockchain application.

As shown in Fig. 1, the simple **HelloBlockchain** application consists of a single workflow with two states, namely **Request** and **Respond**. The data members (or fields) include instance role members (**Requestor** and **Responder**) that range over user addresses. The workflow consists of two actions (or functions) in addition to the constructor function, **SendRequest** and **SendResponse**, both of which take a string as argument.

A transition in the workflow consists of a start state, an action or function, an access control list, and a set of successor states. Figure 1 describes two transitions, one from each of the two states. For example, the application can transition from **Request** to **Respond** if a user belongs to the RESPONDER role (**AR**) and invokes the action **SendResponse**. An "Application Instance Role" (**AIR**) refers to an instance role data member of the workflow that stores a member of a global role (such as **Requestor**). For instance, the transition from **Respond** to **Request** in Fig. 1 uses an **AIR** and is only allowed if the user address matches the value stored in the instance data variable **Requestor**.

2.2   Workbench Application Smart Contract

After specifying the application policy, a user provides a smart contract written in Solidity to implement the workflow. Figure 2 describes a Solidity smart contract that implements the **HelloBlockchain** workflow in the **HelloBlockchain** application. For the purpose of this sub-section, we start by ignoring the portions of the code that are <u>underlined</u>. The contract declares the data members present in the configuration as state variables. Each contract implementing a workflow defines an additional state variable **State** to track the current state of a workflow. The contract consists of the constructor along with two other functions defined in the policy, with matching signatures. The functions set the state variables and update the state variables appropriately to reflect the state transitions.

Although the smart contract drives the application, the policy is used to expose the set of enabled actions at each state for a given user. Discrepancies between the policy and Solidity program can lead to unexpected state transitions. To ensure the correct functioning and security of the application, it is crucial to verify that the Solidity program semantically conforms to the application policy.

```
contract HelloBlockchain {
    enum StateType {Request, Respond} // set of states
    // list of properties
    StateType public State;
    address public Requestor;
    address public Responder;
    string  public RequestMessage;
    string  public ResponseMessage;
    // constructor function
    function HelloBlockchain(string message) constructor_checker() public {
        Requestor = msg.sender;
        RequestMessage = message;
        State = StateType.Request;
    }
    // call this function to send a request
    function SendRequest(string requestMessage) SendRequest_checker() public {
        if (Requestor != msg.sender) revert();
        RequestMessage = requestMessage;
        State = StateType.Request;
    }
    // call this function to send a response
    function SendResponse(string responseMessage) SendResponse_checker() public {
        Responder = msg.sender;
        ResponseMessage = responseMessage;
        State = StateType.Respond;
    }
    <modifier definitions>
}
```

Fig. 2. Solidity contract for HelloBlockchain application.

2.3   Semantic Conformance Verification

Given an application policy and a smart contract, we define the problem
of *semantic conformance* that ensures the smart contract respects the policy
(Sect. 3.2). Moreover, we reduce the semantic conformance verification problem to checking assertions on an instrumented Solidity program. For the
HelloBlockchain application, the instrumentation is provided by adding the
underlined *modifier* invocations in Fig. 2. A *modifier* is a Solidity construct that
allows wrapping a function invocation with code that executes before and after
the function body.

Figure 3 shows the definition of the modifiers used to instrument for conformance checking. Intuitively, we wrap the constructor and functions with checks
to ensure that they implement the FSM state transitions correctly. For example,
if the FSM transitions from state **Respond** to state **Request** upon the invocation of function **SendRequest** by a user with instance role **Requestor**, then we
instrument the definition of **SendRequest** to ensure that any execution starting
in **Respond** with instance role **Requestor** should transition to **Request**.

Finally, given the instrumented Solidity program, we discharge the assertions
statically using a new formal verifier for Solidity called VERISOL. The verifier can
find counterexamples (in the form of a sequence of transactions involving calls to
the constructor and public functions) as well as automatically construct proofs
of semantic conformance. Note that, even though the simple **HelloBlockchain**
example does not contain any unbounded loops or recursion, verifying semantic

```
function nondet() returns (bool); // non-deterministic boolean value

// checker modifiers
modifier constructor_checker() {
  _;
  assert (nondet() /*global role REQUESTOR*/
            ==> State == StateType.Request);
}
modifier SendRequest_checker() {
  StateType oldState = State;
  address oldRequestor = Requestor;
  _;
  assert ((msg.sender == oldRequestor && oldState == StateType.Respond)
            ==> State == StateType.Request);
}
modifier SendResponse_checker() {
  StateType oldState = State;
  _;
  assert ((nondet() /*global role RESPONDER*/ && oldState == StateType.Request)
            ==> State == StateType.Respond);
}
```

Fig. 3. Modifier definitions for instrumented HelloBlockchain application.

conformance still requires reasoning about executions that involve unbounded numbers of calls to the two public functions. We demonstrate that VERISOL is able to find deep violations of the conformance property for well-tested Workbench applications, as well as automatically construct inductive proofs for most of the application samples shipped with Workbench.

3   Semantic Conformance Checking

In this section, we formalize the Workbench application policy and the semantic conformance checking problem, and then explain our approach to checking if an application smart contract is semantically conformant to its policy.

3.1   Formalization of Workbench Application Policies

The Workbench policy for an application allows the user to describe (i) the *data members* and *actions* of an application, (ii) a high-level *state-machine* view of the application, and (iii) role-based *access control* for *state transitions*. The role-based access control provides security for deploying smart contracts in an open and adversarial setting; the high-level state machine naturally captures the essence of a *workflow* that progresses between a set of states based on actions of the user.

More formally, a *Workbench Application Policy* is a pair $(\mathcal{R}, \mathcal{W})$ where $\mathcal{R}$ is a set of *global roles* used for access control, and $\mathcal{W}$ is a set of *workflows* defining a kind of finite state machine. Specifically, a workflow is defined by a tuple $\langle \mathcal{S}, s_0, \mathcal{R}_w, \mathcal{F}, \mathcal{F}_0, ac_0, \gamma \rangle$ where:

- $\mathcal{S}$ is a finite set of *states*, and $s_0 \in \mathcal{S}$ is an *initial state*
- $\mathcal{R}_w$ is a finite set of *instance roles* of the form $(id : t)$, where id is an identifier and t is a role drawn from $\mathcal{R}$
- $\mathcal{F}(id_0, \ldots, id_k)$ is a set of *actions (functions)*, with $\mathcal{F}_0$ denoting an initial action (constructor)
- $ac_0 \subseteq \mathcal{R}$ is the *initiator role* denoting users that can create an instance
- $\gamma \subseteq \mathcal{S} \times \mathcal{F} \times (\mathcal{R}_w \cup \mathcal{R}) \times 2^{\mathcal{S}}$ is a set of transitions. Given a transition $\tau = (s, f, ac, S)$, we write $\tau.s, \tau.f, \tau.ac, \tau.S$ to denote the source state s, action f, access control ac, and target states S of transition τ, respectively

Intuitively, $\mathcal{S}$ defines the different "states" that the contract can be in, and γ describes which state can transition to what other states by performing certain actions. The transitions are guarded by roles (either global or instance roles) that qualify which users are allowed to perform those actions. As mentioned earlier in Sect. 2, each "role" corresponds to a set of users (i.e., addresses on the blockchain). The use of instance roles in the workbench policy allows different instances of the contract to authorize different users to perform certain actions.

3.2   Semantic Conformance

Given a contract $\mathcal{C}$ and a Workbench application policy π, *semantic conformance* between $\mathcal{C}$ and π requires that the contract $\mathcal{C}$ faithfully implements the policy specified by π. In this subsection, we first define some syntactic requirements on the contract, and then formalize what we mean by semantic conformance between a contract and a policy.

Syntactic Conformance. Given a client contract $\mathcal{C}$ and a policy $\pi = (\mathcal{R}, \mathcal{W})$, our syntactic conformance requirement stipulates that the contract for each $w \in \mathcal{W}$ implements all the instance state variables as well as definitions for each of the functions. Additionally, each contract function has a parameter called *sender*, which is a blockchain address that denotes the user or contract invoking this function. Finally, each contract should contain a state variable s_w that ranges over $\mathcal{S}_w$, for each $w \in \mathcal{W}$.

Semantic Conformance. We formalize the semantic conformance requirement for smart contracts using Floyd-Hoare triples of the form $\{\phi\}\ S\ \{\psi\}$ indicating that any execution of statement S starting in a state satisfying ϕ results in a state satisfying ψ (if the execution of S terminates). We can define semantic conformance between a contract $\mathcal{C}$ and a policy π as a set of Hoare triples, one for each pair (m, s) where m is a method in the contract and s is a state in the Workbench policy. At a high-level, the idea is simple: we insist that, when a function is executed along a transition, the resulting state transition should be in accordance with the Workbench policy.

Given a policy $\pi = (\mathcal{R}, \mathcal{W})$ and workflow $w = \langle \mathcal{S}, s_0, \mathcal{R}_w, \mathcal{F}, \mathcal{F}_0, ac_0, \gamma \rangle \in \mathcal{W}$, we can formalize this high-level idea by using the following Hoare triples:

1. **Initiation.**

$$\{sender \in ac_0\} \quad \mathcal{F}_0(v_1, \ldots, v_k) \quad \{s_w = s_0\}$$

The Hoare triple states that the creation of an instance of the workflow with the appropriate access control ac_0 results in establishing the initial state.

2. **Consecution.** Let $\tau = (s_1, f, ac, \mathcal{S}_2)$ be a transition in γ. Then, for each such transition, semantic conformance requires the following Hoare triple to be valid:

$$\{sender \in ac \wedge s_w = s_1\} \quad f(v_1, \ldots, v_k) \quad \{s_w \in \mathcal{S}_2\}$$

Here, the precondition checks two facts: First, the $sender$ must satisfy the access control, and, second, the start state must be s_1. The post-condition asserts that the implementation of method f in the contract results in a state that is valid according to policy π.

3.3   Instrumentation for Semantic Conformance Checking

As mentioned in Sect. 2, our approach checks semantic conformance of Solidity contracts by (a) instrumenting the contract with assertions, and (b) using a verification tool to check that none of the assertions can fail. We explain our instrumentation strategy in this subsection and refer the reader to Sect. 4 for a description of our verification tool chain.

Our instrumentation methodology uses the **modifier** construct in Solidity. A modifier has syntax similar to a function definition in Solidity with a name and list of parameters and a body that can refer to parameters and globals in scope. The general structure of a modifier definition without any parameters is [2]:

```
modifier Foo() { pre-stmt; _; post-stmt;}
```

where **pre-stmt** and **post-stmt** are Solidity statements. When this modifier is applied to a function **Bar** such as

```
function Bar(int x) Foo() {Bar-stmt;}
```

the Solidity compiler transforms the body of **Bar** to execute **pre-stmt** (resp. **post-stmt**) before (resp. after) **Bar-stmt**. This provides a convenient way to inject code at multiple return sites from a procedure and can also inject code before the execution of the constructor.

We now define helper predicates before describing the actual checks. Let $P(ac)$ be a predicate that encodes the membership of $sender$ in the set ac:

$$P(ac) \doteq \begin{cases} false, & ac = \{\} \\ \text{msg.sender} = q, & ac = \{q \in \mathcal{R}_w\} \\ \text{nondet}(), & ac = \{r \in \mathcal{R}\} \\ P(ac^1) \vee P(ac^2), & ac = ac^1 \cup ac^2 \end{cases}$$

Here **nondet** is a side-effect free Solidity function that returns a non-deterministic Boolean value at each invocation. For the sake of static verification, one can declare a function without any definition. This allows us to model the membership check $sender \in ac$ conservatively in the absence of global roles on the blockchain.

We also define a predicate for membership of a contract state in a set of states $\mathcal{S}' \subseteq \mathcal{S}$ using $\alpha(\mathcal{S}')$ as follows:

$$\alpha(\mathcal{S}') \doteq \begin{cases} false, & \mathcal{S}' = \{\} \\ s_w = s, & \mathcal{S}' = \{s \in \mathcal{S}\} \\ \alpha(\mathcal{S}_1) \vee \alpha(\mathcal{S}_2), & \mathcal{S}' = \mathcal{S}_1 \cup \mathcal{S}_2 \end{cases}$$

Using these predicates, the source code transformations are defined as below:
Constructor. We add the following modifier to constructors:

```
modifier constructor_checker() {_; assert (P(ac₀) ⇒ α({s₀}));}
```

Here, the assertion ensures that the constructor sets up the correct initial state when executed by a user with access control ac_0.

Other Functions. For a function g, let $\gamma^g \doteq \{\tau \in \gamma \mid \tau = (s_1, g, ac, \mathcal{S}_2)\}$ be the set of all transitions where g is invoked.

```
modifier g_checker() {
    StateType oldState = sw; // copy old State
    ... // copy old instance role vars
    _;
    assert ⋀τ∈γᵍ (old (P(τ.ac) ∧ α({τ.s1))) ⇒ α(τ.S2));
}
```

Here, the instrumented code first copies the s_w variable and all of the variables in $\mathcal{R}_w$ into corresponding "old" copies. Next, the assertion checks that if the function is executed in a transition τ, then state transitions to one of the successor states in $\tau.\mathcal{S}_2$. The notation $\mathbf{old}(e)$ replaces any occurrences of a state variable (such as s_w) with the "old" copy that holds the value at the entry to the function. As an example, Fig. 3 shows the modifier definitions for our running example `HelloBlockchain` described in Sect. 2. Although we show the $\mathbf{nondet}()$ to highlight the issue of global roles, one can safely replace $\mathbf{nondet}()$ with *true* since the function only appears negatively in any assertion.

4 Formal Verification Using VeriSol

In this section, we present our formal verifier called VERISOL for checking the correctness of assertions in Solidity smart contracts.

4.1 General Methodology

Let $\mathcal{C} = \{\lambda\vec{x_0}.f_0, \lambda\vec{x_1}.f_1, \ldots, \lambda\vec{x_n}.f_n\}$ be a smart contract annotated with assertions where:

- $\lambda\vec{x_0}.f_0$ is the constructor
- $\lambda\vec{x_i}.f_i$ for $i \in [1, n]$ are public functions

Our verification methodology is based on finding a *contract invariant* $\mathcal{I}$ satisfying the following Hoare triples:

(1) $\models \{\texttt{true}\}\ f_0\ \{\mathcal{I}\}$

(2) $\models \{\mathcal{I}\}\ f_i\ \{\mathcal{I}\}$ for all $i \in [1, n]$

Here, the first condition states the contract invariant is established by the constructor, and the second condition states that $\mathcal{I}$ is inductive—i.e., it is preserved by every public function in $\mathcal{C}$. Note that such a contract invariant suffices to establish the validity of all assertions in the contract under *any* possible sequence of function invocations of the contract. To see why this is the case, consider a "harness" that invokes the functions in $\mathcal{C}$ as in Fig. 4.

```
call f_0(*);
while (true) {
    if (*) call f_1(*); else if (*) ...
    else if (*) call f_n(*);
}
```

Fig. 4. Harness for Solidity contracts

This harness first creates an instance of the contract by calling the constructor, and then repeatedly and non-deterministically invokes one of the public functions of $\mathcal{C}$. Observe that the Hoare triples (1) and (2) listed above essentially state that $\mathcal{I}$ is an inductive invariant of the loop in this harness; thus, the contract invariant $\mathcal{I}$ overapproximates the state of the contract under any sequence of the contract's function invocations. Furthermore, when the functions contain assertions, the Hoare triple $\{\mathcal{I}\}\ f_i\ \{\mathcal{I}\}$ can only be proven if $\mathcal{I}$ is strong enough to imply the assertion conditions. Thus, the validity of the Hoare triples in (1) and (2) establishes correctness under all possible usage patterns of the contract.

4.2   Overview

We now describe the design of our tool called VERISOL for checking safety of smart contracts. VERISOL is based on the proof methodology outlined in Sect. 4.1, and its workflow is illustrated in Fig. 5. At a high-level, VERISOL takes as input a Solidity contract $\mathcal{C}$ annotated with assertions and yields one of the following three outcomes:

- *Fully verified:* This means that the assertions in $\mathcal{C}$ are guaranteed not to fail under any usage scenario.
- *Refuted:* This indicates that VERISOL finds at least one transaction sequence of the contract $\mathcal{C}$ under which one of the assertions is guaranteed to fail.
- *Partially verified:* When VERISOL can neither verify nor refute contract correctness, it performs bounded verification to establish that the contract is safe up to k transactions. This essentially corresponds to unrolling the "harness" loop from Fig. 4 for k times and then verifying that the assertions do not fail in the unrolled version.

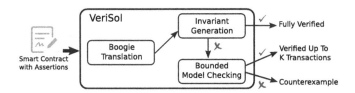

Fig. 5. Schematic workflow of VERISOL.

VERISOL consists of three modules, namely (a) *Boogie Translation* from a Solidity program, (b) *Invariant Generation* to infer a *contract invariant* as well as loop invariants and procedure summaries, and (c) *Bounded Model Checking* to explore assertion failures within all transactions up to a user-specified depth k. In what follows, we discuss each of these components in more detail.

4.3 Solidity to Boogie Translation

In this subsection, we formally describe our translation of Solidity source code to the Boogie intermediate verification language. We start with a brief description of Solidity and Boogie, and then discuss our translation.

Solidity Language. Figure 6 shows a core subset of Solidity that we use for our formalization. At a high level, Solidity is a typed object-oriented programming language with built-in support for basic verification constructs, such as the `require` construct for expressing pre-conditions.

$$
\begin{aligned}
st \in SolTypes &::= integer \mid string \mid address \mid C \\
se \in SolExprs &::= c \mid \mathbf{x} \mid \mathbf{op}(se, \ldots, se) \mid \mathtt{msg.sender} \\
sst \in SolStmts &::= \mathbf{x} := se \mid sst; sst \mid \mathbf{require}(se) \mid \mathbf{assert}(se) \\
&\quad \mid\ \mathbf{if}\ (se)\ \{sst\}\ \mathbf{else}\ \{sst\} \mid \mathbf{while}\ (se)\ \mathbf{do}\ \{sst\} \\
&\quad \mid\ se := \mathbf{f}(\vec{se}) \mid se := se.\mathbf{f}(\vec{se}) \mid se := \mathbf{new}\ C(\vec{se})
\end{aligned}
$$

Fig. 6. A subset of Solidity language. C denotes a contract and $\mathbf{f}$ denotes a function.

Types in our core language include integers, strings, addresses, and contracts. As is standard, expressions in Solidity include constants, local variables, *state variables* (i.e., fields in standard object-oriented language terminology), unary/binary operators (denoted **op**), and `msg.sender` that yields the address of the contract or user that initiates the current function invocation. Statements in our core Solidity language include assignments, conditionals, loops, requires, assertions, internal and external function calls, and contract instance creation[3]. Solidity differentiates between two types of function calls: internal

---

[3] We omit several aspects of the language such as arrays and mappings due to space limit. More details can be found in the extended version of this paper [30].

and external. An *internal* call $se := f(\vec{se})$ invokes the function f and keeps
msg.sender unchanged. An *external* call $se := se_0.f(\vec{se})$ invokes function f in
the contract instance pointed by se_0 (which may include this), and uses this
as the msg.sender for the callee.

$$bbt \in BoogieElemTypes ::= \textbf{int} \mid \textbf{Ref} \qquad bt \in BoogieTypes ::= bbt \mid [bbt]\, bt$$

$$e \in Exprs ::= c \mid \textbf{x} \mid \textbf{op}(e, \ldots, e) \mid \textbf{uf}(e, \ldots, e) \mid \textbf{x}[e] \mid \forall i : bbt :: e$$
$$st \in Stmts ::= \textbf{skip} \mid \textbf{havoc x} \mid \textbf{x} := e \mid \textbf{x}[e] := e$$
$$\mid \textbf{assume } e \mid \textbf{assert } e \mid \textbf{if } (e) \; \{st\} \textbf{ else } \{st\}$$
$$\mid st; st \mid \textbf{while } (e) \textbf{ do } \{st\} \mid \textbf{call } \vec{\textbf{x}} := f(e, \ldots, e)$$

Fig. 7. A subset of Boogie language.

Boogie Language. Since our goal is to translate Solidity to Boogie, we also give
a brief overview of the Boogie intermediate verification language. As shown in
Fig. 7, types in Boogie include integers (**int**), references (**Ref**), and arrays/maps.
Expressions (*Exprs*) consist of constants, variables, arithmetic and logical operators (**op**), uninterpreted functions (**uf**), map lookups, and quantified expressions. Statements (*Stmts*) in Boogie consist of skip, variable and map assignment, sequential composition, conditionals, and loops. The **havoc x** statement
assigns an arbitrary value of appropriate type to a variable **x**. A procedure call
(**call** $\vec{\textbf{x}} := f(e, \ldots, e)$) returns a vector of values that can be stored in local variables. The **assert** and **assume** statements behave as no-ops when their argu-
ments evaluate to true and terminate execution otherwise. An assertion failure
is considered as a failing execution, whereas an assumption failure blocks.

From Solidity to Boogie Types. We define a function $\mu : SolTypes \rightarrow$
BoogieTypes that translates a Solidity type to a type in Boogie as follows:

$$\mu(st) \doteq \begin{cases} \textbf{int}, & st \in \{integer, string\} \\ \textbf{Ref}, & st \in \{address\} \cup ContractNames \end{cases}$$

Specifically, we translate Solidity integers and strings to Boogie integers;
addresses, and contract names to Boogie references. Note that we represent Solidity strings as integers in Boogie because Solidity only allows equality checks on
strings.

From Solidity to Boogie Expressions. We present our translation from Solid-
ity to Boogie expressions using judgments of the form $\vdash e \hookrightarrow \chi$ in Fig. 8, where
e is a Solidity expression and χ is the corresponding Boogie expression. While
Solidity local variables and the expression msg.sender are mapped directly into
Boogie local variables and parameters respectively, state variables in Solidity are
translated into map lookups. Specifically, for each state variable **x** in contract
C, we introduce a mapping $\textbf{x}^C$ from contract instances to the value stored in
its state variable **x**. Thus, reads from state variable **x** are modeled as $\textbf{x}^C[\text{this}]$
in Boogie. Next, we translate string constants in Solidity to Boogie integers

$$\frac{x \in \mathit{LocalVars}}{\vdash x \hookrightarrow x} \text{ (Var1)} \qquad \frac{x \in \mathit{StateVars(C)}}{\vdash x \hookrightarrow x^C[\mathbf{this}]} \text{ (Var2)}$$

$$\frac{\mathit{Type}(c) \neq \mathit{string}}{\vdash c \hookrightarrow c} \text{ (Const1)} \qquad \frac{\mathit{Type}(c) = \mathit{string} \quad c' = \mathit{Hash}(c)}{\vdash c \hookrightarrow \mathit{StrToInt}(c')} \text{ (Const2)}$$

$$\frac{v = \mathbf{sender}}{\vdash \mathbf{msg.sender} \hookrightarrow v} \text{ (Sender)} \qquad \frac{\vdash e_i \hookrightarrow \chi_i \quad i = 1, \dots, n}{\vdash \mathbf{op}(e_1, \dots, e_n) \hookrightarrow \mathbf{op}(\chi_1, \dots, \chi_n)} \text{ (Op)}$$

Fig. 8. Inference rules for encoding Solidity expressions to Boogie expressions. $\mathit{Type}(e)$ is a function that returns the static type of Solidity expression e.

using an uninterpreted function called *StrToInt* that is applied to a hash of the string[4]. As mentioned earlier, this string-to-integer translation does not cause imprecision because Solidity only allows equality checks between variables of type string.

From Solidity to Boogie statements. Figure 9 presents the translation from Solidity to Boogie statements using judgments of the form $\vdash s \rightsquigarrow \omega$ indicating that Solidity statement s is translated to Boogie statement ω. Since most rules in Fig. 9 are self-explanatory, we only explain our translation for function calls. Functions in Solidity have two implicit parameters, namely **this** for the receiver object and **msg.sender** for the Blockchain address of the caller. Thus, when translating Solidity calls to their corresponding Boogie version, we explicitly pass these parameters in the Boogie version. However, recall that the value of the implicit **msg.sender** parameter varies depending on whether the call is external or internal. For internal calls, **msg.sender** remains unchanged, whereas for external calls, **msg.sender** becomes the current receiver object. For both types of calls, our translation introduces a conditional statement to deal with dynamic dispatch. Specifically, our Boogie encoding introduces a map τ to store the dynamic type of receiver objects at allocation sites, and the translation of function calls invokes the correct version of the method based on the content of τ for the receiver object. In the case of contract creation (labeled NewCont in Fig. 9), the Boogie code we generate updates the τ map mentioned previously in addition to allocating new memory. Specifically, using the global auxiliary **Alloc** map to indicate whether a reference is allocated or not, we obtain a freshly allocated reference v. Then we initialize $\tau[v]$ to be C and also call C's constructor as required by Solidity semantics.

---

[4] We assume that the hash function is collision-free. In our implementation, we enforce this by keeping a mapping from each string constant to a counter.

$$\frac{\vdash e \hookrightarrow \chi}{\vdash \mathbf{require}(e) \rightsquigarrow \mathbf{assume} \; \chi} \; \text{(Req)} \qquad \frac{\vdash e \hookrightarrow \chi}{\vdash \mathbf{assert}(e) \rightsquigarrow \mathbf{assert} \; \chi} \; \text{(Asrt)}$$

$$\frac{\vdash s_1 \rightsquigarrow \omega_1 \quad \vdash s_2 \rightsquigarrow \omega_2}{\vdash s_1; s_2 \rightsquigarrow \omega_1; \omega_2} \; \text{(Seq)} \qquad \frac{\vdash e \hookrightarrow \chi \quad \vdash s_1 \rightsquigarrow \omega_1 \quad \vdash s_2 \rightsquigarrow \omega_2}{\vdash \mathbf{if} \; (e) \; \{s_1\} \; \mathbf{else} \; \{s_2\} \rightsquigarrow \mathbf{if} \; (\chi) \; \{\omega_1\} \; \mathbf{else} \; \{\omega_2\}} \; \text{(Cond)}$$

$$\frac{\vdash e_1 \hookrightarrow \chi_1 \quad \vdash e_2 \hookrightarrow \chi_2}{\vdash e_1 := e_2 \rightsquigarrow \chi_1 := \chi_2} \; \text{(Asgn)} \qquad \frac{\vdash e \hookrightarrow \chi \quad \vdash s \rightsquigarrow \omega}{\vdash \mathbf{while} \; (e) \; \mathbf{do} \; \{s\} \rightsquigarrow \mathbf{while} \; (\chi) \; \mathbf{do} \; \{\omega\}} \; \text{(Loop)}$$

$$\frac{\begin{array}{c} \vdash e_r \hookrightarrow \chi_r \quad \vdash e_i \hookrightarrow \chi_i \quad i = 1, \ldots, n \quad \text{fresh } v \quad C_j <: \mathit{Type}(\mathbf{this}) \quad j = 1, \ldots, m \\ \omega \equiv \mathbf{if} \; (\tau[\mathbf{this}] = C_1) \; \{\mathbf{call} \; v := f^{C_1}(\mathbf{this}, \chi_1, \ldots, \chi_n, \mathbf{sender}); \; \chi_r := v\} \; \mathbf{else \; if} \ldots \\ \mathbf{else \; if} \; (\tau[\mathbf{this}] = C_m) \; \{\mathbf{call} \; v := f^{C_m}(\mathbf{this}, \chi_1, \ldots, \chi_n, \mathbf{sender}); \; \chi_r := v\} \end{array}}{\vdash e_r := f(e_1, \ldots, e_n) \rightsquigarrow \omega} \; \text{(ICall)}$$

$$\frac{\begin{array}{c} \vdash e_r \hookrightarrow \chi_r \quad \vdash e_i \hookrightarrow \chi_i \quad i = 0, \ldots, n \quad \text{fresh } v \quad C_j <: \mathit{Type}(e_0) \quad j = 1, \ldots, m \\ \omega \equiv \mathbf{if} \; (\tau[\chi_0] = C_1) \; \{\mathbf{call} \; v := f^{C_1}(\chi_0, \chi_1, \ldots, \chi_n, \mathbf{this}); \; \chi_r := v\} \; \mathbf{else \; if} \; \ldots \\ \mathbf{else \; if} \; (\tau[\chi_0] = C_m) \; \{\mathbf{call} \; v := f^{C_m}(\chi_0, \chi_1, \ldots, \chi_n, \mathbf{this}); \; \chi_r := v\} \end{array}}{\vdash e_r := e_0.f(e_1, \ldots, e_n) \rightsquigarrow \omega} \; \text{(ECall)}$$

$$\frac{\begin{array}{c} \vdash e_r \hookrightarrow \chi_r \quad \vdash e_i \hookrightarrow \chi_i \quad i = 1, \ldots, n \quad \text{fresh } v \\ \omega \equiv \mathbf{havoc} \; v; \; \mathbf{assume} \; \neg \mathtt{Alloc}[v]; \; \mathtt{Alloc}[v] := \mathbf{true}; \\ \mathbf{assume} \; \tau[v] = C; \; \mathbf{call} \; f_0^C(v, \chi_1, \ldots, \chi_n, \mathbf{this}); \; \chi_r := v \end{array}}{\vdash e_r := \mathbf{new} \; C(e_1, \ldots, e_n) \rightsquigarrow \omega} \; \text{(NewCont)}$$

Fig. 9. Inference rules for encoding Solidity statements to Boogie statements. $\mathit{Type}(e)$ is a function that returns the static type of Solidity expression e. Symbol f^C denotes the function f in contract C, and f_0^C denotes the constructor of contract C. The $<:$ relation represents the sub-typing relationship.

4.4   Invariant Generation

As mentioned earlier, translating Solidity code into Boogie allows VERISOL to leverage the existing ecosystem around Boogie, including efficient verification condition generation [25]. However, in order to completely automate verification (even for loop and recursion-free contracts), we still need to infer a suitable contract invariant as discussed in Sect. 4.2.

VERISOL uses monomial predicate abstraction [17, 22, 23] to automatically infer contract invariants. Specifically, the inference algorithm conjectures the conjunction of all candidate predicates as an inductive invariant and progressively weakens it based on failure to prove a candidate predicate inductive. This algorithm converges fairly fast even on large examples but relies on starting with a superset of necessary predicates. In the current implementation of VERISOL, we obtain candidate invariants by instantiating the predicate template $e_1 \bowtie e_2$ where $\bowtie$ is either equality or disequality. Here, expressions e_1, e_2 can be instantiated with variables corresponding to roles and states in the Workbench policy as well as constants. We have found these candidate predicates to be sufficiently general for automatically verifying semantic conformance of most Workbench contracts; however, additional predicates may be required for other types of contracts.

Table 1. Experimental results. ✓ denotes fully verified, × denotes refuted, and M denotes fully verified with manual effort.

Name	Description	Orig SLOC	Inst SLOC	Init Stat	After Fix	Time (s)
AssetTransfer	Selling high-value assets	192	444	×	✓	2.1
BasicProvenance	Keeping record of ownership	43	95	✓	✓	1.5
BazaarItemListing	Multiple workflow scenario for selling items	98	175	×	✓	2.3
DefectCompCounter	Product counting for manufacturers	31	68	✓	✓	1.3
DigitalLocker	Sharing digitally locked files	129	260	×	✓	1.7
FreqFlyerRewards	Calculating frequent flyer rewards	47	90	✓	✓	1.3
HelloBlockchain	Request and response (Fig. 1)	32	78	✓	✓	1.3
PingPongGame	Multiple workflow for two-player games	74	136	×	M	2.1
RefrigTransport	Provenance scenario with IoT monitoring	118	187	✓	✓	2.2
RoomThermostat	Thermostat installation and use	42	99	✓	✓	1.3
SimpleMarketplace	Owner and buyer transactions	62	118	✓	✓	1.4
Average	–	79	159	–	–	1.7

4.5 Bounded Model Checking

If VERISOL fails to verify contract correctness using monomial predicate abstraction, it employs an assertion-directed bounded verifier, namely CORRAL [24], to look for a transaction sequence leading to an assertion violation.

CORRAL analyzes the harness in Fig. 4 by unrolling the loop k times and uses a combination of *abstraction refinement* techniques (including lazy inlining of nested procedures) to look for counterexamples in a scalable manner. Thus, when VERISOL fails to verify the property, it either successfully finds a counterexample or verifies the lack of any counterexample with k transactions.

5 Evaluation

In this section, we evaluate the effectiveness and efficiency of our approach to checking semantic conformance against Workbench application policies. All experiments are conducted on a machine with Intel Xeon(R) E5-1620 v3 CPU and 32 GB of physical memory, running the Ubuntu 14.04 operating system.

Benchmarks. We have collected all sample smart contracts that are shipped with Workbench and their corresponding application policies on the Github repository of Azure Blockchain [6]. These smart contracts and their policies depict various workflow scenarios that are representative in real-world enterprise use cases. The smart contracts exercise various features of Solidity such as arrays, nested contract creation, external calls, enum types, and mutual recursion. For each smart contract C and its application policy π, we perform program instrumentation as explained in Sect. 3.3 to obtain contract C'. Note that no assertion failure of C' is equivalent to the semantic conformance between C and π, so we include such instrumented smart contracts in our benchmark set.

Main Results. Table 1 summarizes the results of our experimental evaluation. Here, the "Description" column describes the contract's usage scenario. The next two columns give the number of lines of Solidity code before and after the instrumentation described in Sect. 3.3. The last three columns present the main verification results: In particular, "Init Stat" shows the result of applying VERISOL on the original smart contract, and "After Fix" presents the result of VERISOL after we manually fix the bug (if any). Finally, "Time" shows the running time of VERISOL in seconds when applied to the fixed contracts.

Our experimental results demonstrate that VERISOL is useful for checking semantic conformance between Workbench contracts and the policies. In particular, VERISOL finds bugs in 4 out of 11 well-tested contracts and precisely pinpoints the trace leading to the violation. Our results also demonstrate that VERISOL can effectively automate semantic conformance proofs, as it can successfully verify all the contracts after fixing the original bug. Moreover, for 10 out of the 11 contracts, the invariant inference techniques sufficed to make the proofs completely push-button. Our candidate templates for contract invariant did not suffice for the **PingPongGame** contract mainly due to the presence of mutually recursive functions between two contracts. This required us to manually provide a function summary for the mutually recursive procedures that states an invariant over the state variable s_w of the sender contract (e.g. $s_w[\texttt{msg.sender}] = s_1 \lor s_w[\texttt{msg.sender}] = s_2$ where s_i are states of the sender contract). This illustrates that we can achieve the power of the sound Boogie modular verification to perform non-trivial proofs with modest manual overhead. We are currently working on extending the templates for contract invariant inference to richer templates for inferring postconditions for recursive procedures.

Bug Analysis. The four bugs found by VERISOL can be categorized into two classes: (i) incorrect state transition, and (ii) incorrect initial state. We briefly discuss these two classes of bugs.

Incorrect State Transition. This class of bugs arises when the implementation of a function in the contract violates the state transition stated by the policy. VERISOL has found such non-conformance in the **AssetTransfer** and **PingPongGame** contracts. Let us consider **AssetTransfer** [7] as a concrete example. In this contract, actions are guarded by the membership of **msg.sender** within one of the roles or instance role variables. VERISOL found the transition from state `BuyerAccepted` to state `Accepted` in the `Accept` function had no matching transitions in the policy. Specifically, the policy allows a transition from `BuyerAccepted` to `SellerAccepted` when invoking the function `Accept` and `msg.sender` equals the instance role variable `InstanceOwner`. However, the implementation of function `Accept` transitions to the state `Accepted` instead of `SellerAccepted`. From the perspective of the bounded verifier, this is a fairly deep bug, as it requires at least 6 transactions to reach the state `BuyerAccepted` from the initial state.

Incorrect Initial State. This class of bugs arises when the initial state of a smart contract is not established as instructed by the corresponding policy. We have found such non-conformance in `DigitalLocker` and `BazaarItemListing`. For instance, the policy of `DigitalLocker` requires the initial state to be `Requested`, but the implementation ends up incorrectly setting the initial state to `DocumentReview`. In the `BazaarItemListing` benchmark, the developer fails to set the initial state of the contract despite the policy requiring it to be set to `ItemAvailable`.

6 Related Work

In this section, we discuss prior work on ensuring the safety and security of smart contracts. Existing techniques can be roughly categorized into several categories, including static approaches for finding vulnerable patterns, formal verification techniques, and runtime checking. In addition, there has been work on formalizing the semantics of EVM in a formal language such as the $\mathcal{K}$ Framework [20]. There are also several works that discuss a survey and taxonomy of vulnerabilities in smart contracts [14,26,28].

Static Analysis. The static analysis tools are based on a choice of data-flow analysis or symbolic execution to find variants of known vulnerable patterns. Such patterns include reentrancy, transaction ordering dependencies, sending ether to unconstrained addresses, use of block time-stamps, mishandled exceptions, calling `suicide` on an unconstrained address, etc. Tools based on symbolic execution include Oyente [26], MAIAN [28], Manticore [10], and Mythril++ [11]. Several data-flow based tools also exist such as Securify [29] and Slither [12]. MadMax [18] uses static analysis to find vulnerabilities related to out-of-gas exceptions. These tools neither check semantic conformance nor verify assertions. Instead, they mostly find instances of known vulnerable patterns. On the other hand, VERISOL does not reason about gas consumption since it analyzes Solidity code, and it also needs the vulnerabilities to be expressed as formal specifications.

Formal Verification. F* [16] and Zeus [21] use formal verification for checking correctness of smart contracts. These approaches translate Solidity to the formal verification languages of F* and LLVM respectively and then apply F*-based verifiers and constrained horn clause solvers to check the correctness of the translated program. Although the F* based approach is fairly expressive, the tool only covers a small subset of Solidity without loops and requires substantial user guidance to discharge proofs of user-specified assertions. The design of Zeus shares similarities with VERISOL in that it translates Solidity to an intermediate language and uses SMT based solvers to discharge the verification problem. However, one of the key contributions of this paper is the semantic conformance checking problem for smart contracts, which Zeus does not address. Unfortunately, we were unable to obtain a copy of Zeus, making it difficult for us to perform an experimental comparison for discharging assertions in Solidity code.

Other Approaches. In addition to static analyzers and formal verification tools, there are also other approaches that enforce safe reentrancy patterns at runtime by borrowing ideas from linearizability [19]. Another related work is FSolidM [27], which provides an approach to specify smart contracts using a finite state machine with actions written in Solidity. Although there is a similarity in their state machine model with our Workbench policies, they do not consider access control, and the actions do not have nested procedure calls or loops. Finally, the FSolidM tool does not provide any static or dynamic verification support.

7 Conclusion

In this work, we described one of the first uses of automated formal verification for smart contracts in an industrial setting. We formalized the semantic conformance checking problem between Workbench contracts and application policies, and proposed to use program instrumentation to enforce such policies. We also developed a new verifier VERISOL using the Boogie tool chain and demonstrated its effectiveness and efficiency for smart contract verification and bug-finding.

References

1. Explaining the DAO exploit for beginners in solidity (2016). https://medium.com/@MyPaoG/explaining-the-dao-exploit-for-beginners-in-solidity-80ee84f0d470
2. Solidity: Function modifiers (2016). https://solidity.readthedocs.io/en/v0.4.24/structure-of-a-contract.html#function-modifiers
3. Forecast: Blockchain business value, worldwide, 2017–2030 (2017). https://www.gartner.com/en/documents/3627117
4. Microsoft azure blockchain (2017). https://azure.microsoft.com/en-us/solutions/blockchain/
5. Parity: The bug that put $169m of ethereum on ice? Yeah, it was on the todo list for months (2017). https://www.theregister.co.uk/2017/11/16/parity_flaw_not_fixed
6. Applications and smart contract samples for workbench (2018). https://github.com/Azure-Samples/blockchain/tree/master/blockchain-workbench/application-and-smart-contract-samples
7. Asset transfer sample for azure blockchain workbench (2018). https://github.com/Azure-Samples/blockchain/tree/master/blockchain-workbench/application-and-smart-contract-samples/asset-transfer
8. Azure blockchain content and samples (2018). https://github.com/Azure-Samples/blockchain

9. Azure blockchain workbench (2018). https://azure.microsoft.com/en-us/features/blockchain-workbench/
10. Manticore (2018). https://github.com/trailofbits/manticore
11. Mythril classic: Security analysis tool for ethereum smart contracts (2018). https://github.com/ConsenSys/mythril-classic
12. Slither, the solidity source analyzer (2018). https://github.com/trailofbits/slither
13. Verisol: A formal verifier and analysis tool for solidity smart contracts (2018). https://github.com/Microsoft/verisol
14. Atzei, N., Bartoletti, M., Cimoli, T.: A survey of attacks on ethereum smart contracts (SoK). In: Maffei, M., Ryan, M. (eds.) POST 2017. LNCS, vol. 10204, pp. 164–186. Springer, Heidelberg (2017). https://doi.org/10.1007/978-3-662-54455-6_8
15. Barnett, M., Chang, B.-Y.E., DeLine, R., Jacobs, B., Leino, K.R.M.: Boogie: a modular reusable verifier for object-oriented programs. In: de Boer, F.S., Bonsangue, M.M., Graf, S., de Roever, W.-P. (eds.) FMCO 2005. LNCS, vol. 4111, pp. 364–387. Springer, Heidelberg (2006). https://doi.org/10.1007/11804192_17
16. Bhargavan, K., et al.: Formal verification of smart contracts: short paper. In Proceedings of the 2016 ACM Workshop on Programming Languages and Analysis for Security, PLAS@CCS 2016, Vienna, Austria, 24 October 2016, pp. 91–96 (2016)
17. Flanagan, C., Leino, K.R.M.: Houdini, an annotation assistant for ESC/Java. In: Oliveira, J.N., Zave, P. (eds.) FME 2001. LNCS, vol. 2021, pp. 500–517. Springer, Heidelberg (2001). https://doi.org/10.1007/3-540-45251-6_29
18. Grech, N., Kong, M., Jurisevic, A., Brent, L., Scholz, B., Smaragdakis, Y.: MadMax: surviving out-of-gas conditions in ethereum smart contracts. PACMPL 2(OOPSLA), 116:1–116:27 (2018)
19. Grossman, S., et al.: Online detection of effectively callback free objects with applications to smart contracts. PACMPL 2(POPL), 48:1–48:28 (2018)
20. Hildenbrandt, E., et al.: KEVM: a complete formal semantics of the ethereum virtual machine. In 31st IEEE Computer Security Foundations Symposium, CSF 2018, Oxford, United Kingdom, 9–12 July 2018, pp. 204–217 (2018)
21. Kalra, S., Goel, S., Dhawan, M., Sharma, S.: ZEUS: analyzing safety of smart contracts. In: 25th Annual Network and Distributed System Security Symposium, NDSS 2018, San Diego, California, USA, 18–21 February 2018 (2018)
22. Lahiri, S.K., Qadeer, S.: Complexity and algorithms for monomial and clausal predicate abstraction. In: Schmidt, R.A. (ed.) CADE 2009. LNCS (LNAI), vol. 5663, pp. 214–229. Springer, Heidelberg (2009). https://doi.org/10.1007/978-3-642-02959-2_18
23. Lahiri, S.K., Qadeer, S., Galeotti, J.P., Voung, J.W., Wies, T.: Intra-module inference. In: Bouajjani, A., Maler, O. (eds.) CAV 2009. LNCS, vol. 5643, pp. 493–508. Springer, Heidelberg (2009). https://doi.org/10.1007/978-3-642-02658-4_37
24. Lal, A., Qadeer, S., Lahiri, S.K.: A solver for reachability modulo theories. In: Madhusudan, P., Seshia, S.A. (eds.) CAV 2012. LNCS, vol. 7358, pp. 427–443. Springer, Heidelberg (2012). https://doi.org/10.1007/978-3-642-31424-7_32
25. Rustan, K., Leino, M.: Efficient weakest preconditions. Inf. Process. Lett. 93(6), 281–288 (2005)
26. Luu, L., Chu, D.H., Olickel, H., Saxena, P., Hobor, A.: Making smart contracts smarter. In: Proceedings of the 2016 ACM SIGSAC Conference on Computer and Communications Security, Vienna, Austria, 24–28 October 2016, pp. 254–269 (2016)

27. Mavridou, A., Laszka, A.: Tool demonstration: Fsolidm for designing secure ethereum smart contracts. In: Principles of Security and Trust - 7th International Conference, POST 2018, Held as Part of the European Joint Conferences on Theory and Practice of Software, ETAPS 2018, Thessaloniki, Greece, 14–20 April 2018, Proceedings, pp. 270–277 (2018)
28. Nikolic, I., Kolluri, A., Sergey, I., Saxena, P., Hobor, A.: Finding the greedy, prodigal, and suicidal contracts at scale. In: Proceedings of the 34th Annual Computer Security Applications Conference, ACSAC 2018, San Juan, PR, USA, 03–07 December 2018, pp. 653–663 (2018)
29. Tsankov, P., et al.: Securify: practical security analysis of smart contracts. In: Proceedings of the 2018 ACM SIGSAC Conference on Computer and Communications Security, CCS 2018, Toronto, ON, Canada, 15–19 October 2018, pp. 67–82 (2018)
30. Wang, Y., et al.: Formal specification and verification of smart contracts in azure blockchain (2018). https://arxiv.org/abs/1812.08829/

Ghost Code in Action: Automated Verification of a Symbolic Interpreter

Benedikt Becker and Claude Marché[✉]

Inria & LRI (CNRS Univ. Paris-Sud), Université Paris-Saclay, Orsay, France
{benedikt.becker,claude.marche}@inria.fr

Abstract. Symbolic execution is a basic concept for the static analysis of programs. It amounts to representing sets of concrete program states as a logical formula relating the program variables, and interpreting sets of executions as a transformation of that formula. We are interested in formalising the correctness of a symbolic interpreter engine, expressed by an over-approximation property stating that symbolic execution covers all concrete executions, and an under-approximation property stating that no useless symbolic states are generated. Our formalisation is tailored for automated verification, that is the automated discharge of verification conditions to SMT solvers. To achieve this level of automation, we appropriately annotate the code of the symbolic interpreter with an original use of both *ghost* data and *ghost* statements.

Keywords: Deductive program verification · Symbolic execution · Automated theorem proving · Ghost code

1 Introduction

Symbolic execution is one of the basic approaches for analysing program code. It amounts to representing a set of program states as a symbolic formula on the program variables, and interpreting each concrete execution in one of these states as one unique transformation of that formula. This technique allows one to detect if an undesired program state is reachable from a given set of initial inputs. In such a basic form, symbolic execution is a common idea behind more elaborated approaches to the static analysis of programs, such as *model checking* and *abstract interpretation*, and also for *test generation*. Formalisations of such approaches exist, for example the Verasco abstract interpreter [10] is formally specified and verified using the Coq proof assistant [3], but we are not aware of simpler, more basic formalisation of a symbolic execution engine. In the light of advanced verification efforts such as Verasco, the verification of a symbolic execution engine may seem an easy task. However, instead of using a proof assistant like Coq, we aim in this work at the use of *automated verifiers*, where proofs are not constructed interactively but carried out by automated theorem provers. In this work we use the Why3 environment [4] to achieve this task.

This work has been partially supported by the ANR project CoLiS, contract number ANR-15-CE25-0001.

© Springer Nature Switzerland AG 2020
S. Chakraborty and J. A. Navas (Eds.): VSTTE 2019, LNCS 12031, pp. 107–123, 2020.
https://doi.org/10.1007/978-3-030-41600-3_8

Informal Presentation of Symbolic Execution. Let us consider the toy program below from a mini-language in the style of IMP [11].

```
y := x - y - 1;
if y < 10 then x := y - 1 else y := 4 - x
```

Symbolically executing such a program means considering at once a set of possible inputs, a *symbolic state*, defined by a mapping from program variables to logical variables and a logical constraint. For example, let's consider

$$(x \mapsto u, y \mapsto v \mid 0 \leq u \leq 7 \wedge 1 \leq v \leq 11)$$

as an initial symbolic state for our toy program. The symbolic execution of the first assignment produces the new symbolic state

$$(x \mapsto u, y \mapsto w \mid \exists v.\ 0 \leq u \leq 7 \wedge 1 \leq v \leq 11 \wedge w = u - v - 1)$$

which represents the collection of concrete states that can be reached from any concrete state satisfying the initial constraint. The symbolic execution of the if statement results in a pair of symbolic states corresponding to the two branches:

$$
\begin{aligned}
& (x \mapsto t, y \mapsto w \mid \exists u, v.\ 0 \leq u \leq 7 \wedge 1 \leq v \leq 11 \wedge \\
& \qquad\qquad\qquad\qquad w = u - v - 1 \wedge w < 10 \wedge t = w - 1) \\
\cup\ & (x \mapsto u, y \mapsto t \mid \exists v, w.\ 0 \leq u \leq 7 \wedge 1 \leq v \leq 11 \wedge \\
& \qquad\qquad\qquad\qquad w = u - v - 1 \wedge w \geq 10 \wedge t = 4 - u)
\end{aligned}
$$

Using a constraint solver that is able to detect if a constraint is unsatisfiable, it is possible to discard some of these symbolic execution branches.

Handling Loops. Loops can be handled similarly to conditionals by executing all possible paths of concrete execution. In most cases, however, an infinite set of symbolic states will be produced, and symbolic execution will be non-terminating even on terminating programs. A simple solution is to restrict the number of loop iterations by a limit N given as a parameter of the symbolic execution, resulting in a N-bounded symbolic execution, also called *loop-k* [1].

When using a loop limit, we would like to distinguish between the executions that terminate normally and executions that reach the loop limit. For example, the symbolic execution of the program

```
y := 1;
while x > 1 do y := y * x; x := x - 1 done
```

with loop limit $N = 3$ and initial state $(x \mapsto v_1 \mid \textbf{true})$, results in two sets of symbolic states, where intermediate logical variables are existentially quantified in the constraint. One set of symbolic states represent normal *behaviour*:

$$(x \mapsto v_1, y \mapsto v_2 \mid v_1 \leq 1 \wedge v_2 = 1)$$
$$\cup \quad (x \mapsto v_3, y \mapsto v_4 \mid \exists\, v_1, v_2.\ v_1 = 2 \wedge v_2 = 1 \wedge v_3 = 1 \wedge v_4 = 2)$$
$$\cup \quad (x \mapsto v_5, y \mapsto v_6 \mid \exists\, v_1, v_2, v_3, v_4.\ v_1 = 3 \wedge v_2 = 1 \wedge$$
$$v_3 = 2 \wedge v_4 = 2 \wedge v_5 = 1 \wedge v_6 = 6)$$

and one represents the abnormal behaviour obtained from reaching the loop limit:

$$(x \mapsto v_5, y \mapsto v_6 \mid \exists\, v_1, v_2, v_3, v_4.\ v_1 > 3 \wedge v_2 = 1 \wedge$$
$$v_3 > 2 \wedge v_4 = 2 \wedge v_5 > 1 \wedge v_6 = 6)$$

In the remainder of this article we consider an additional abnormal behaviour obtained when trying to evaluate a variable that is not bound in the context. Symbolic execution thus produces a triple of finite sets of symbolic states, respectively for each of the Normal, LoopLimit and UnboundVar behaviours.

Introduction to Ghost Annotations. Adding *ghost annotations* to a program is a powerful versatile approach to proving advanced program properties [7]. A ghost annotation can be used at the level of data structures, e.g. as a ghost field in a record, or at the level of the code, e.g. as an assignment to a ghost variable. Ghost annotations may even be required to simply express a property, and they can greatly improve the degree of automation when using automated verifiers [5]. An essential property of ghost code is that it must never interfere with the execution of regular code [7], a property that is ensured statically in the verifier Why3 [4] we use in this work.

A specific use case of ghost code is the handling of existential quantifiers, for example in the post-condition of a program. Assume one has a program with a post-condition of the following form:

$$\texttt{function } f\ (x) \texttt{ returns } y$$
$$\texttt{ensures } \{\ \forall z.\ P(x, z) \rightarrow \exists t.\ Q(x, y, z, t)\ \}$$

Proving a quantified post-condition of this form is generally out of reach of automated provers. A workaround is to turn the quantified variables into ghost parameters and results of the function:

$$\texttt{function } f\ (x, \texttt{ ghost } z) \texttt{ returns } (y, \texttt{ ghost } t)$$
$$\texttt{requires } \{\ P(x, z)\ \}$$
$$\texttt{ensures } \{\ Q(x, y, z, t)\ \}$$

This reformulation is logically equivalent to the former one because the VC generation will universally quantify over parameters and existentially quantify over results. An important advantage of the ghost reformulation is that ghost code can be added to the body of f to compute an appropriate value of t. Moreover, when f is defined recursively, appropriate values of z can be passed to the recursive calls.

Literals:	$\bar{n} \in \bar{\mathbb{N}}$
Variables:	$x \in PVar$
Expressions:	$e ::= \bar{n} \mid x \mid e - e$
Instructions:	$i ::= \texttt{skip} \mid x := e \mid i;i \mid \texttt{if } e \texttt{ then } i \texttt{ else } i \mid \texttt{while } e \texttt{ do } e$

Fig. 1. Syntax of the IMP language

Structure of This Paper. In Sect. 2, we present the toy mini-IMP language for which we formalise our symbolic execution engine. We present its syntax and the formal semantics of its concrete execution. As a first exercise, we develop a concrete interpreter and prove its correctness. In Sect. 3, we introduce our symbolic interpreter engine and a formalisation of the expected properties, and present a technique based on ghost annotations to prove the properties using automated theorem provers. We conclude by a discussion of related and future work in Sect. 4.

Our Why3 development of the concrete and symbolic interpreters, and the material required to replay the proofs and compile and execute the interpreters, is available at http://toccata.lri.fr/gallery/symbolic_imp.en.html.

2   Presentation of the IMP Language

We consider a simple, imperative language with close resemblance to the *imp* language [11]. The abstract syntax of this language, called IMP, is shown in Fig. 1, and features two syntactic categories: expressions and instructions. An expression has type integer and is either an integer literal, a program variable from an infinite set *PVar*, or a subtraction operation. An instruction is either a variable assignment, or it combines other instructions into a sequence, a conditional, or a WHILE loop. Expressions are used as tests in conditionals and loops, where non-zero values represent the Boolean value TRUE.

2.1   Formal Semantics

We formalise the natural semantics of the IMP language using inductive rules, encoded by inductive predicates in Why3.

The natural semantics of expressions is defined by a judgement $e/\Gamma \Downarrow \alpha$ with the inductive rules shown in Fig. 2. Expressions are evaluated in the context of a *concrete variable environment* $\Gamma : PVar \twoheadrightarrow \mathbb{Z}$, a partial function from program variables to integers with domain $\mathrm{dom}(\Gamma)$. The behaviour of an expression is either normal and carries an integer, or it indicates the use of an unbound variable. A literal evaluates with normal behaviour to its integer value. A variable evaluates with normal behaviour to its value in the variable environment, if the variable is defined. The binary operation has normal behaviour and evaluates to the subtraction of the values of its operands, if both operands have normal behaviour. The evaluation of an unbound variable triggers the behaviour UnboundVar, which is propagated across binary operations.

Expression behaviour: $\alpha ::= \mathsf{Normal}\ \mathbb{Z}\ |\ \mathsf{UnboundVar}$

LITERAL

$$\overline{\bar{n}/\Gamma \Downarrow \mathsf{Normal}\ n}$$

VAR
$$\frac{x \in \mathrm{dom}(\Gamma) \qquad \Gamma[x] = n}{x/\Gamma \Downarrow \mathsf{Normal}\ n}$$

VAR-ERR
$$\frac{x \notin \mathrm{dom}(\Gamma)}{x/\Gamma \Downarrow \mathsf{UnboundVar}}$$

SUB
$$\frac{e_1/\Gamma \Downarrow \mathsf{Normal}\ n_1 \qquad e_2/\Gamma \Downarrow \mathsf{Normal}\ n_2}{e_1 - e_2/\Gamma \Downarrow \mathsf{Normal}\ (n_1 - n_2)}$$

SUB-ERR-1
$$\frac{e_1/\Gamma \Downarrow \mathsf{UnboundVar}}{e_1 - e_2/\Gamma \Downarrow \mathsf{UnboundVar}}$$

SUB-ERR-2
$$\frac{e_1/\Gamma \Downarrow \mathsf{Normal}\ n_1 \qquad e_2/\Gamma \Downarrow \mathsf{UnboundVar}}{e_1 - e_2/\Gamma \Downarrow \mathsf{UnboundVar}}$$

Fig. 2. Semantics of expressions, which is formalized an inductive predicate in Why3

Instruction behaviour: $\beta ::= \mathsf{Normal}\ |\ \mathsf{UnboundVar}\ |\ \mathsf{LoopLimit}$

SKIP

$$\overline{\mathtt{skip}/\Gamma \Downarrow^N \mathsf{Normal}/\Gamma}$$

ASSIGN
$$\frac{e/\Gamma \Downarrow \mathsf{Normal}\ n}{x := e/\Gamma \Downarrow^N \mathsf{Normal}/\Gamma[x \leftarrow n]}$$

ASSIGN-ERR
$$\frac{e/\Gamma \Downarrow \mathsf{UnboundVar}}{x := e/\Gamma \Downarrow^N \mathsf{UnboundVar}/\Gamma}$$

SEQ
$$\frac{i_1/\Gamma \Downarrow^N \mathsf{Normal}/\Gamma_1 \qquad i_2/\Gamma_1 \Downarrow^N \beta/\Gamma_2}{i_1 ; i_2/\Gamma \Downarrow^N \beta/\Gamma_2}$$

SEQ-ERR
$$\frac{i_1/\Gamma \Downarrow^N \beta/\Gamma_1 \qquad \beta \neq \mathsf{Normal}}{i_1 ; i_2/\Gamma \Downarrow^N \beta/\Gamma_1}$$

COND-TRUE
$$\frac{e/\Gamma \Downarrow \mathsf{Normal}\ n \qquad n \neq 0 \qquad i_1/\Gamma \Downarrow^N \beta/\Gamma'}{\text{if } e \text{ then } i_1 \text{ else } i_2/\Gamma \Downarrow^N \beta/\Gamma'}$$

COND-FALSE
$$\frac{e/\Gamma \Downarrow \mathsf{Normal}\ 0 \qquad i_2/\Gamma \Downarrow^N \beta/\Gamma'}{\text{if } e \text{ then } i_1 \text{ else } i_2/\Gamma \Downarrow^N \beta/\Gamma'}$$

COND-ERR
$$\frac{e/\Gamma \Downarrow \mathsf{UnboundVar}}{\text{if } e \text{ then } i_1 \text{ else } i_2/\Gamma \Downarrow^N \mathsf{UnboundVar}/\Gamma}$$

WHILE
$$\frac{e, i/\Gamma \Downarrow^{0/N} \beta/\Gamma'}{\text{while } e \text{ do } i/\Gamma \Downarrow^N \beta/\Gamma'}$$

Fig. 3. Semantics rules for instructions

The natural semantics of instructions is defined by a judgement $i/\Gamma \Downarrow^N \beta/\Gamma'$. The inductive rules are shown in Fig. 3. A concrete variable environment Γ constitutes the program state, which can be modified by the evaluation of an instruction to Γ'. The value $N \in \mathbb{N} \cup \{\infty\}$ specifies an optional iteration limit for WHILE loops, where $N = \infty$ disables the iteration limit. N is a parameter and

WHILE-LIMIT
$$\frac{n = N}{e, i/\Gamma \Downarrow^{n/N} \text{LoopLimit}/\Gamma}$$

WHILE-FALSE
$$\frac{n < N \qquad e/\Gamma \Downarrow \text{Normal } 0}{e, i/\Gamma \Downarrow^{n/N} \text{Normal}/\Gamma}$$

WHILE-LOOP
$$\frac{n < N \qquad e/\Gamma_1 \Downarrow \text{Normal } m \qquad m \neq 0}{i/\Gamma_1 \Downarrow^N \text{Normal}/\Gamma_2 \qquad e, i/\Gamma_2 \Downarrow^{(n+1)/N} \beta/\Gamma_3}{e, i/\Gamma_1 \Downarrow^{n/N} \beta/\Gamma_3}$$

WHILE-TEST-ERR
$$\frac{n < N \qquad e/\Gamma \Downarrow \text{UnboundVar}}{e, i/\Gamma \Downarrow^{n/N} \text{UnboundVar}/\Gamma}$$

WHILE-BODY-ERR
$$\frac{n < N \qquad e/\Gamma_1 \Downarrow \text{Normal } m \qquad m \neq 0 \qquad i/\Gamma_1 \Downarrow^N \beta/\Gamma_2 \qquad \beta \neq \text{Normal}}{e, i/\Gamma_1 \Downarrow^{n/N} \beta/\Gamma_2}$$

Fig. 4. Semantics rules for an optionally bounded while loop

kept constant across the evaluation of instructions. The instruction behaviour β is either normal, indicates an unbound variable in a sub-expression, or the reaching of the loop limit. An assignment changes the value of the variable in the environment to the value of an expression, if the expression evaluates with normal behaviour. Expressions are used as tests in conditionals and WHILE loops, and the integer 0 is interpreted as the Boolean value FALSE, and any non-zero value is interpreted as TRUE. Abnormal behaviour (UnboundVar, LoopLimit) of sub-expressions and sub-instructions is propagated to the behaviour of the instruction.

The semantics of loops is defined by a judgement $e, i/\Gamma \Downarrow^{n/N} \beta/\Gamma'$ for a test expression e and a loop body i. The inductive rules are shown in Fig. 4. When the loop counter $n \in \mathbb{N}$ reaches the loop limit N, the evaluation of the loop terminates with behaviour LoopLimit. All other rules require the number of previous iterations smaller than the loop limit. The evaluation of a loop terminates with normal behaviour when the test expression evaluates to zero. Otherwise, and if the evaluation of the loop body has normal behaviour, the evaluation of the loop continues with an increased loop counter, and the result of the continuation determines the result of the loop. Abnormal behaviour in the test expression or loop body is propagated to the behaviour of the loop.

2.2   Concrete Execution

A concrete interpreter of the IMP language is implemented in the programming language of Why3. A global, imperative variable environment from module Env (Listing 1) constitutes the program state. The type of the variable environment is left abstract in the Why3 program, and can be used only through the functions of module Env. These are specified via post-conditions in terms of the partial function Γ that represents the environment in the logical specifications. The

```
module Env
   type env = abstract { mutable Γ: PVar ↦ ℤ }

   val empty (_:unit) : env ensures { ∀x. x ∉ dom(result.Γ) }

   val set (e:env) (x:PVar) (n:ℤ) : unit
     writes { e }
     ensures { e.Γ = (old e.Γ)[x ← n] }

   exception Unbound_var

   val find (e:env) (x:PVar) : ℤ
     ensures { x ∈ dom(e.Γ) ∧ result = (e.Γ x) }
     raises { Unbound_var → x ∉ dom(e.Γ) }
end
```

Listing 1. The imperative variable environment Env

interpretation of expressions and instructions is implemented by two functions that map the language constructs of the IMP language to the corresponding language constructs of Why3 (see Listing 2). The functions of the interpreter return normally in case of a normal evaluation, and exceptions are raised for unbound variables. The interpretation of loops is unbound in the concrete interpreter.

The soundness of the concrete interpreter with respect to the formal semantics without loop limit ($N = \infty$) is expressed by post-conditions for normal behaviour (keyword ensures) and exceptional behaviour (keyword raises) (see Listing 2). Each post-condition contains a semantic judgement that describes the transformation of the global variable environment before running the interpreter (old env) to the variable environment after running the interpreter (env). A loop invariant is required to verify the soundness of the while loop in Why3 that executes the loops of IMP. A ghost variable Γ_0 retains the initial variable environment and a mutable ghost variable n acts as an iteration counter. The loop invariant then states that the result of the loop when starting in the current program state (env.Γ) is the result of the loop when starting in the initial variable environment Γ_0.

Why3 splits the proof into 8 verification goals for interp_exp (covering also the termination) and 16 goals for interp_ins, corresponding to the execution paths of the interpreter functions. All verification conditions were automatically proven by either CVC4 or Alt-Ergo in fractions of a second after applying basic interactive proof steps in Why3 [6].

```
let env = Env.empty () (* A global, imperative variable environment *)

let rec interp_exp (e : expression) : int
  variant { e }
  ensures { e/env.Γ ⇓ Normal result }
  raises  { Env.Unbound_var → e/env.Γ ⇓ UnboundVar }
= match e with
    | Lit  n → n
    | Var  x → Env.find env x
    | Sub  e₁ e₂ → interp_exp e₁ - interp_exp e₂
  end

let rec interp_ins (i : instruction) : unit
  writes  { env.Γ }
  ensures { i/(old env.Γ) ⇓∞ Normal/env.Γ }
  raises  { Env.Unbound_var → i/(old env.Γ) ⇓∞ UnboundVar/env.Γ }
= match i with
    | Skip → ()
    | Assign x e → Env.set env x (interp_exp e)
    | Seq i₁ i₂ → interp_ins i₁; interp_ins i₂
    | If e i₁ i₂ → if interp_exp e ≠ 0 then interp_ins i₁ else interp_ins i₂
    | While e i →
      let ghost Γ₀ = env.Γ in let ghost ref n = 0 in
      while interp_exp e ≠ 0 do
        invariant { ∀β/Γ′. e,i/env.Γ ⇓ⁿ/∞ β/Γ′ → e,i/Γ₀ ⇓⁰/∞ β/Γ′ }
        interp_ins i; n ← n + 1
      done
  end
```

Listing 2. A concrete interpreter for the IMP language

3   Symbolic Execution

Following the informal presentation of symbolic execution in Sect. 1, we recall that a symbolic state $(\sigma \mid C)$ has two components: a symbolic environment $\sigma : PVar \rightarrowtail SVar$, which is a partial function from program variables to symbolic variables with domain $\mathrm{dom}(\sigma)$, and a constraint C on symbolic variables. Finite sets of symbolic states are designated by symbol Σ. A symbolic interpreter is a function $\mathtt{sym\_interp\_ins\_}N(\sigma \mid C)(i)$ that is parameterised by a loop limit $N \in \mathbb{N}$, and takes an initial symbolic state and an instruction as arguments. The symbolic interpreter returns a set Σ_* of symbolic result states $(\sigma \mid C)_\beta$, i.e., symbolic states annotated with a behaviour $\beta \in \{\mathsf{Normal}, \mathsf{UnboundVar}, \mathsf{LoopLimit}\}$. For any behaviour β, Σ_β designates the symbolic states in Σ_* with behaviour β.

The constraint language for IMP is shown in Fig. 5. A constraint is either trivially true, the equality or disequality between two symbolic expressions, the conjunction of two constraints, or an existential quantification of a variable over a constraint. A symbolic expression corresponds to a program expression with

Symbolic variables: $v \in SVar$
Symbolic expressions: $se ::= n \mid v \mid se - se$
                         $\in Sym\text{-}expr$
Constraints: $C ::= \top \mid se = se \mid se \neq se \mid C \wedge C \mid \exists v.C$
                         $\in Constraint$

Fig. 5. Constraint language for the symbolic interpretation of IMP

symbolic variables in place of program variables. The application of a symbolic environment to a program expression, $\sigma(e)$, is defined by the natural extension of the symbolic environment to program expressions. The application results in a symbolic expression, if the symbolic environment is defined on all variables occurring in the expression, and is undefined otherwise.

An interpretation, $\rho : SVar \rightharpoonup \mathbb{Z}$, is a partial function from symbolic variables to integers with domain $\mathrm{dom}(\rho)$. The application of an interpretation to a symbolic expression, $\rho(se)$, is defined as the natural extension of ρ to symbolic expressions, if all variables in se are in $\mathrm{dom}(\rho)$, and undefined otherwise. An interpretation ρ is a solution of a constraint C, denoted $\rho \models C$, if the domain of ρ contains all symbolic variables in C and the formula obtained from C by substituting all symbolic variables by their values in ρ, is true. A solution $\rho \models C$ to the constraint of a symbolic state $(\sigma \mid C)$ defines a concrete variable environment by composition with the symbolic environment, $\Gamma = \rho \circ \sigma$. These concrete environments are the instances of the symbolic state.

3.1   Correctness Properties of a Symbolic Interpreter

The correctness of a concrete interpreter is defined by two properties: that every evaluation result derivable by the semantic rules is produced by the interpreter (completeness), and that every result of the interpreter is derivable by the semantic rules (soundness). Symbolic interpretation, however, describes program execution non-deterministically: the initial symbolic state represents a potentially infinite set of initial concrete environments, and the result states represent all concrete environments resulting from all initial environments. The correctness of a symbolic interpreter is defined by two properties that relate the instances of the symbolic states with semantic judgements of the concrete semantics: *over-approximation* and *under-approximation*. Simplified, a symbolic execution is an over-approximation of the concrete execution, if executing an instruction in an instance of the initial symbolic state results in an instance of one of the symbolic result states. Over-approximation is also called *coverage* [2]. A symbolic interpretation is an under-approximation, if every instance of the symbolic result states is the evaluation result of an instance of the initial symbolic state. Under-approximation is also called *precision* [2].

Given the symbolic result states Σ_* resulting from the symbolic execution `interp_ins_N`$(\sigma \mid C)(i)$, the correctness properties can be formalised as follows.

Property 1 (Over-approximation). *The symbolic execution is an over-approximation of the concrete semantics, if for any solution ρ of the initial constraint, $\rho \models C$, and concrete evaluation result $\beta/_{\Gamma'}$ with $i/_{\rho \circ \sigma} \Downarrow^N \beta/_{\Gamma'}$, there exists a symbolic result state $(\sigma' \mid C')_\beta \in \Sigma_*$ and a solution $\rho' \models C'$ such that $\Gamma' = \rho' \circ \sigma'$.*

Property 2 (Under-approximation). *The symbolic execution is an under-approximation of the concrete semantics, if for any symbolic result state $(\sigma' \mid C')_\beta \in \Sigma_*$ and solution $\rho' \models C'$, there exists a solution ρ of the initial constraint, $\rho \models C$, such that $i/_{\rho \circ \sigma} \Downarrow^N \beta/_{\rho' \circ \sigma'}$.*

Reformulation Using Ghost Annotations. The correctness properties contain existential quantifications over solutions for the initial and result symbolic states. As explained in Sect. 1, existential quantifications can be challenging for automatic theorem provers, but are a typical use case of ghost annotations. We thus associate each symbolic state with a ghost interpretation. A ghost-extended symbolic state, $(\sigma \mid C; \rho)$ thus consists of a symbolic environment, a constraint, and a ghost interpretation. From now on, we will only refer to ghost-extended symbolic states. When used in a symbolic interpreter the ghost interpretations do not influence the symbolic execution, but only support proving the properties. They allow for substituting universally or existentially quantified solutions in the properties by the ghost interpretations associated with the initial symbolic state or a resulting symbolic state.

Given the set of extended symbolic result states Σ_* resulting from a symbolic execution `interp_ins`$_N(\sigma \mid C; \rho)(i)$, the above correctness properties can be reformulated equivalently as follows:

Property 3 (Ghost-reformulated Over-approximation). *The symbolic execution is an over-approximation of the concrete semantics, if, assuming that the interpretation ρ of the initial state is a solution of the initial constraint, $\rho \models C$, and given a concrete evaluation result $\beta/_{\Gamma'}$ with $i/_{\rho \circ \sigma} \Downarrow^N \beta/_{\Gamma'}$, there exists a symbolic result state $(\sigma' \mid C'; \rho')_\beta \in \Sigma_*$ such that $\rho' \models C'$ and $\Gamma' = \rho' \circ \sigma'$.*

Property 4 (Ghost-reformulated Under-approximation). *The symbolic execution is an under-approximation of the concrete semantics, if for symbolic result state $(\sigma' \mid C'; \rho')_\beta \in \Sigma_*$ such that $\rho' \models C'$, it holds that $\rho \models C$ and $i/_{\rho \circ \sigma} \Downarrow^N \beta/_{\rho' \circ \sigma'}$.*

3.2   Implementation of the Symbolic Interpreter

We implemented a symbolic interpreter for IMP in the Why3 programming language with main function `sym_interp_ins` (see Listing 3), which is recursively defined over the structure of the instruction. The reformulated correctness properties are formalised as post-conditions of the function.

```
val sym_interp_ins_N(σ | C; ρ)(i) : Σ_*
    ensures { (* Over-approximation *) ρ ⊨ C → ∀β/Γ'. (i/ρ∘σ ⇓^N β/Γ') →
        ∃(σ' | C'; ρ')_β ∈ result. ρ' ⊨ C' ∧ Γ' = ρ' ∘ σ' }
    ensures { (* Under-approximation *)
        ∀(σ' | C'; ρ')_β ∈ result. ρ' ⊨ C' → ρ ⊨ C ∧ (i/ρ∘σ ⇓^N β/ρ'∘σ') }
```

Listing 3. Signature of the basic symbolic interpreter function with correctness properties encoded as post-conditions

Assignment and Quantification over a Variable. To execute an assignment $x := e$, the variable x is assigned in the symbolic environment to a fresh symbolic variable v, and an equality constraint between v and the symbolic expression corresponding to e is added, if the symbolic environment is defined on all variables in e (see Listing 4, Line 21 et seq.). The interpretation ρ is updated by assigning the fresh variable to the value of the symbolic expression in the interpretation. If the program variable was already bound to a variable v' in σ, then the variable v' becomes inaccessible from the symbolic environment and the remaining program. The constraint is replaced by an existential quantification over v'. More precisely, we apply the function existentially_quantify (Line 25) to delegate the construction of the quantification to a constraint solver, which allows for simplifying the constraint by quantifier elimination. The requirements for function existentially_quantify are expressed by its post-conditions: it does not introduce any new variables and it produces a constraint equivalent to an explicit existential quantification.

If the symbolic environment is undefined on any variable in e, the initial symbolic state annotated with behaviour UnboundVar comprises the singleton result set (Line 29).

Updating the ghost interpretation when executing an assignment implies that the interpretation retains values of symbolic variables that satisfy the constraint, and that the interpretation serves as an environment of witnesses to existentially quantified variables. This original aspect must be reflected by the following definition of the predicate $\rho \models C$, in which the last case, the one of existential quantifiers, is to be particularly emphasised:

$$\rho \models C \text{ iff. } \text{vars}(C) \subseteq \text{dom}(\rho) \land \begin{cases} \top & \text{when } C = \top \\ \rho(se_1) = \rho(se_2) & \text{when } C = (se_1 = se_2) \\ \rho(se_1) \neq \rho(se_2) & \text{when } C = (se_1 \neq se_2) \\ \rho \models C_1 \land \rho \models C_2 & \text{when } C = C_1 \land C_2 \\ \rho \models C_1 & \text{when } C = \exists v.C_1 \end{cases}$$

The case of the existential quantifier is non-standard: instead of pretending that "there exists a value for the quantified variable v such that ...", we go even further in the use of ghost annotations by requiring that the ghost interpretation ρ already holds the adequate value for v. This choice is crucial to facilitate the application of automatic theorem provers. A drawback, however, is that we lose invariance with respect to α-renaming, because the witnesses in the interpretation are identified by their exact variable names. This requires extra

```
 1   val fresh (ghost ρ) : SVar
 2     ensures { result ∉ dom(ρ) }
 3
 4   val existentially_quantify (v) (C) : Constraint
 5     ensures { vars(result) ⊆ vars(∃ v. C) }
 6     ensures { ∀ρ.  ρ ⊨ result ↔ ρ ⊨ ∃ v. C }
 7
 8   predicate ρ ⊑ ρ' =
 9     dom(ρ) ⊆ dom(ρ') ∧ ∀ v ∈ dom(ρ). ρ(v) = ρ'(v)
10
11   type sym_state = (σ | C; ghost ρ)
12     invariant { codom(σ) ∪ vars(C) ⊆ dom(ρ) }
13
14   let rec sym_interp_ins_N (σ | C; ρ)(i) : Σ_*
15     ensures { ... (* Over−approximation and under−approximation *) }
16     ensures { (* Result interpretations extend the initial interpretation *)
17       ∀(σ' | C'; ρ')_β ∈ result → ρ ⊑ ρ' }
18     = match i with ...
19     | Assign x e →
20       try
21         let se = σ(e) in
22         let v = fresh ρ in
23         let σ' = σ[x ← v] in
24         let C' =
25           if x ∈ dom(σ) then existentially_quantify (σ(x)) (C ∧ (v = se))
26           else C ∧ (v = se) in
27         let ghost ρ' = ρ[v ← ρ(se)] in
28         {(σ' | C'; ρ')_Normal}
29       with UnboundVar (* from σ(e) *) → {(σ | C; ρ)_UnboundVar} end
```

Listing 4. Symbolic execution of the assignment, with additional post-condition and state invariant to ensure the correct use of the interpretation as an environment of witnesses to existentially quantified variables

care with the concept of "fresh" variables: these have to be fresh even with respect to existentially quantified variables. We ensure this property in the implementation by three means:

1. The function `fresh` has an interpretation as a ghost argument and ensures that the resulting variable is not in the domain of the interpretation (Listing 4, Line 2).
2. An invariant of the symbolic state ensures that the domain of the interpretation covers all variables in the codomain of the symbolic environment and all variables in the constraint, including existentially quantified variables (Line 12).
3. The symbolic execution function always *extends* the interpretation, i.e., the domain of the initial interpretation is a subset of the domains of the resulting interpretation, and all values of the initial interpretation are retained in the resulting interpretations (defined by predicate ⊑, Line 9). This property is ensured by a post-condition (Line 17).

```
let rec sym_interp_ins_N(s)(i) =
  match i with ...
  | Seq i₁ i₂ →
    let Σ* = sym_interp_ins_N(s)(i₁) in
    let Σ'* = sym_interp_ins'_N(Σ_Normal)(i₂) in
    Σ_UnboundVar ∪ Σ_LoopLimit ∪ Σ'*
```

Listing 5. Symbolic execution of sequences

Sequences and Sets of Initial States. The concrete semantics of the sequence of two instructions specifies that the first instruction is evaluated first, and the second instruction is evaluated only if the behaviour of the first instruction was normal. Similarly, the symbolic execution of a sequence starts by executing the first instruction (see Listing 5). The second instruction is executed in the context of the resulting symbolic states annotated with behaviour Normal, using an auxiliary function $\texttt{sym\_interp\_ins'}_N(\Sigma)(i) : \Sigma_*$ that operates on a set of initial states Σ, applies $\texttt{sym\_interp\_ins}$ on each element of Σ, and joins the resulting symbolic state sets. The result of the execution of the sequence is the union of the symbolic result states representing abnormal behaviour in the first instruction, and the symbolic result state set from the second instruction.

Conditionals and State Pruning. Listing 6 shows the symbolic execution of the conditional instruction. The test expression e is converted into a symbolic expression se by applying the symbolic environment. The exception UnboundVar, raised when a variable in e is undefined in σ, results in a singleton set of the initial state annotated with behaviour UnboundVar. The instructions i_1 and i_2 are interpreted in symbolic states that extend the initial symbolic state by constraints stating that se is different from 0, or equal to 0, respectively. If the constraint corresponding to one of the branches is unsatisfiable, the branch is pruned by assuming an empty set. Our symbolic interpreter uses a potentially incomplete procedure maybe_sat for testing unsatisfiability of a constraint. If maybe_sat C returns False then constraint C does not have a solution. It may or may not have a solution if the procedure returns True.

Loops. The function $\texttt{sym\_interp\_loop}_{n/N}(\sigma \mid C;\ \rho)(e, i) : (\Sigma_\beta)_\beta$ executes a loop with test expression e and body i (see Listing 7). When the loop counter n reaches the loop limit N, the initial symbolic state is returned as a singleton state set annotated with behaviour LoopLimit. Otherwise, the loop is executed. The normal termination of the loop is represented by the singleton set of the initial symbolic state with the additional constraint that the symbolic test expression is false and annotated with behaviour Normal. The loop body is executed in the symbolic state with the additional constraint that the symbolic test expression is true. The continuation of the loop is executed by a call to function $\texttt{sym\_interp\_loop'}$ that executes the loop in the context of a set of symbolic states with an increased loop counter. If the constraint representing the termination

```
val maybe_sat (C : Constraint) : 𝔹
  ensures { result = False → ∄ρ. ρ ⊨ C }

let rec sym_interp_ins_N(σ | C; ρ)(i) =
  match i with ...
  | If e i₁ i₂ →
    try
      let se = σ(e) in
      let Σ_* = (* then-branch *)
        if maybe_sat (C ∧ (se ≠ 0))
        then sym_interp_ins_N(σ | C ∧ (se ≠ 0); ρ)(i₁)
        else ∅ in (* prune then-branch *)
      let Σ'_* = (* else-branch *)
        if maybe_sat (C ∧ (se = 0))
        then sym_interp_ins_N(σ | C ∧ (se = 0); ρ)(i₂)
        else ∅ in (* prune else-branch *)
      Σ_* ∪ Σ'_*
    with UnboundVar (* from σ(e) *) → {(σ | C; ρ)_UnboundVar} end
```

Listing 6. Symbolic execution of conditions with state pruning

(or continuation) of the loop is unsatisfiable according to function `maybe_sat`, the termination (or further execution) of the loop is pruned.

3.3   Proofs of the Symbolic Properties

Post-conditions ensure the under-approximation, over-approximation, and extension of interpretations of the functions implementing the symbolic interpreter, namely `sym_interp_ins` and `sym_interp_loop`, and their variants operating on sets of initial symbolic states. The post-conditions, required lemmas, and termination criteria of the symbolic interpreter functions amount to 31 verification goals, to which we applied 86 lightweight interactive transformations [6]. Most transformations were required to separate the post-conditions of function `sym_interp_loop` by its execution paths into verification conditions that are within reach of automatic theorem provers. The resulting proof tree has 186 leaf verification conditions, which were discharged to the automatic theorem provers CVC4 1.6, Alt-Ergo 2.2.0, and Eprover 2.2. Each goal was verified by one prover, trying the three provers in the given order. The use and processing times of the provers is given in table Table 1 (on a machine with four cores Intel i7-8650U@1.90 GHz, 16 GB RAM, and running Debian 9.9).

```
with sym_interp_loop_{n/N}(σ | C; ρ)(e, i) : Σ_* =
  if n = N (* loop limit reached *)
  then {(σ | C; ρ)_LoopLimit}
  else
    try
      let se = σ(e) in
      let Σ_*^loop = (* continue loop *)
        if maybe_sat (C ∧ (se ≠ 0)) then
          let Σ_* = sym_interp_cmd_N(σ | C ∧ (se ≠ 0); ρ)(i) in
          let Σ'_* = sym_interp_loop'_{(n+1)/N}(Σ_Normal)(e, i) in
          Σ_UnboundVar ∪ Σ_LoopLimit ∪ Σ'_*
        else ∅ in (* prune loop continuation *)
      let Σ_*^term = (* loop termination *)
        if maybe_sat (C ∧ (se = 0))
        then {(σ | C ∧ (se = 0); ρ)_Normal}
        else ∅ in (* prune loop termination *)
      Σ_*^loop ∪ Σ_*^term
    with UnboundVar (* from σ(e) *) → {(σ | C; ρ)_UnboundVar} end
```

Listing 7. Symbolic execution of loops

Table 1. The use of different automatic theorem provers in the verification conditions of the symbolic interpreter functions with processing time in seconds.

Prover	Verification conditions	Fastest	Slowest	Average
CVC4 1.6	162	0.03	2.57	0.26
Alt-Ergo 2.2.0	20	0.03	3.59	0.42
Eprover 2.2	4	0.09	0.31	0.20

3.4   Execution and Test of the Symbolic Interpreter

The Why3 environment offers an *extraction* feature that allows one to automatically generate OCaml code from a Why3 program. An OCaml program was extracted from our symbolic interpreter, and compiled together with handwritten OCaml code to experiment with that interpreter. All ghost annotations are removed during extraction.

To perform the extraction, some information must be given to Why3, under the form of an *extraction driver*, a simple file that explain how the abstract symbols of the Why3 code must be mapped to OCaml. In particular, the constraint solver required to execute the code must be provided by an external OCaml library: we use the one from the Alt-Ergo prover. The abstract type of symbolic variables is substituted by an OCaml type that is private to a module. The substitution of the function `fresh` creates universally fresh variables to comply with the post-condition given in the Why3 program. The resulting code was tested against simple examples. The performance of the generated code is satisfactory in the sense that the Why3 extraction procedure, which erases the ghost code, produces an OCaml code that is as efficient as a code that would have been written by hand.

For reproducibility, the source code of the formal semantics, the concrete interpreter, the symbolic interpreter, the proof session to replay the proofs, and the extraction driver are available at http://toccata.lri.fr/gallery/symbolic_imp. en.html. See the file `README.md` for the required dependencies.

4   Conclusions, Related Work and Future Work

We presented in this article a formalisation of two correctness properties of symbolic interpreter engines, over-approximation and under-approximation. We employed advanced *ghost* annotations of data and code of the symbolic interpreter to discharge the generated verification conditions to automated theorem provers.

A natural question is whether our approach can scale to a symbolic execution tool on a more complex language. First, we believe that our technique using ghost code for automating proofs is already well demonstrated on the essential constructions of assignment, conditionals and loops, so that it should apply similarly on languages with similar control structures. Indeed, we believe the complexity of symbolic execution tools for complex languages relies more on the complexity of data, which must be handled by the constraints and not the symbolic engine itself. Second, as a matter of fact, we recently finish to transfer the correctness properties and proof techniques developed in this article to the CoLiS language [8]. The CoLiS language is an intermediate language for a subset of the POSIX shell language with formally defined and easily understandable semantics. It has been developed to statically analyse Debian maintainer scripts, and we aim at identifying errors in maintainer scripts by symbolically executing the corresponding CoLiS scripts. Indeed we have already been able to identify issues in some of those scripts. We represent the file system symbolically using *feature tree constraints* [9]. Program variables, however, are statically known in Debian maintainer scripts, and represented concretely. This results in simplified correctness properties, where the only variable of the symbolic environment represents successive values of the file system's root node.

Acknowledgement. We would like to thank Nicolas Jeannerod, Ralf Treinen, Mihaela Sighireanu and Yann Regis-Gianas, partners of the CoLiS project, for their input and remarks on the design of the symbolic interpreter and the formulation of expected properties. We also thank Burkhart Wolff for his feedback about related work on symbolic execution.

References

1. Albert, E., Arenas, P., Gómez-Zamalloa, M., Rojas, J.M.: Test case generation by symbolic execution: basic concepts, a CLP-based instance, and actor-based concurrency. In: Bernardo, M., Damiani, F., Hähnle, R., Johnsen, E.B., Schaefer, I. (eds.) SFM 2014. LNCS, vol. 8483, pp. 263–309. Springer, Cham (2014). https://doi.org/10.1007/978-3-319-07317-0_7

2. Arusoaie, A., Lucanu, D., Rusu, V.: A Generic Framework for Symbolic Execution: Theory and Applications. Research Report RR-8189, Inria, September 2015. https://hal.inria.fr/hal-00766220

3. Bertot, Y., Castéran, P.: Interactive Theorem Proving and Program Development. Texts in Theoretical Computer Science. Springer, Heidelberg (2004). https://doi.org/10.1007/978-3-662-07964-5

4. Bobot, F., Filliâtre, J.C., Marché, C., Paskevich, A.: Let's verify this with Why3. Int. J. Softw. Tools Technol. Transf. (STTT) **17**(6), 709–727 (2015). https://doi.org/10.1007/s10009-014-0314-5. http://hal.inria.fr/hal-00967132/en, see also http://toccata.lri.fr/gallery/fm2012comp.en.html

5. Clochard, M., Marché, C., Paskevich, A.: Deductive verification with ghost monitors, November 2018. https://hal.inria.fr/hal-01926659. Working paper

6. Dailler, S., Marché, C., Moy, Y.: Lightweight interactive proving inside an automatic program verifier. In: Proceedings of the Fourth Workshop on Formal Integrated Development Environment, F-IDE, Oxford, UK, 14 July 2018 (2018). https://hal.inria.fr/hal-01936302

7. Filliâtre, J.C., Gondelman, L., Paskevich, A.: The spirit of ghost code. Formal Methods Syst. Des. **48**(3), 152–174 (2016). https://doi.org/10.1007/s10703-016-0243-x. https://hal.archives-ouvertes.fr/hal-01396864v1

8. Jeannerod, N., Marché, C., Treinen, R.: A formally verified interpreter for a shell-like programming language. In: Paskevich, A., Wies, T. (eds.) VSTTE 2017. LNCS, vol. 10712, pp. 1–18. Springer, Cham (2017). https://doi.org/10.1007/978-3-319-72308-2_1. https://hal.archives-ouvertes.fr/hal-01534747

9. Jeannerod, N., Treinen, R.: Deciding the first-order theory of an algebra of feature trees with updates. In: Galmiche, D., Schulz, S., Sebastiani, R. (eds.) IJCAR 2018. LNCS (LNAI), vol. 10900, pp. 439–454. Springer, Cham (2018). https://doi.org/10.1007/978-3-319-94205-6_29. https://hal.archives-ouvertes.fr/hal-01760575

10. Jourdan, J.H., Laporte, V., Blazy, S., Leroy, X., Pichardie, D.: A formally-verified C static analyzer. In: 42nd ACM SIGPLAN-SIGACT Symposium on Principles of Programming Languages, pp. 247–259. ACM, Mumbai, January 2015. https://doi.org/10.1145/2676726.2676966. https://hal.inria.fr/hal-01078386

11. Winskel, G.: The Formal Semantics of Programming Languages: An Introduction. MIT Press, Cambridge (1993)

DCSynth: Guided Reactive Synthesis with Soft Requirements

Amol Wakankar[1,2($\boxtimes$)], Paritosh K. Pandya[3], and Raj Mohan Matteplackel[3]

[1] Homi Bhabha National Institute, Mumbai, India
amolk@barc.gov.in
[2] Bhabha Atomic Research Centre, Mumbai, India
[3] Tata Institute of Fundamental Research, Mumbai, India

Abstract. In this paper, we propose a technique for guided synthesis of a controller from regular requirements which are specified using an interval temporal logic QDDC. We find that QDDC is well suited for guided synthesis due to its superiority in dealing with both qualitative and quantitative specifications. Our framework allows specification consisting of both *hard* and *soft* requirements as QDDC formulas. We have developed a method and a tool DCSynth, which computes a controller that *invariantly* satisfies the *hard requirement* and it *H-optimally* meets the *soft requirement*. Soft requirements can be used to specify quality attributes. The proposed technique is also useful in dealing with conflicting (i.e. unrealizable) requirements by making some of them as *soft* requirements. Case studies are carried out to demonstrate the effectiveness of the soft requirement guided synthesis in obtaining high quality controllers. The quality of the synthesized controllers is compared by measuring both the *guaranteed* as well as the *expected case* behaviour of the controlled system. Tool DCSynth facilitates such comparison.

1 Introduction

Reactive synthesis aims at algorithmically constructing a controller (say a Mealy Machine) from a given temporal logic specification of its desired behaviour. Considerable amount of research has gone into the area of reactive synthesis and several tools are available for experimenting with reactive synthesis [14]. However, existing tools do not have the capability to guide the synthesis towards the most desirable controller. In practice, user specification may be incomplete. It may also contain certain requirements which cannot be mandatorily satisfied, but they are desirable. We term the desirable properties as *soft* requirements.

In this work, we propose a specification consisting of *hard requirements*, which are mandatory and need to be satisfied *invariantly*, as well as *soft requirements*, which are desirable and should be satisfied at as many points in the execution as possible. We choose to specify the hard and soft requirements as regular properties in logic *Quantified Discrete Duration Calculus* (**QDDC**) [20,21]. QDDC is the discrete time variant of Duration Calculus proposed by Zhou *et al.* [7,8].

© Springer Nature Switzerland AG 2020
S. Chakraborty and J. A. Navas (Eds.): VSTTE 2019, LNCS 12031, pp. 124–142, 2020.
https://doi.org/10.1007/978-3-030-41600-3_9

Regular properties can conceptually be specified by a deterministic finite state automaton (DFA). At any point in the execution, a regular property holds provided the past behaviour upto the point is accepted by its DFA. The study of synthesis of controllers for such properties was pioneered by Ramadge and Wonham [18,25,26]. QDDC is an interval temporal logic, which has the expressive power of regular languages. Section 2 presents the syntax and semantics of this logic. Prior work [17,20,21] shows that any formula in QDDC can be effectively translated into a language equivalent DFA over finite words. Logic QDDC's bounded counting features, interval based modalities, regular expression like primitives and second order quantification constructs allow complex qualitative and quantitative properties (such as latency, resource constraints) to be specified succinctly and modularly. (See the example below as well as papers [19,21,22] for more illustrations.) Paper [19] also gives a comparison with other logics such as LTL and PSL. It should be noted that QDDC does not allow specification of general liveness properties; however, time bounded liveness can be specified. The following example motivates the need for soft requirement guided synthesis.

Example 1 (Arbiter for Mutually Exclusive Shared Resource). The arbiter has an input r_i (denoting request for access) and an output a_i (denoting acknowledgement for access) for each client $1 \leq i \leq n$. The specification consists of the following two requirements, given as QDDC formulas together with their intuitive explanation. Section 2 gives the formal syntax and semantics of QDDC.
$-$*Mutual Exclusion Requirement* R_1: $[[\ \wedge_{i \neq j}\ \neg(a_i \wedge a_j)\ ]]$, states that at every point, the access to the shared resource should be mutually exclusive.
$-$*k-cycle Response Requirement* R_2: $\wedge_i$ $[](\ (([[r_i]]\ \&\& \ (slen >= (k-1)))\ \Rightarrow\ (scount\ a_i > 0))$, states that in any observation interval spanning k or more cycles if request from i^{th} client (r_i) is *continuously* high during the interval, then that client should get at least one access (a_i) within the observation interval. Modality $[]D$ states that sub-formula D should hold for all observation intervals. Term $slen$ gives the length of the observation interval and the term $(scount\ P)$ counts the number of occurrences of proposition P within the observation interval. The requirement $R2$ is asserted for each client $1 \leq i \leq n$.

When $k < n$ no controller can satisfy both the requirements (as their conjunction is unrealizable); e.g. consider the case where all clients request all the time. We may want to opt for an implementation, which mandatorily satisfies $R1$ and it tries to meet the $R2$ "as much as possible". This can be specified in our framework, by making requirement $R2$ as a *soft requirement*. $\square$

This paper introduces a tool *DCSynth* which allows synthesis of controllers from *regular properties* (QDDC formulas). The specification in *DCSynth* is a tuple (I, O, D^h, D^s), where D^h and D^s are QDDC formulas over a set of input and output propositions (I, O). Here, D^h and D^s are the **hard** and the **soft** requirement, respectively[1]. We use the term *supervisor* for a non-blocking Mealy

---

[1] The tool supports more general lexicographically ordered list of soft requirements. However, we omit the general case for brevity.

machine which may non-deterministically produce one or more outputs for each input. A supervisor may be *refined* to a sub-supervisor by resolving (pruning) the non-deterministic choice of outputs. The sub-supervisor may use additional memory for making the choice. We define a determinism ordering on supervisors in the paper. A *controller* is a deterministic supervisor. Ramadge and Wonham [25, 26] investigated the synthesis of the *maximally permissive* supervisor for a regular specification. The maximally permissive supervisor is a unique (up to language equivalence) supervisor, which encompasses all the behaviors invariantly satisfying the specified regular property (see Definition 6). The well known safety synthesis algorithm applied to the DFA for D^h gives us the maximally permissive supervisor $MPS(D^h)$ [10]. If no such supervisor exists, the specification is reported as unrealizable.

Any controller obtained by arbitrarily resolving the nondeterministic choices for outputs in $MPS(D^h)$ is correct-by-construction. This results in several controllers with distinct behaviours and qualities. Thus, only correct-by-construction synthesis is not sufficient [2]. Some form of guidance must be provided to the synthesis method to choose among the possible controllers. We use the soft requirements to provide such guidance. Our synthesis method tries to choose a controller, which satisfies the soft requirements (D^s) "as much as possible". Soft requirements can also specify the desirable requirements, which cannot be met invariantly. For example, in a Mine-pump controller, as soft requirement "keep the pump off unless mandated by the hard requirement" specifies an energy efficient controller. Specification of scheduling, performance and quality constraints are often such desirable properties. Moreover, a specification may consist of a conjunction of conflicting requirements. In this case, all the requirements cannot be invariantly met simultaneously. The user may resolve the conflicts by making some of these requirements as soft. Therefore, soft requirements give us a capability to synthesize meaningful and practical controllers.

In DCSynth, we formalize the notion of a controller meeting the soft requirement D^s "as much as possible", by synthesizing a sub-supervisor of $MPS(D^h)$ (guaranteeing invariance of D^h), which maximizes the expected value of count of D^s in next H moves when averaged over all the inputs. The classical value iteration algorithm due to Bellman [1] allows us to compute this H-optimal sub-supervisor. This can be further refined to a controller as desired. *Thus, our synthesis method gives a controller which, (a) invariantly satisfies D^h and (b) it is H-optimal for D^s amongst all controllers meeting condition (a).*

The above synthesis method is implemented in tool DCSynth. An efficient representation of DFA using Multi-Terminal BDDs, originally introduced by the tool MONA [16], is used for representing both automata and supervisors. We adapt the safety synthesis algorithm and the value iteration algorithm so that they work symbolically over this MONA DFA representation.

We illustrate our specification method and synthesis tool with the help of two case studies[2]. We define metrics to compare the controllers for their *guaranteed*

---

[2] DCSynth can be downloaded at [30] along with the specification files for experiments.

and *expected behaviour*. The tool DCSynth facilitates measurement of both these metrics. Thus, the main contributions of this paper are as follows:

- We develop a technique for the synthesis of controllers from QDDC requirements. This extends the past work on model checking of logic QDDC [6,17,20,21,29] with synthesis abilities.
- We propose a method for guided synthesis of controllers based on **soft requirements** which are met in a H-optimal fashion. Conceptually, this enhances the Ramadge-Wonham framework with optimal controller synthesis.
- We present a tool DCSynth for guided synthesis, which
  - represents and manipulates automata/supervisors using BDD-based semi-symbolic DFA and uses eager minimization for efficient synthesis.
  - provides facility to compare both the guaranteed and expected case behaviours of the candidate controllers.
- We analyze the impact of soft requirements on the quality of the synthesized controllers experimentally using case studies.

The rest of the paper is arranged as follows. Section 2 describes the syntax and semantics of QDDC. Important definitions are presented in Sect. 3. Syntax of DCSynth specification and the controller synthesis method are presented in Sect. 4. Section 5 discusses case studies and experimental results. The paper is concluded with a discussion and related work in Sects. 6 and 7.

2   Quantified Discrete Duration Calculus (QDDC) Logic

Let PV be a finite non-empty set of propositional variables. Let σ be a non-empty finite word over the alphabet 2^{PV}. It has the form $\sigma = P_0 \cdots P_n$ where $P_i \subseteq PV$ for each $i \in \{0, \ldots, n\}$. Let $len(\sigma) = n + 1$, $dom(\sigma) = \{0, \ldots, n\}$, $\sigma[i, j] = P_i \cdots P_j$ and $\sigma[i] = P_i$.

Propositional formulas over variables PV is defined as usual with &&, ||, ! denoting conjunction, dis-junction and negation, respectively. We omit this definition. It may be noted that a textual syntax accepted by our tool is used in place of usual mathematical symbols. Derived operators such as => and <=> are defined as usual. Let $\Omega(PV)$ be the set of all propositional formulas over variables PV. Let $i \in dom(\sigma)$. Then the satisfaction of propositional formula φ at point i, denoted $\sigma, i \models \varphi$, is defined as usual and omitted here for brevity.

The syntax of a QDDC formula over variables PV is given by:

$$D := \langle \varphi \rangle \mid [\varphi] \mid [[\varphi]] \mid D ^\frown D \mid !D \mid D \mid\mid D \mid D \text{ \&\& } D \mid$$
$$ex \ p. \ D \mid all \ p. \ D \mid slen \bowtie c \mid scount \ \varphi \bowtie c$$

where $\varphi \in \Omega(PV)$, $p \in PV$, $c \in \mathbb{N}$ and $\bowtie \in \{<, \leq, =, \geq, >\}$.

An *interval* over a word σ is of the form $[b, e]$ where $b, e \in dom(\sigma)$ and $b \leq e$. Let $Intv(\sigma)$ be the set of all intervals over σ. Let σ be a finite, non-empty word over 2^{PV} and let $[b, e] \in Intv(\sigma)$ be an interval. Then the satisfaction relation of a QDDC formula D over Σ and interval $[b, e]$ written as $\sigma, [b, e] \models D$, is defined inductively as follows:

$$\sigma, [b, e] \models \langle \varphi \rangle \quad \text{iff} \quad b = e \text{ and } \sigma, b \models \varphi,$$
$$\sigma, [b, e] \models [\varphi] \quad \text{iff} \quad b < e \text{ and } \forall b \leq i < e : \sigma, i \models \varphi,$$
$$\sigma, [b, e] \models [[\varphi]] \quad \text{iff} \quad \forall b \leq i \leq e : \sigma, i \models \varphi,$$
$$\sigma, [b, e] \models D_1 \char`^ D_2 \quad \text{iff} \quad \exists b \leq i \leq e : \sigma, [b, i] \models D_1 \text{ and } \sigma, [i, e] \models D_2,$$

with Boolean combinations $!D$, $D_1 \parallel D_2$ and D_1 && D_2 defined in the expected way. For $p \in PV$, we call a word σ' a p-variant of a word σ if $\forall i \in dom(\sigma), \forall q \neq p : q \in \sigma'[i] \Leftrightarrow q \in \sigma[i]$. Then $\sigma, [b, e] \models ex\ p.\ D \Leftrightarrow \sigma', [b, e] \models D$ for some p-variant σ' of σ and $(all\ p.\ D) \Leftrightarrow (!ex\ p.\ !D)$.

Entities $slen$ and $scount$ are called $terms$. The term $slen$ gives the length of the interval in which it is measured, $scount\ \varphi$ where $\varphi \in \Omega(PV)$, counts the number of positions in the interval under consideration where φ holds. Formally, for $\varphi \in \Omega(PV)$ we have $slen(\sigma, [b, e]) = e - b$ and $scount(\sigma, \varphi, [b, e]) = \sum_{i=b}^{i=e} \begin{cases} 1, \text{ if } \sigma, i \models \varphi, \\ 0, \text{ otherwise.} \end{cases}$

We also define the following derived constructs: $pt = \langle true \rangle$, $ext = !pt$, $\langle \rangle \mathbf{D} = true \char`^ D \char`^ true$, $[]D = (!\langle \rangle !D)$ and $\mathbf{pref(D)} = !((!D)\char`^ true)$. Thus, $\sigma, [b, e] \models []D$ iff $\sigma, [b', e'] \models D$ for all sub-intervals $b \leq b' \leq e' \leq e$ and $\sigma, [b, e] \models pref(D)$ iff $\sigma, [b, e'] \models D$ for all prefix intervals $b \leq e' \leq e$.

Definition 1 (Language of a QDDC formula). *Let* $\sigma, i \models D$ *iff* $\sigma, [0, i] \models D$, *and* $\sigma \models D$ *iff* $\sigma, len(\sigma) - 1 \models D$. *We define* $L(D) = \{\sigma \mid \sigma \models D\}$, *the set of behaviours accepted by* D. *Formula* D *is called valid, denoted* $\models D$, *iff* $L(D) = (2^{PV})^+$. □

Thus, a formula D holds at a point i in a behaviour provided the **past** of the point i satisfies D.

Theorem 1. *[21] For every formula* D *over variables* PV *we can construct a DFA* $\mathcal{A}(D)$ *over alphabet* 2^{PV} *such that* $L(\mathcal{A}(D)) = L(D)$. *We call* $\mathcal{A}(D)$ *a formula automaton for* D *or the monitor automaton for* D. □

A tool DCVALID implements this formula automaton construction in an efficient manner by internally using the tool MONA [16]. It gives *minimal, deterministic* automaton (DFA) for the formula D. We omit the details here. The reader may refer to several papers on QDDC for detailed description and examples of QDDC specifications as well as its model checking tool DCVALID [6, 19–21, 29].

3   Supervisor and Controller

In this section we present QDDC formulas and automata where variables $PV = I \cup O$ are partitioned into disjoint sets of input variables I and output variables O. It is known that supervisors and controllers can be expressed as Mealy machines with special properties. Here we show how Mealy machines can be represented as special form of Deterministic finite automata (DFA). This representation allows us to use the MONA DFA library [16] to compute supervisors and controllers efficiently using our tool DCSynth.

Definition 2 (Output-nondeterministic Mealy Machine). *A total and Deterministic Finite Automaton (DFA) over input-output alphabet $\Sigma = 2^I \times 2^O$ is a tuple $A = (Q, \Sigma, s, \delta, F)$ having conventional meaning, where $\delta : Q \times 2^I \times 2^O \to Q$. An* **output-nondeterministic Mealy machine** *is a DFA with a unique reject (or non-final) state r which is a sink state i.e., $F = Q - \{r\}$ and $\delta(r, i, o) = r$ for all $i \in 2^I$, $o \in 2^O$.* □

The intuition behind this definition is that the transitions from $q \in F$ to r are forbidden (and kept only for making the DFA total). The language of any such Mealy machine is prefix-closed. Recall that for a Mealy machine, $F = Q - \{r\}$. A Mealy machine is **deterministic** if $\forall s \in F$, $\forall i \in 2^I$, $\exists$ at most one $o \in 2^O$ such that $\delta(s, i, o) \neq r$.

Definition 3 (Non-blocking Mealy Machine). *An output-nondeterministic Mealy machine is called* **non-blocking** *if $\forall s \in F$, $\forall i \in 2^I.\exists o \in 2^O$ such that $\delta(s, i, o) \in F$. It follows that for all input sequences a non-blocking Mealy machine can produce one or more output sequence without ever getting into the reject state.* □

For a Mealy machine M over variables (I, O), its language $L(M) \subseteq (2^I \times 2^O)^*$. A word $\sigma \in L(M)$ can also be represented as pair $(ii, oo) \in ((2^I)^*, (2^O)^*)$ such that $\sigma[k] = ii[k] \cup oo[k], \forall k \in dom(\sigma)$. Here σ, ii, oo must have the same length. Note that in the rest of this paper, we do not distinguish between σ and (ii, oo). Also, for any input sequence $ii \in (2^I)^*$, we define $M[ii] = \{oo \mid (ii, oo) \in L(M)\}$.

Definition 4 (Controllers and Supervisors). *An output-nondeterministic Mealy machine which is non-blocking is called a* **supervisor**. *A deterministic supervisor is called a* **controller**. □

The non-deterministic choice of outputs in a supervisor denotes unresolved decision. The determinism ordering defined below allows supervisors to be refined into controllers.

Definition 5 (Determinism Order and Sub-supervisor). *Given two supervisors S_1 and S_2, we say $S_1 \leq_{det} S_2$ (S_2 is more deterministic than S_1), iff $L(S_2) \subseteq L(S_1)$. We call S_2 to be a sub-supervisor of S_1.* □

Note that being supervisors, they both are non-blocking and hence $\emptyset \subset S_2[ii] \subseteq S_1[ii]$ for any $ii \in (2^I)^*$. The supervisor S_2 may make use of additional memory for resolving and pruning the non-determinism in S_1.

For technical convenience, we define a notion of *indicator variable* for a QDDC formula (regular property). The idea behind this is that the indicator variable w witnesses the truth of a formula D at any point in execution. Let,

$$Ind(D, w) = pref(EP(w) \Leftrightarrow D)$$

Here, $\mathbf{EP}(\mathbf{w}) = (true^\smallfrown\langle w\rangle)$, i.e. $EP(w)$ holds at a point i, if variable w is true at that point i. Hence, w will be $true$ exactly on those points where D is $true$. The formula automaton $\mathcal{A}(Ind(D,w))$ gives us a controller with input-output alphabet $(I\cup O, w)$ such that it outputs $w = 1$ on a transition iff the past satisfies D. Since our formula automata are minimal DFA, $\mathcal{A}(Ind(D,w))$ characterizes the least memory needed to track the truth of formula D.

4   DCSynth Specification and Controller Synthesis

This section defines the DCSynth specification. It also presents the algorithm used in our tool DCSynth for soft requirement guided controller synthesis from a DCSynth specification. The process of synthesizing a controller as discussed in Sect. 4.4 uses three main algorithms given in Sects. 4.1–4.3.

4.1   Invariance Properties and Maximally Permissive Supervisor

A QDDC formula D specifies a regular property which may hold intermittently during a behaviour (see Definition 1). An important class of properties, denoted by **inv** D, states that D must hold invariantly during the system behaviour.

Definition 6. *Let* **S realizes inv D** *denote that a supervisor S realizes the invariance of QDDC formula D. We define* **S realizes inv D** *provided* $L(S) \subseteq L(D)$. *Recall that, by the definition of supervisors, S must be non-blocking. A supervisor S for a formula D is called* **maximally permissive** *iff* $S \leq_{det} S'$ *holds for any supervisor S' such that S' **realizes** inv D. This S (when it exists) is unique up to language equivalence of automata, and the minimum state maximally permissive supervisor is denoted as* **MPS(D)**. □

Now, we discuss how $MPS(D)$ for a given QDDC formula D is computed.

1. Language equivalent DFA $\mathcal{A}(D) = \langle S, 2^{I\cup O}, s_0, \delta, F\rangle$ is constructed for formula D (Theorem 1). The standard safety synthesis algorithm (see [12]) over $\mathcal{A}(D)$ gives us the desired $MPS(D)$ as outlined in the following steps.
2. We first compute the *largest* set of winning states $G \subseteq F$ with the following property: state $s \in G$ iff $\forall i\exists o : \delta(s,(i,o)) \in G$. Let $Cpre(\mathcal{A}(D), X) = \{s \mid \forall i\exists o : \delta(s,(i,o)) \in X\}$. Then we iteratively compute G as follows:
   > G=F;
   > **do**
   >> G1=G;
   >> G=Cpre($\mathcal{A}(D)$, G1);
   > **while** (G != G1);
3. If initial state $s_0 \notin G$, then the specification is *unrealizable*. Otherwise, $MPS(D)$ is obtained by declaring G as the set of final states and retaining all the transitions in $\mathcal{A}(D)$ between states in G and redirecting the remaining transitions of $\mathcal{A}(D)$ to a unique reject state r which is made a sink state.

Proposition 1. *For a given QDDC formula D the above algorithm computes the maximally permissive supervisor MPS(D).*   □

The proposition follows straightforwardly by combining Theorem 1 with the correctness of standard safety synthesis algorithm [12]. We omit a detailed proof.

4.2 Maximally Permissive H-Optimal Supervisor (MPHOS)

Given a supervisor S and a desired QDDC formula D which should hold "as much as possible" (both are over input-output variables (I, O)), we give a method for constructing an "optimal" sub-supervisor of S, which maximizes the expected value of count of D holding in next H moves when averaged over all the inputs.

First consider $\mathcal{A}^{Arena} = S \times \mathcal{A}(Ind(D, w))$ which is a supervisor over input-output variables $(I, O \cup \{w\})$. It augments S by producing an additional output w which witnesses the truth of D. (See the end of Sect. 3.) It has the property: $L(\mathcal{A}^{Arena}) \downarrow (I \cup O) = L(S)$. Also for $\sigma \in L(\mathcal{A}^{Arena})$ and $i \in dom(\sigma)$ we have $w \in \sigma[i]$ iff $\sigma[0 : i] \models D$. Thus, every transition of $\mathcal{A}^{Arena}$ is labelled with w iff D holds on taking the transition. Let the weight of transitions labelled with w be 1 and 0 otherwise. Thus, for $o \in 2^{(O \cup \{w\})}$ let $wt(o) = 1$ if $w \in o$ and 0 otherwise. Technically, this makes $\mathcal{A}^{Arena}$ a weighted automaton.

In the supervisor $\mathcal{A}^{Arena} = (Q, \Sigma, s, \delta, Q - \{r\})$, where r is the unique reject state, we define for $(q \in Q) \neq r$ and $i \in 2^I$, set $LegalOutputs(q, i) = \{o \mid \delta(q, i) \neq r\}$. We also define a deterministic selection rule as function f s.t. $f(q, i) \in LegalOutputs(q, i)$ and a non-deterministic selection rule F as function F s.t. $F(q, i) \in \{O \subseteq LegalOutputs(q, i) \mid O \neq \emptyset\}$. Let H be a natural number. Then H-horizon policy π is a sequence $F_1, F_2, \ldots, F_H$ of non-deterministic selection rules. A deterministic policy will use only deterministic selection rules. A policy is stationary (memory-less) if each F_i is the same independently of i.

Given a state s, a policy π and an input sequence $ii \in (2^I)^H$ (of length H), we define $L(\mathcal{A}^{Arena}, ii, s)$ as all runs of $\mathcal{A}^{Arena}$ over the input ii starting from state s and $L^{\pi}(\mathcal{A}^{Arena}, ii, s)$ as all runs over input ii starting from s and following the selection rule F_i at step i. Each run has the form (ii, oo). Let $Value(ii, oo) = \Sigma_{1 \leq i \leq H} \; wt(oo[i]))$. Thus, $Value(ii, oo)$ gives the count of D holding during behaviour fragment (ii, oo). Then, we define $VMIN^{\pi}(s, ii) = min\{Value(ii, oo) \mid (ii, oo) \in L^{\pi}(\mathcal{A}^{Arena}, ii, s)\}$, which gives the minimum possible count of D among all the runs of S under policy π on input ii, starting with state s. We also define, $VMAX(s, ii) = max\{Value(ii, oo) \mid (ii, oo) \in L(\mathcal{A}^{Arena}, ii, s)\}$, which gives the maximum achievable count. Note that $VMAX$ is independent of any policy.

Given a horizon value (natural number) H, $\mathcal{A}^{Arena}$ and a non-deterministic H-horizon policy π, we define utility values $ValAvgMin^{\pi}(s)$ and $ValAvgMax(s)$ for each state s of $\mathcal{A}^{Arena}$ as follows.

$$ValAvgMax(s) = \mathbb{E}_{ii \in (2^I)^H} \; VMAX(s, ii)$$
$$ValAvgMin^{\pi}(s) = \mathbb{E}_{ii \in (2^I)^H} \; VMIN^{\pi}(s, ii)$$

Thus, intuitively, $ValAvgMax(s)$ gives the maximal achievable count of D from state s, when averaged over all inputs of length H Similarly,

$ValAvgMin^{\pi}(s)$ gives the minimal such count for D under policy π, when averaged over all inputs of length H. We will construct a horizon-H policy $\pi^* = argmax_{\pi}\ ValAvgMin^{\pi}(s)$. This will turn out to be a stationary policy given by a selection rule F^*. This rule can be implemented as a supervisor denoted by $MPHOS(\mathcal{A}^{Arena}, H)$. We now give its construction.

The well known value iteration algorithm allows us to efficiently compute $ValAvgMax(s)$ as recursive function $Val(s, H)$ below.

$$Val(s, 0) = 0$$
$$Val(s, p+1) = \mathbb{E}_{i \in 2^I}\ max_{o \in 2^{(O \cup \{w\})}\ :\ \delta(s,(i,o)) \neq r} \{wt(o)\ +\ Val(\delta(s, (i, o)), p)\}$$

We omit the straightforward proof that $Val(s, H) = ValAvgMax(s)$ (see [24]).

Having computed this, the optimal selection rule F^* giving stationary policy π^* is given as follows: For each state $s \in \mathcal{A}^{Arena}$ and each input $i \in 2^I$,

$$F^*(s, i) = argmax_{o \in 2^O}\{wt(o)\ +\ Val(s, H)$$
$$|\ \delta_{\mathcal{A}^{Arena}}(s, (i, o)) = s' \wedge s' \neq r\}$$

Note that $F^*(s, i)$ is non-deterministic as more than one output o may satisfy the $argmax$ condition. The following well-known lemma states that the stationary policy π^* using the selection rule F^* is H-optimal.

Lemma 1. *For all states s of $\mathcal{A}^{Arena}$, $ValAvgMin^{\pi^*}(s) = ValAvgMax(s)$ always holds. Therefore, for all states s of $\mathcal{A}^{Arena}$ and for any H-horizon policy π, $ValAvgMin_H^{\pi}(s) \leq ValAvgMin^{\pi^*}(s)$ also holds.* $\square$

We omit the proof of these well known properties from optimal control of Markov Decision Processes (see [24]).

Supervisor $\mathcal{A}^{Arena}$ is pruned to retain only the transitions with the outputs in set $F^*(s, i)$ (as these are all equally optimal). This gives us *Maximally Permissive H-Optimal Sub-supervisor of $\mathcal{A}^{Arena}$* w.r.t. D, denoted by $MPHOS(\mathcal{A}^{Arena}, H)$ or equivalently $MPHOS(S, D, H)$. The following proposition follows immediately from the construction of $MPHOS(S, D, H)$ and Lemma 1.

Proposition 2. *1. $S \leq_{det} MPHOS(S, D, H)$, for all H.*
2. $MPHOS(S, D, H)$ is maximally permissive H-optimal sub-supervisor of S.
3. Any sub-supervisor S' of $MPHOS(S, D, H)$ i.e. $MPHOS(S, D, H) \leq_{det} S'$ is also H-Optimal. $\square$

4.3   From Supervisor to Controller

A controller Cnt can be obtained from a supervisor S by resolving output non-determinism in S. We give a rather straightforward mechanism for this. We allow the user to specify a preference ordering Ord on the set of output variables 2^O. A given supervisor S is determinized by retaining only the highest ordered output among those permitted by S. This is denoted $Det_{Ord}(S)$. The output ordering is specified by giving a lexicographically ordered list of output variable literals. This facility is used to determinize $MPHOS$ and MPS supervisors as required.

Example 2. For a supervisor S over variables $(I, \{o_1, o_2\})$, an example output order can be given as lexicographically ordered list $(o_1 > !o_2)$. Then, for any transition the determinization step will try to select the highest ordered output (which is allowed by S) from the list $\{(o_1 = true, o_2 = false), (o_1 = true, o_2 = true), (o_1 = false, o_2 = false), (o_1 = false, o_2 = true)\}$. □

4.4 DCSynth Specification and Controller Synthesis

A **DCSynth specification** is a tuple (I, O, D^h, D^s), where I and O are the set of *input* and *output* variables, respectively. Formula D^h called the *hard require-ment* and formula D^s called the *soft requirement* are QDDC formulas over the set of propositions $PV = I \cup O$. Let H be a natural number called Horizon. The objective in DCSynth is to synthesize a deterministic controller which (a) *invariantly* satisfies the hard requirement D^h, and (b) it is H Optimal w.r.t. D^s amongst all the controllers satisfying (a).

Given a specification (I, O, D^h, D^s), a horizon value H (a natural number) and a total ordering Ord on the set of outputs 2^O, the controller synthesis in DCSynth can be given as Algorithm 1.

Algorithm 1 : *Controller Synthesis*
Input: $S = (I, O, D^h, D^s)$. *Horizon H, Output ordering Ord*
Output: *Controller Cnt for S.*

1. $\mathcal{A}^{mps} = MPS(D^h)$
2. $\mathcal{A}^{mphos} = MPHOS(\mathcal{A}^{mps}, D^s, H)$
3. $Cnt = Det_{ord}(\mathcal{A}^{mphos})$.
4. *Encode the automaton Cnt in an implementation language.*

Step 1 uses the MPS construction given in Sect. 4.1. Step 2 uses the MPHOS construction given in Sect. 4.2 whereas Step 3 uses the determinization method of Sect. 4.3.

Proposition 3. *The controller Cnt output by Algorithm 1 invariantly satisfies D^h, and it intermittently, but H-optimally, satisfies D^s.*

Proof. By Proposition 1, $\mathcal{A}^{mps}$ realizes **inv** D^h. Then, by Proposition 2, $\mathcal{A}^{mphos}$ and Cnt are sub-supervisors of $\mathcal{A}^{mps}$ and hence they also realize **inv** D^h. More-over, by Lemma 1, we get that $\mathcal{A}^{mphos}$ is H-optimal w.r.t. D^s. Hence, by Propo-sition 2, we get that Cnt which is a sub-supervisor of $\mathcal{A}^{mphos}$ is also H-Optimal with respect to D^s.   □

At all stages of above synthesis, the automata/supervisors $\mathcal{A}(D^h)$, $\mathcal{A}(D^s)$, $\mathcal{A}^{mps}$ and $\mathcal{A}^{mphos}$ and Cnt are all represented as semi-symbolic automata (SSDFA) using the DFA data structure of tool MONA [16]. In this representation, the transition function is represented as a multi-terminal BDD. The MONA DFA library provides a rich set of automata operations including product, projection, determinization and minimization over the SSDFA. The algorithms discussed in Sects. 4.1, 4.2 and 4.3 are implemented over SSDFA. Moreover, these algorithms are adapted to work without actually expanding the specification automata in to game graph. At each stage of the computation, the automata and supervisors are aggressively minimized, which leads to significant improvement in the scalability and computation time of the tool.

5   Case Studies and Experiments

For a DCSynth specification, D^h and D^s can be any QDDC formulas. While invariance of D^h is guaranteed by the synthesis algorithm, the quality of the controller is governed by optimizing the outputs for which the soft requirement D^s holds. For example, D^s may specify outputs which save energy, giving an energy efficient controller. The soft requirement can also be used to improve the robustness [2] of the controller (see [23]). Below, we consider the specifications structured as assumptions and commitments pair. We also compare the performance of the synthesized controllers using our tool DCSynth.

5.1   Types of Controller Specification

For many examples, the controller specification can be given as a pair (A, C) of QDDC formulas over input-output variables (I, O). Here, **commitment** C is a formula specifying the desired behaviour which must ideally hold invariantly. But this may be unrealizable, and a suitable **assumption** A on the behaviour of environment may have to be made for C to hold. In case the assumption A does not hold, it is still desirable that controller satisfies C, intermittently but "as much as possible". Given this assumption-commitment pair (A, C), we specify four types of derived controller specifications (I, O, D^h, D^s) as follows.

Type	Hard Requirement D^h	Soft Requirement D^s
Type0	C	$true$
Type1	$(A \Rightarrow C)$	$true$
Type2	$true$	C
Type3	$(A \Rightarrow C)$	C

Type0 controller gives the best guarantee but it may be unrealizable. Type1 controller provides a firm but conditional guarantee. Type2 controller tries to achieve C in H-optimal fashion irrespective of any assumption and Type3 Controller provides firm conditional guarantee and it also tries to satisfy C in H-optimal fashion even when the assumption does not hold.

5.2 Performance Metrics: Measuring Quality of Controllers

Given multiple controllers targeted at meeting a commitment C as often as possible, we identify two measures of comparing their performance. (i) *Expected Case Performance measure* computes the probability of commitment holding when averaged over random inputs. (ii) *Must Dominance* compares whether one controller always meets the commitment whenever the second controller does so. This is a measure of worst case performance.

(i) Expected Case Performance: Given a controller Cnt over input-output alphabet (I, O) and a QDDC formula (regular property) C over variables $I \cup O$, we can construct a *Discrete Time Markov Chain (DTMC)*, denoted as $M_{unif}(Cnt, C)$, whose analysis allows us to measure the probability of C holding in long runs of Cnt under random independent and identically distributed(iid) inputs. This value is designated as $\mathbb{E}_{unif}(Cnt, C)$. The construction of the desired DTMC is as follows. The product $Cnt \times \mathcal{A}(C)$ gives a finite state automaton with the same behaviours as Cnt. Moreover, it is in accepting state when C holds for the past behaviour. (Here $\mathcal{A}(C)$ works as a total deterministic monitor automaton for C without restricting Cnt). By assigning uniform discrete probabilities to all the inputs from any state, we obtain the DTMC $M_{unif}(Cnt, C)$ along with a designated set of accepting states, such that the DTMC is in accepting state precisely when C holds. Standard techniques from Markov chain analysis allow us to compute the *Expected value* of being in the set of accepting states on long runs of the DTMC. This gives us the desired value $\mathbb{E}_{unif}(Cnt, C)$. A leading probabilistic model checking tool MRMC allows this computation [15]. In DCSynth, we provide a facility to compute $M_{unif}(Cnt, C)$ in a format accepted by the tool MRMC. Hence, using DCSynth and MRMC, we can compute $\mathbb{E}_{unif}(Cnt, C)$.

(ii) Guaranteed Performance as Must-Dominance: Consider two supervisors S_1, S_2 and a regular property C. Define that S_i guarantees C for an input sequence ii, provided for every output sequence $oo \in S_i[ii]$ produced by S_i on ii we have that (ii, oo) satisfies C. We say that S_2 *must dominance* S_1 with respect to the property C provided for every input sequence ii, if S_1 guarantees C then S_2 also guarantees C. Thus, S_2 provides a superior must guarantee of C than S_1.

Definition 7 (Must Dominance). *Given two supervisors S_1, S_2 and a formula C over input-output alphabet (I, O), the must dominance of S_2 over S_1 is defined as $S_1 \leq^C_{dom} S_2$ iff $MustInp(S_1, C) \subseteq MustInp(S_2, C)$, where $MustInp(S_i, C) = \{ii \in (2^I)^+ \mid \forall oo \in (2^O)^+ . ((ii, oo) \in L(S_i)) \Rightarrow (ii, oo) \models C\}$.* □

We establish *must dominance* relations among MPHOS supervisors of various types of specifications discussed in Sect. 5.1.

Lemma 2. *For any QDDC formulas A and C, and any horizon H, the following must dominance relations will hold*

1. $MPHOS_1(A, C)) \leq_{dom}^C MPHOS_3(A, C)) \leq_{dom}^C MPHOS_0(A, C))$

2. $MPHOS_2(A, C)) \leq_{dom}^C MPHOS_0(A, C))$

where, $MPHOS_i(A, C)$ denote the maximally permissive H-optimal supervisor $\mathcal{A}^{MPHOS}$ of Algorithm 1 for the specification $Type_i(A, C)$.

Proof. By definition, $MPHOS_0(A, C)$ invariantly satisfies C for all input sequences. Hence, $MustInp(MPHOS_0(A, C), C) = (2^I)^*$, which immediately gives us that $S \leq_{dom}^C MPHOS_0(A, C))$ for any supervisor S.

Now we prove the remaining relation $MPHOS_1(A, C)) \leq_{dom}^C MPHOS_3(A, C))$. Let $S = MPS(A \Rightarrow C)$. Then, $MPHOS_1(A, C)) = MPHOS(S, true, H) = S$. The second equality holds as soft requirement *true* does not cause any pruning of outputs in H-optimal computation. By definition $MPHOS_3(A, C) = MPHOS(S, C, H)$. By Proposition 2, $S \leq_{det} MPHOS(S, C, H)$ which gives us the required result.   □

It may be noted that in general, $MPHOS_2(A, C)$ is theoretically incomparable with $MPHOS_1(A, C)$ and $MPHOS_3(A, C)$, as $MPHOS_2(A, C)$ is a supervisor that does not have to meet any hard requirement, but it optimally meets the soft requirements irrespective of the assumption. However, for specific (A, C) instances, some additional must-dominance relations may hold between $MPHOS_2(A, C)$ and the other supervisors.

5.3   Case Studies: Mine-Pump and Arbiter Specifications

Mine-pump: The Mine-pump controller (see [21]) has two input sensors: high water level sensor $HH2O$ and methane leakage sensor $HCH4$; and one output, $PUMPON$ to keep the pump on. The objective of the controller is to *safely* operate the pump in such a way that the water level never remains high continuously for more that w cycles. Thus, Mine-pump controller specification has input and output variables $(\{HH2O, HCH4\}, \{PUMPON\})$.

We have following **assumptions** on the *mine* and the *pump*. Their conjunction is denoted by $MineAssume(\epsilon, \zeta, \kappa)$ with integer parameters ϵ, ζ, κ. Being of the form $[]D$ each formula states that the property D (described in text) holds for all observation intervals in past.

- *Pump capacity:* $([]!(slen = \epsilon \ \&\& \ ([PUMPON \ \&\& \ HH2O]^{\wedge}\langle HH2O\rangle)))$. If the pump is continuously on for ϵ cycles with water level also continuously high, then water level will not be high at the $\epsilon + 1$ cycle.
- *Methane release:* $[](([HCH4]^{\wedge}[!HCH4]^{\wedge}\langle HCH4\rangle) \Rightarrow (slen > \zeta))$ and $[]([[HCH4]] \Rightarrow slen < \kappa)$. The minimum separation between the two leaks of methane is ζ cycles and the leak cannot persist for more than κ cycles.

The **commitments** are as follows. The conjunction of commitments is denoted by $MineCommit(w)$ and they hold intermittently in absence of assumption.

Table 1. Synthesis from Mine-pump(8, 2, 6, 2) and Arb(5, 3, 2) specifications in DCSynth. The last column gives the expected value of commitment in long run on random inputs.

Sr	DCSynth Specification		Synthesis (States/Time)			
	Controller	Output	MPS	MPHOS	Controller	Expected
No	type	Ordering	Stats	Stats	Stats	Value
Mine-pump(8, 2, 6, 2)						
1	$Type0$	-	Unrealizable			
2	$Type1$	$PUMPON$	70/0.00045	70/0.00254	21/0.00220	0.0
3	$Type2$	$PUMPON$	1/0.00004	10/0.00545	10/0.00033	0.99805
4	$Type3$	$PUMPON$	70/0.00045	75/0.044216	73/0.00081	0.99805
5	$Type1$	$!(PUMPON)$	70/0.00045	70/0.00254	47/0.00230	0.0
6	$Type2$	$!(PUMPON)$	1/0.00004	10/0.00545	10/0.00019	0.99805
7	$Type3$	$!(PUMPON)$	70/0.00045	75/0.044216	73/0.00082	0.99805
Arb(5, 3, 2)						
1	$Type0$	-	Unrealizable			
2	$Type1$	$ArbDef$	13/0.000226	13/0.004794	11/0.007048	0.0
3	$Type2$	$ArbDef$	1/0.00001	207/1.864346	201/0.058423	0.9930985
4	$Type3$	$ArbDef$	13/0.000213	207/1.897907	201/0.057062	0.9930985

- *Safety conditions:* $true^\wedge\langle\langle((HCH4 \;||\; !HH2O) \Rightarrow !PUMPON)\rangle\rangle$ states that if there is a methane leak or absence of high water in current cycle, then pump should be off in the current cycle. Formula $!(true^\wedge([[HH2O]] \;\&\&\; slen = w))$ states that, water level does not remain continuously high in last $w+1$ cycles.

The Mine-Pump specification denoted by $MinePump(w, \epsilon, \zeta, \kappa)$ is given by the assumption-commitment pair $(MineAssume(\epsilon, \zeta, \kappa), MineCommit(w))$. The four types of DCSynth specifications of Sect. 5.1 are synthesized.

Arbiter: Due to space limitations, the detailed specification of the arbiter, introduced in Example 1, is given in full paper [31]. The arbiter is denoted as $Arb(n, k, r)$, where n denotes the number of clients, k is the response time (time for which a client should keep the request high continuously to get the guaranteed access). The arbiter works under the assumption that in past in any cycle the maximum number of request that can be true simultaneously is r.

5.4   Experimental Evaluation

Given an assumption-commitment pair (A, C) the four types of DCSynth specifications can be derived as given in Sect. 5.1. Given any such specification, a horizon value H, and an ordering of outputs, a controller can be synthesized using our tool DCSynth as described in Sect. 4.4.

For the *Mine-pump* instance $MinePump(8, 2, 6, 2)$, we synthesized controllers for all the four derived specification types with horizon value $H = 50$

and output ordering $PUMPON$. These controllers choose to get rid of water aggressively by keeping the pump on whenever possible. Similarly, controllers were also synthesized with the output ordering $!PUMPON$. These controllers save energy by keeping the pump off whenever possible. Note that, in our synthesis method, hard and soft requirements are fulfilled before applying the output orderings.

For Arbiter instance $Arb(5,3,2)$ also, the controllers were synthesized for all the four derived specification types with horizon value $H = 50$ and output ordering $ArbDef = (a_1 > a_2 > a_3 > a_4 > a_5)$. This ordering tries to give acknowledgment such that client i has priority higher than client j for all $i < j$.

Table 1 gives the performance of the tool DCSynth in synthesizing these controllers. The table gives the time taken at each step of the synthesis, and the sizes of the computed supervisors/controllers. The experiments were conducted on Ubuntu 16.04, with Intel i5 64 bit (2.5 GHz) machine and 4 GB memory.

Experimental Evaluation of Expected Case Performance: The last column of Table 1 gives the expected value of commitment holding in long run over random inputs. This value is computed as outlined in Sect. 5.2.

It can be observed from Table 1 that in both the examples, the controllers for *Type1* (i.e., when soft-requirements are not used) specifications have 0 expected value of commitment C. This is because of the strong assumptions used in guaranteeing C, which themselves have expected value 0. In such a case, whenever the assumption fails, the synthesis algorithm has no incentive to try to meet C. On the other hand, with soft requirement C in *Type2* and *Type3* specifications, the H-optimal controllers have the expected value of C above 99%. This remarkable increase in the *expected value* of Commitment shows that H-optimal synthesis is very effective in figuring out controllers which meet the desirable property C as much as possible, irrespective of the assumption.

Experimental Evaluation of Must-Dominance: Given supervisors S_1, S_2 for an assumption-commitment pair (A, C), since both S_1, S_2 are finite state Mealy machines and C is a regular property, an automata theoretic technique can automatically check whether $S_1 \leq^C_{dom} S_2$. This technique is implemented in our tool DCSynth. If $S_1 \leq^C_{dom} S_2$ does not hold, the tool provides a counter example.

For our case studies, we experimentally compare must dominance of supervisors $MPHOS_i(A, C)$ as defined in Lemma 2. Recall that $MPHOS_i(A, C)$ denotes the maximally permissive H-optimal supervisor for the specification $Type_i(A, C)$. The results obtained (with $H = 50$) are as follows.

1. Mine-pump instance $Minepump(8,2,6,2)$ is abbreviated as MP:
$$MPHOS_1(MP) <^C_{dom} MPHOS_3(MP) =^C_{dom} MPHOS_2(MP)$$
2. Arbiter instance $Arb(5,3,2)$ is abbreviated as ARB:
$$MPHOS_1(ARB) <^C_{dom} MPHOS_2(ARB) =^C_{dom} MPHOS_3(ARB)$$

As expected $MPHOS_3$ must dominates $MPHOS_1$, because $MPHOS_3$ is a sub-supervisor of $MPHOS_1$. What is interesting and surprising is that in both the case studies, the $MPHOS_2$ and $MPHOS_3$ supervisors are found to be syntactically identical. This is not theoretically guaranteed, as $Type2$ and $Type3$ supervisors are must-incomparable in general. However, in these examples, the H-optimal $MPHOS_2$ already provides all the must-guarantees of the hand-crafted $MPHOS_3$ hard requirements. The H-optimization of C seems to exhibit startling ability to guarantees C without human intervention. It will be our attempt to validate this with more examples in future. So far we have considered commitment as soft requirement. In general, the soft requirement can be used to optimize MPS w.r.t. any regular property of interest, where as the hard requirements gives the necessary must guarantees. Such soft requirements may embody performance and quality goals. Hence, it is advisable to use the combination of hard and soft requirement based on the criticality of each requirement.

6   Discussion Along with Related Work

Reactive synthesis from Linear Temporal Logic (LTL) specification is a widely studied area [2] and many tools [4,11] supported by theoretical foundations are available. The leading tools like Acacia+ [4] and BoSy [11] mainly focus on the future fragment of LTL. In contrast, this paper focuses on *invariance* of complex regular properties, denoted by **inv** D^h where D^h is a QDDC formula. For such a property, a maximally permissive supervisor (MPS) can be synthesized. Formally, logics LTL and QDDC have incomparable expressive power; namely star-free omega-regular versus regular languages, respective. There is increasing evidence that regular properties form an important class of requirements [9,18,19]. The IEEE standard PSL extends LTL with regular properties [13]. Wonham and Ramadge in their seminal work [25,26] first studied the synthesis of MPS from regular properties. In their supervisory control theory, MPS can in fact be synthesized for a richer property class $AGEF\ D^h$ [10]. Tool DCSynth can be easily extended to support such properties too. Riedweg *et al.* [28] give some sub-classes of Quantified Mu-Calculus for which MPS can be computed. However, none of these works address soft requirement guided synthesis.

   Most of the reactive synthesis tools focus on correct-by-construction synthesis from hard requirements, e.g. none of the tools in recent competition on reactive synthesis [14], address the issue of guided synthesis which is our main focus. In our approach, we refine the MPS (for hard requirements) to a sub-supervisor optimally satisfying the soft requirements. Since LTL does not admit MPS (see [10] for an example), it is unclear how our approach can extend to LTL.

   In quantitative synthesis, a weighted arena is assumed to be available, and algorithms for optimal controller synthesis for diverse objectives such as Mean-payoff [3] or energy [5] have been investigated. In our case, we first synthesize the weighted arena from given hard and soft requirements. Moreover, we use H-optimality as the synthesis criterion. This criterion has been widely used in reinforcement learning as well as optimal control of MDPs [1,24]. In other related work, techniques for optimal controller synthesis are discussed by Ding *et al.* [9], Wongpiromsarn *et al.* [32] and Raman *et al.* [27], where they have explored the use of receding horizon model predictive control along with temporal logic properties.

Since our focus is on the quality of the controllers, we have also defined measurement techniques for comparing the controllers for their guaranteed (based on must dominance) and expected case performance. For the expected case measurement, we have assumed that inputs are *iid*. However, the method can easily accommodate a finite state Markov model governing the occurrences of inputs.

DCSynth uses an BDD-based symbolic representation, inherited from tool MONA [16] for storing automata, supervisors and controllers. The use of eager minimization allows us to handle complex properties (See [31]). Experiments show that the main bottleneck to scalability is the monitor construction step.

7   Conclusions

We have presented a technique for guided synthesis of controllers from hard and soft requirements specified in logic QDDC. The technique is implemented in our tool DCSynth. Case studies show that combination of hard and soft requirements provides, capability to deal with desirable and/or conflicting requirements. For example, in the context of assumption-commitment based specification, hard requirements provide *conditional guarantees* on the synthesized controller, whereas the soft requirements improve the expected case performance. Hence, the combination of hard and soft requirements as formulated in $Type3$ specifications offers a superior choice of controller specification. We have also explored the experimental ability to compare the controllers using *expected value* and *must dominance* metrics. This helps us in designing better performing controllers.

References

1. Bellman, R.E.: Dynamic Programming. Princeton University Press, Princeton (1957)
2. Bloem, R., et al.: Synthesizing robust systems. Acta Inf. **51**(3–4), 193–220 (2014). https://doi.org/10.1007/s00236-013-0191-5
3. Bloem, R., Chatterjee, K., Henzinger, T.A., Jobstmann, B.: Better quality in synthesis through quantitative objectives. In: Bouajjani, A., Maler, O. (eds.) CAV 2009. LNCS, vol. 5643, pp. 140–156. Springer, Heidelberg (2009). https://doi.org/10.1007/978-3-642-02658-4_14
4. Bohy, A., Bruyère, V., Filiot, E., Jin, N., Raskin, J.-F.: Acacia+, a tool for LTL synthesis. In: Madhusudan, P., Seshia, S.A. (eds.) CAV 2012. LNCS, vol. 7358, pp. 652–657. Springer, Heidelberg (2012). https://doi.org/10.1007/978-3-642-31424-7_45
5. Bouyer, P., Markey, N., Randour, M., Larsen, K.G., Laursen, S.: Average-energy games. Acta Informatica **55**(2), 91–127 (2018). https://doi.org/10.1007/s00236-016-0274-1
6. Chakravorty, G., Pandya, P.K.: Digitizing interval duration logic. In: Hunt, W.A., Somenzi, F. (eds.) CAV 2003. LNCS, vol. 2725, pp. 167–179. Springer, Heidelberg (2003). https://doi.org/10.1007/978-3-540-45069-6_17

7. Zhou, C., Hansen, M.R.: Duration Calculus - A Formal Approach to Real-Time Systems. Monographs in Theoretical Computer Science. An EATCS Series. Springer, Heidelberg (2004). https://doi.org/10.1007/978-3-662-06784-0
8. Zhou, C., Hoare, C.A.R., Ravn, A.P.: A calculus of durations. Inf. Process. Lett. **40**(5), 269–276 (1991). https://doi.org/10.1016/0020-0190(91)90122-X
9. Ding, X.C., Lazar, M., Belta, C.: LTL receding horizon control for finite deterministic systems. Automatica **50**(2), 399–408 (2014). https://doi.org/10.1016/j.automatica.2013.11.030
10. Ehlers, R., Lafortune, S., Tripakis, S., Vardi, M.Y.: Supervisory control and reactive synthesis: a comparative introduction. Discrete Event Dyn. Syst. **27**(2), 209–260 (2017). https://doi.org/10.1007/s10626-015-0223-0
11. Faymonville, P., Finkbeiner, B., Tentrup, L.: BoSy: an experimentation framework for bounded synthesis. In: Majumdar, R., Kunčak, V. (eds.) CAV 2017. LNCS, vol. 10427, pp. 325–332. Springer, Cham (2017). https://doi.org/10.1007/978-3-319-63390-9_17
12. Grädel, E., Thomas, W., Wilke, T. (eds.): Automata Logics, and Infinite Games. LNCS, vol. 2500. Springer, Heidelberg (2002). https://doi.org/10.1007/3-540-36387-4
13. IEC: IEC 62531:2012(e) (IEEE std 1850–2010): Standard for property specification language (PSL). IEC 62531:2012(E) (IEEE Std 1850–2010), pp. 1–184, June 2012. https://doi.org/10.1109/IEEESTD.2012.6228486
14. Jacobs, S., et al.: The 4th reactive synthesis competition (SYNTCOMP 2017): benchmarks, participants & results. CoRR abs/1711.11439 (2017). http://arxiv.org/abs/1711.11439
15. Katoen, J., Zapreev, I.S., Hahn, E.M., Hermanns, H., Jansen, D.N.: The INS and outs of the probabilistic model checker MRMC. Perform. Eval. **68**, 89–220 (2011). https://doi.org/10.1016/j.peva.2010.04.001
16. Klarlund, N., Møller, A., Schwartzbach, M.I.: MONA implementation secrets **2088**, 182–194 (2001). https://doi.org/10.1007/3-540-44674-5_15
17. Krishna, S.N., Pandya, P.K.: Modal strength reduction in quantified discrete duration calculus. In: Sarukkai, S., Sen, S. (eds.) FSTTCS 2005. LNCS, vol. 3821, pp. 444–456. Springer, Heidelberg (2005). https://doi.org/10.1007/11590156_36
18. Lafortune, S., Rudie, K., Tripakis, S.: Thirty years of the ramadge-wonham theory of supervisory control: a retrospective and future perspectives [conference reports]. IEEE Control Syst. Mag. **38**(4), 111–112 (2018). https://doi.org/10.1109/MCS.2018.2830083
19. Matteplackel, R.M., Pandya, P.K., Wakankar, A.: Formalizing timing diagram requirements in discrete duration calculus. In: Cimatti, A., Sirjani, M. (eds.) SEFM 2017. LNCS, vol. 10469, pp. 253–268. Springer, Cham (2017). https://doi.org/10.1007/978-3-319-66197-1_16
20. Pandya, P.K.: Model checking CTL*[DC]. In: Margaria, T., Yi, W. (eds.) TACAS 2001. LNCS, vol. 2031, pp. 559–573. Springer, Heidelberg (2001). https://doi.org/10.1007/3-540-45319-9_38
21. Pandya, P.K.: Specifying and deciding quantified discrete-time duration calculus formulae using DCVALID. In: RTTOOLS (affiliated with CONCUR 2001) (2001)
22. Pandya, P.K.: The saga of synchronous bus arbiter: on model checking quantitative timing properties of synchronous programs. Electr. Notes Theor. Comput. Sci. **65**(5), 110–124 (2002). https://doi.org/10.1016/S1571-0661(05)80445-1
23. Pandya, P.K., Wakankar, A.: Specification and reactive synthesis of robust controllers. CoRR abs/1905.11157 (2019). http://arxiv.org/abs/1905.11157

24. Puterman, M.L.: Markov Decision Processes: Discrete Stochastic Dynamic Programming, 1st edn. Wiley, Hoboken (1994)
25. Ramadge, P., Wonham, W.: Supervisory control of a class of discrete event processes. SIAM J. Control Optim. **25**(1), 206–230 (1987). https://doi.org/10.1137/0325013
26. Ramadge, P., Wonham, W.: The control of discrete event systems. Proc. IEEE **77**, 81–98 (1989). https://doi.org/10.1109/5.21072
27. Raman, V., Donzé, A., Sadigh, D., Murray, R.M., Seshia, S.A.: Reactive synthesis from signal temporal logic specifications. In: HSCC, HSCC 2015, pp. 239–248. ACM (2015). https://doi.org/10.1145/2728606.2728628
28. Riedweg, S., Pinchinat, S.: Quantified mu-calculus for control synthesis. In: Rovan, B., Vojtáš, P. (eds.) MFCS 2003. LNCS, vol. 2747, pp. 642–651. Springer, Heidelberg (2003). https://doi.org/10.1007/978-3-540-45138-9_58
29. Sharma, B., Pandya, P.K., Chakraborty, S.: Bounded validity checking of interval duration logic. In: Halbwachs, N., Zuck, L.D. (eds.) TACAS 2005. LNCS, vol. 3440, pp. 301–316. Springer, Heidelberg (2005). https://doi.org/10.1007/978-3-540-31980-1_20
30. Wakankar, A., Pandya, P.K., Matteplackel, R.M.: DCSynth 1.0. TIFR, Mumbai (2018). http://www.tcs.tifr.res.in/~pandya/dcsynth/dcsynth.html
31. Wakankar, A., Pandya, P.K., Matteplackel, R.M.: DCSynth: a tool for guided reactive synthesis with soft requirements, VSTTE 2019. CoRR abs/1903.03991 (2019, in press). http://arxiv.org/abs/1903.03991
32. Wongpiromsarn, T., Topcu, U., Murray, R.M.: Receding horizon temporal logic planning. IEEE Trans. Automat. Contr. **57**(11), 2817–2830 (2012). https://doi.org/10.1109/TAC.2012.2195811

Refinement Type Contracts
for Verification of Scientific Investigative
Software

Maxwell Shinn[✉][ID]

Yale University, New Haven, CT 06520, USA
maxwell.shinn@yale.edu

Abstract. Our scientific knowledge is increasingly built on software output. User code which defines data analysis pipelines and computational models is essential for research in the natural and social sciences, but little is known about how to ensure its correctness. The structure of this code and the development process used to build it limit the utility of traditional testing methodology. Formal methods for software verification have seen great success in ensuring code correctness but generally require more specialized training, development time, and funding than is available in the natural and social sciences. Here, we present a Python library which uses lightweight formal methods to provide correctness guarantees without the need for specialized knowledge or substantial time investment. Our package provides runtime verification of function entry and exit condition contracts using refinement types. It allows checking hyperproperties within contracts and offers automated test case generation to supplement online checking. We co-developed our tool with a medium-sized ($\approx$3000 LOC) software package which simulates decision-making in cognitive neuroscience. In addition to helping us locate trivial bugs earlier on in the development cycle, our tool was able to locate four bugs which may have been difficult to find using traditional testing methods. It was also able to find bugs in user code which did not contain contracts or refinement type annotations. This demonstrates how formal methods can be used to verify the correctness of scientific software which is difficult to test with mainstream approaches.

Keywords: Formal methods · Scientific software · Contracts · Refinement types · Python · Runtime verification

1 Introduction

Over the last several decades, software engineering has made great strides in developing tools and processes for verifying the correctness of computer software. Although verification has been strikingly successful across many different domains, it has not been widely applied to scientific software. It has been estimated that 5%–100% of scientific software output is incorrect due to undetected

© Springer Nature Switzerland AG 2020
S. Chakraborty and J. A. Navas (Eds.): VSTTE 2019, LNCS 12031, pp. 143–160, 2020.
https://doi.org/10.1007/978-3-030-41600-3_10

software bugs [44], and this is evident from the many retractions caused by undetected bugs[1]. Some of these retractions were covered in depth by the popular press. In one case, a researcher discovered that the results defining his career were built on a software bug, forcing him to retract five of his most important papers from top journals [33]. In another case, a software bug reversed the results of highly influential economics research which was widely cited in public policy decisions [23]. Section 2 will provide concrete examples which illustrate common sources of such bugs.

One ubiquitous class of scientific software has received little to no attention from the verification community: this software is user code which is characterized by (a) small amounts of code (usually 50–500 LOC) (b) written by domain experts with little to no formal training in software engineering [8,19,39], which is (c) run a limited number of times, (d) has specifications that change unpredictably on a daily or hourly basis, (e) is used almost exclusively by the original developer, and (f) has no testing oracle because the output of the software is the object of investigation [21,29,44]. We refer to this class of software as "investigative software". Investigative software is written on a daily basis by countless researchers across the natural and social sciences. Some common examples of investigative software include: scripts to load experimental data and perform statistical tests using statistical libraries; simulations of a computational model; a pipeline which performs complicated preprocessing operations on input data; or a script used internally to make business decisions. This paper presents a tool which is used to verify investigative software.

Testing and verifying correctness of investigative software is difficult due to many technical and cultural factors including unclean data, the lack of a testing oracle, and the insufficiency of standard testing procedures for the structure and goals of scientific programs [25–28,30,40]. There already exist methods in the scientific community for checking program correctness, but they have serious limitations which limit their utility as discussed in Sect. 7; as a result, investigative software is most commonly validated by determining whether the program's output matches the expectations of the scientist, posing a fundamental violation of the scientific method [40]. A more convenient and effective method for ensuring the quality of scientific software is needed.

Formal methods are able to check the correctness of investigative software. However, state of the art formal verification tools are time-consuming to implement and require substantial formal methods expertise, which make their use impractical for investigative software. A survey estimated that scientists spend about 30% of their time writing software [19], so the need to formally verify this code is a substantial hurdle to productivity.

By contrast, runtime verification is easy to use and especially well-suited to investigative software. It requires little training to use, yet is able to achieve many of the same goals; because investigative software is usually developed by its sole user, it doesn't matter whether bugs are caught during development or detected at runtime through verification condition violations. This reflects the

---

[1] See http://retractionwatch.com/.

fact that investigative software development often cannot be meaningfully separated from data analysis [25,31,34,40]. Researchers need access to lightweight formal methods to improve the correctness of their software without slowing down the research process.

We created Paranoid Scientist[2], a Python library for verifying the correctness of investigative software. Paranoid Scientist employs runtime verification to check software correctness. Developers specify function behavior through entry and exit conditions, thereby creating function contracts which must be satisfied by each function execution [2,20]. Contracts are specified in two parts. First, each function argument and the return value are specified modularly using refinement types [14,46], which are types defined by predicates. Second, additional constraints such as a dependence of the return type on the function arguments or the function argument types on each other are specified using predicates written in pure Python. These constraints may also depend on previous calls to the function in order to check hyperproperties. In addition to runtime checking, Paranoid Scientist may further use the refinement type contracts to automatically generate test cases. Critically, Paranoid Scientist uses simple syntax and is intuitive to those without a background in formal methods or software engineering. We ran our tool on real-world investigative software and found that it was able to catch four undetected bugs while imposing a 1.05–6.41 factor performance penalty.

2   Motivating Examples

We provide two motivating examples from real-world investigative software written for research in the biomedical sciences.

Incorrect Function Usage. Figure 1a shows an example bug in a function designed to find the reverse complement of a DNA sequence. Briefly, DNA is the primary medium for long-term information storage in biological organisms. Each strand is composed of long sequences of four "base" molecules—adenine (A), guanine (G), cytosine (C), and thymine (T). For chemical stability, each strand of DNA within an organism is usually bound to a "reverse complement" strand whereby the A and T bases and the G and C bases are swapped and the resulting sequence is reversed. By contrast, RNA is a biological medium for short-term information storage. It shares a nearly identical structure with DNA, but replaces T with uracil (U). Consequently, when forming the RNA reverse complement, A is swapped with U instead of T.

The function `complement_sequence` in Fig. 1a uses a simple mechanism to compute the reverse complement DNA sequence. It accepts a list of characters and, using Python's equivalent of the Unix program "tr", it converts all A to T, G to C, C to G, and T to A, and then reverses the result. While this function behaves as intended, an erroneous usage of the function occurs when the user tries to find the reverse complement of an RNA sequence instead of a DNA sequence. The function accepts the valid RNA sequence UCG and returns another valid

---

[2] https://github.com/mwshinn/paranoidscientist.

```
1  # Find the reverse  complement of       1  # Perform CPU-intensive preprocessing
2  # DNA. Assumes 'seq' is a list of       2  timeseries = preprocess_ts(timeseries)
3  # chars "A", "G", "C", and "T".         3  # Find timeseries pairwise correlations
4  def complement_sequence(seq):           4  corr_matrix = corrcoef(timeseries)
5      # Convert 'seq' to string and       5  # Fisher z-transform (arctanh).
6      # use regex translate               6  # Assumes abs(correlation) <= 1
7      c_str = ''.join(seq).translate(     7  norm = fisher_transform(corr_matrix)
8          str.maketrans('AGCT', 'TCGA'))  8  save_csv("matrix.csv", norm)
9      return list(reversed(c_str))        9
10                                         10 corr_matrix = load_csv("matrix.csv")
11 # Correct usage, return ['G','A','T']   11 # BUG: normalized before saving,
12 complement_sequence(['A','T','C'])      12 # these values violate assumptions
13 # BUG: Called for RNA instead of DNA,   13 # of the fisher_transform function.
14 # Return ['C','G','U'], however U       14 norm = fisher_transform(corr_matrix)
15 # is not its own complement.            15 # Convert matrix to undirected graph
16 complement_sequence(['U','C','G'])      16 G = matrix_to_graph(norm)
```

(a) Incorrect function usage example   (b) NaN propagation example

Fig. 1. Two examples illustrate real-world bugs in investigative software. (a) A function designed to process DNA sequences is invoked with an RNA sequence. Due to their similarity, a valid but incorrect output is returned for the RNA sequence. (b) NaN values can be silently propagated. This code constructs an undirected graph weighted by transformed pairwise correlations of brain scan timeseries. The `fisher_transform` function is accidentally applied twice, the second execution of which generates a matrix with some NaN values which are silently ignored in the `matrix_to_graph` function.

RNA sequence CGU without error. However, CGU is not the reverse complement of UCG, because the U should be replaced with an A. The `complement_sequence` function is only designed to operate on DNA sequences, and thus cannot properly deal with the RNA base U.

Paranoid Scientist is able to ensure correctness in this example. An annotated version of the `complement_sequence` function is shown in Fig. 2a. Most importantly for this example, the `@accepts` decorator checks that the argument value is a list consisting only of values A, G, C, and T. This means that passing an RNA sequence to the function in Fig. 1a will raise an error, because the "U" element in the list is invalid for DNA. Even if entry conditions were not specified, the "U" would have been caught as an invalid output type by the return type specification in the `@returns` decorator, and by the exit condition in the `@ensures` decorator which specifies that all values of the input must be different than the corresponding values of the reversed output. These properties are checked at runtime to ensure the function is receiving correct input and producing correct output.

NaN Propagation. Another example bug is shown in Fig. 1b, which is a condensed version of a bug from real-world investigative software. This code is the final step in a pipeline which converts a functional magnetic resonance imaging (fMRI) scan—a type of brain scan which allows researchers to look at brain activity over time—to an undirected graph where edges represent strong correlations in brain activity [4]. First, several computationally-intensive preprocessing steps are applied to the timeseries, and then the pairwise Pearson correlation of each region is computed. Pearson correlation is a value from -1 to 1 inclusive,

```
1  @accepts(List(Set('AGCT')))              1  @accepts(NDArray(t=Range(-1, 1)))
2  @returns(List(Set('AGCT')))              2  @returns(NDArray(t=Number))
3  @ensures("all(seq[i] != return[::-1][i] \ 3  @ensures("return.shape == \
4      for i in range(0, len(seq)))")       4      corr_values.shape")
5  def complement_sequence(seq):            5  def fisher_transform(corr_values):
6      ...                                  6      ...
```

(a) Annotations for Figure 1a   (b) Annotations for Figure 1b

Fig. 2. Two examples of Paranoid Scientist annotations which could detect the bugs in Fig. 1a and b. (a) Ensure that the `complement_sequence` function accepts and returns DNA sequences. (b) Ensure that the `fisher_transform` function only receives values for which it is defined, and that it always returns a number (i.e. not NaN or $\pm$inf).

which is converted to a more statistically-informative value from negative infinity to infinity using the Fisher z-transform, or equivalently hyperbolic arctangent. This is then saved to a file so that the computationally intensive steps do not need to be repeated.

After saving, the timeseries can be reloaded and turned into an undirected graph. However, before doing so, the `fisher_transform` function is erroneously applied a second time. The second time it is called, the inputs hold values from negative infinity to infinity. This is outside of the domain of the hyperbolic arctangent function, causing it to return NaN for inputs less than -1 or greater than 1. In practice, this gives reasonable values for small- and medium-valued correlations but NaN for large correlations. These NaN values are masked by the function `matrix_to_graph`, returning a graph which does not show evidence of the NaN values; this creates a graph which appears to be correct for all but the largest correlations. This bug therefore created subtle changes in the resulting graph topology which were not noticed immediately, causing several weeks of work analyzing the resulting graphs to be lost.

Paranoid Scientist is able to detect this bug. Figure 2b shows annotations for the `fisher_transform` function. This function takes any N-dimensional array (`NDArray`) with values ranging from -1 to 1, and returns an N-dimensional array of the same shape with elements which are numbers. NaN is not a valid number. These annotations would have been sufficient to catch the bug in Fig. 1b. Alternatively, annotations which specified the valid input of `matrix_to_graph` would have also been able to detect this bug.

If either of these two bugs had appeared in software which had an oracle, there is a high probability that the difference in behavior would manifest as an observable bug and the behavior could be corrected [29]. Investigative software is written because the result is unknown, so in these cases the bugs may never have been found.

3   Package Summary

3.1   Refinement Types

Function entry and exit conditions are specified in part by refinement types. In our tool, refinement types are defined by a predicate which checks whether an input is an element of the type. Predicates are constructed by Python functions using purely Python code, and thus may reach arbitrary levels of complexity without depending on a domain specific language. This allows types to be defined in terms of their scientific purpose and conceptual properties instead of as datatypes [46]. These refinement types are akin to what one would write when documenting the function. For example, one type defined by default is "Number", which can be a float or an int but not NaN or ±inf. Types can also represent more complex properties. For example, a discrete probability distribution is a list with non-negative elements which sum to 1, and a correlation matrix is a symmetric positive semidefinite matrix with 1 on the diagonal. A list of all types included by default is included in the Appendix. Any class can be used in place of a type by checking whether the passed value is a subclass of the given class. Alternatively, classes can define a method to determine whether the passed value is an instance of the class, described in further detail in Sect. 3.3.

3.2   Entry and Exit Conditions

In addition to refinement types, additional entry and exit conditions may be specified for conditions involving multiple function arguments or involving function arguments and the return value. For example, there may be a constraint that the first argument is greater than or equal to the second argument, or that the function returns a matrix with the number of rows and columns specified by the input arguments. Conditions are specified as a string which is evaluated as Python code.

Function properties may depend on more than a single execution of the function. For example, function concavity and function monotonicity are hyperproperties which cannot be determined at runtime when considering a single function execution. Paranoid Scientist saves in memory a list of arguments and return values from previous function executions. All future function executions are compared against these past values. For functions which are executed many times, a naive implementation would cause serious performance and memory penalties, limiting the practicality of this feature. We address this problem by saving only a subset of function calls and using reservoir sampling [48] to test against a uniform distribution across all function calls; as a result, verification of hyperproperties is not performed across all previous calls but rather checked across a sample of previous calls which is uniformly-distributed across time. An example of one such hyperproperty is shown in Fig. 3.

```
1    @accepts(Number)
2    @returns(Number)
3    @ensures("t >= t' --> return >= return'") # Monotonic function
4    def cube(t):
5        return t**3
```

Fig. 3. Example of a hyperproperty. For any two executions of this function, Paranoid Scientist will check that the monotonicity hyperproperty is satisfied.

3.3 Syntax

Refinement types for function arguments and return values are specified using the @accepts and @returns function decorators, respectively. Further entry and exit conditions are passed as strings of Python code to the @requires and @ensures function decorators, respectively. The strings are evaluated using a namespace which includes the function arguments and additional user-specified libraries. In @ensures, the special value return represents the return value of the function. For testing hyperproperties, function arguments and return values from previous executions can be accessed by appending one or more backtick characters as a suffix, a notation which is reminiscent of the "prime" symbol from mathematics. Additionally, syntactic sugar is available for the two common idioms "implies" with the --> syntax and "if and only if" with the <--> syntax.

In addition to the default types, refinement types may be defined manually. Types are classes which define two methods: one to test values for adherence to the type, and a second to generate values of the type for use in automated testing, as described below. The type definition may optionally accept arguments to specify parameterizable behavior or generics. Any existing class can also be used as a type by using the class name in place of a refinement type. In these cases, Paranoid Scientist only tests whether the element is an instance of the class, where adherence to the Liskov substitution principle is assumed by default, i.e. subclasses are also considered to be elements of their parent class. For more precise control over the checking, class methods may be defined analogous to the methods for testing and generating values in stand-alone refinement types, allowing a single class to serve both as a normal class and also as a refinement type.

3.4 Automated Testing

The use of entry and exit conditions for each function makes it possible to perform unit tests automatically. A stand-alone command line utility takes the program to be checked as input and individually tests each function in the program with values generated using a specialized method from the refinement type specifications, similar to fuzz testing [12]. These generated values are passed as arguments to each function as long as the values satisfy the function's entry conditions. Because investigative software very seldom includes tests, this increases robustness.

Not all functions can be tested. Those with unspecified types, strict entry conditions, or arguments which cannot be automatically generated will not produce any test cases. Likewise, some tests run for a very long time under certain parameterizations; these are killed after some designated time duration to balance correctness with the practical constraints of testing. Paranoid Scientist will report to the user a list of the functions which could not be tested so that these may be targeted for further testing.

More detailed information about syntax and automated testing is available in the package documentation.

4   Performance Evaluation

We evaluate the runtime performance of Paranoid Scientist on several examples programs drawn from investigative software in cognitive neuroscience.

Design matrix construction (`design`) Construct a design matrix for a generalized linear model, similar to the analysis performed in [35].

Nodal versatility (`versatility`) Compute the versatility [42] of a node in an undirected graph with respect to a community detection algorithm.

Decision-making simulation (`pyddm_sim`) Simulate decision-making using the PyDDM software package (see Sect. 5).

Decision-making fitting (`pyddm_fit`) Fit a decision-making model to simulated data using the PyDDM software package (see Sect. 5).

Performance benchmarks are shown in Table 1. Overall, annotations comprised between 25–30% of the lines of code. There is a performance penalty for runtime verification, and this penalty varies depending on the details of the code. This penalty falls within the ranges suggested for "deliverable" (a 3x slowdown) or "usable" (10x slowdown or less) in runtime checks [45].

These examples were derived from real-world investigative software. Notably, a previously undetected bug was found in the `design` example when Paranoid Scientist annotations were added to it, which caused incorrect binning of data before performing the regression analysis.

Table 1. Performance benchmarks. Runtime for each example program is shown with standard error of the mean over 10 runs.

	design	versatility	pyddm_sim	pyddm_fit
Total LOC	162	86	5	20
Program LOC	117	68	5	20
Annotation LOC	45	18	(user code)	(user code)
% Code annotations	28%	26%	0%	0%
Runtime w/ checking (s)	8.452 ± 0.052	29.047 ± 0.158	13.685 ± 0.057	4.726 ± 0.160
Runtime w/o checking (s)	3.239 ± 0.022	27.606 ± 0.205	2.136 ± 0.013	3.066 ± 0.121
Slowdown factor	2.61	1.05	6.41	1.54

5   Case Study

We used our tool while developing PyDDM[3], a decision-making simulator for cognitive neuroscience. PyDDM's development was initially intended for a specific series of studies and was later released to other research groups [15]. Overall, Paranoid Scientist annotations comprised about 10% of the codebase. Over 95% of these annotations require refinement types which cannot be checked using existing static type checkers for Python. Hyperproperties were specified for less than 5% of function exit conditions.

We briefly describe the motivation for PyDDM. PyDDM aids in the study of a simple form of decision-making whereby two options are presented and the subject must choose one of the two based on either preference or matching a given stimulus. This type of decision-making is often studied using the drift-diffusion model (DDM), which posits that all decisions consist of some underlying evidence signal plus noise in continuous time [38]. The process of making a decision relies on integrating evidence for each option over time and coming to the final decision when the total integrated evidence surpasses some confidence criterion. Decision-making is usually studied for simple decisions over a short duration of time ($< 5\,\mathrm{s}$), such as for determining whether a sock is black or dark blue, but the model can also be used for decisions which may span days or weeks, such as deciding between two job offers. In either case, there is a trade-off between the time it takes to make the decision and the accuracy expected.

The DDM represents evidence integration as a diffusion process governed by the first passage time of a stochastic differential equation across a boundary. Analytical solutions for the DDM are fast to compute, but only specific versions of the model can be solved analytically. Recent experiments have found that humans and animals exhibit behavior which differs from these specific versions of the model. In order to explain experimental data, it is necessary to use a more general version of the model which can only be solved numerically. PyDDM provides a consistent interface to a collection of analytical and numerical algorithms for solving the generalized DDM, selecting the best routine for each model.

As a result, PyDDM contains a mix of optimized routines for finding solutions to stochastic differential equations, and a set of object-oriented interfaces to make these routines convenient to use. This includes predefined models for the most common use cases. Consequently, PyDDM must be used in conjunction with user code written by neuroscience researchers who may have limited experience in software engineering. Thus, the goals of verification are two-fold: detecting errors in PyDDM itself, and detecting errors in PyDDM user code.

5.1   Detecting Errors in PyDDM

We found four non-trivial bugs in PyDDM using Paranoid Scientist. Briefly, the bugs were:

---

[3] https://github.com/mwshinn/PyDDM.

1. Under certain circumstances, a small function which was assumed to return a positive number would return a negative number due to a typo in a mathematical equation. This was caught by a return type of "Positive".
2. An algorithm assumed that the output of a previous step in the processing pipeline yielded a vector with 0 as the first element. It was intuitive that this should be the case. When the numerical algorithm was upgraded, this no longer held true. Only one distant branch in the pipeline relied on this value being zero. This was caught by a precondition specifying the first element of the array should be 0.
3. When a model of a particular form was fit to data, a discretization approximation in a non-central portion of the code would exploit the limited numerical resolution of the simulation in order to select unnatural parameters which in turn artificially inflated the model's performance metrics. This was caught by a postcondition which checked that the distribution would integrate to 1.
4. Particular inputs caused numerical instabilities in one of the three simulation methods and made the probability distribution contain values slightly less than 0. This was caught by a precondition on a different function which required all elements of the input array to be greater than 0.

Bugs (1) and (2) would have been very difficult to detect without our tool, and detecting bug (3) would have required manually examining a large amount of intermediate output. These three bugs would have slightly impacted scientific results. Bug (4) would have likely been noticed eventually but would have caused a substantial time investment to locate. In addition to these bugs, Paranoid Scientist was able to detect an internal inconsistency in how data were stored. Though this did not manifest in a bug which affected results, it had the potential to do so in the future.

5.2   Detecting Errors Using Traditional Methodology

In addition to Paranoid Scientist annotations, unit tests and manual code review were used to catch bugs in PyDDM. One non-trivial bug was found in unit testing which was not detected by Paranoid Scientist, but this bug did not impact results:

1. When the core simulator's representation of a probability distribution was extended to include support for storing the distribution of incomplete trials, this unexpectedly modified the behavior of a distant piece of the code which utilized that representation.

Additionally, two non-trivial bugs were detected through code review which neither Paranoid Scientist nor unit/integration tests were able to catch; these bugs also did not impact results:

1. When constructing a diffusion matrix as a part of the core simulation routine, certain rare but important cases utilized the previous timestep instead the next timestep.
2. A simulation algorithm is automatically chosen for each model, but this choice was suboptimal for a small number of models.

5.3 Detecting Errors in User Code

In addition to PyDDM's core library code, a key feature is its extensibility with user code to define new models. Due to the complexity of models which can be defined by users, it is important to catch errors in user code even if the users do not use Paranoid Scientist annotations.

Paranoid Scientist was able to find three bugs in user code, even though this code did not have Paranoid Scientist annotations. All three of these would have impacted results:

1. Two subjects completed an experimental task with different task parameters, but parameters were mixed because the expression `if subject == 1` should have been `if subject != 1`. This caused a parameterization which was valid on its own but not within the context of the data. This was caught by a precondition which checked that one parameter was less than or equal to all elements of a data array.
2. A user-defined function to generate discrete probability distributions sometimes produced an invalid distribution. This was caught by a precondition checking that the distribution summed to 1.
3. Boundaries were initialized randomly according to a normal distribution. However, sometimes these bounds would be erroneously initialized such that some mass of the initial probability distribution had already crossed the bounds. This was caught by a precondition which checked that two input vectors were the same size.

6 Limitations

Runtime checking imposes penalties on the program's speed. Paranoid Scientist has not been optimized for speed, though such optimization is possible in the future. Previous work has demonstrated improved performance of runtime checks through a client–server architecture [10] and through optional contracts [11]. Performance could also be improved by producing a certificate during runtime which can be checked after execution.

Paranoid Scientist is compatible with all Python features and does not require the programmer to limit herself to a Python subset or to use a wrapper of the Python executable. Nevertheless, some less-commonly used Python features may cause problems if incorporated into contracts due to the present implementation of runtime checking, especially if these features are stateful. For example, Python objects are allowed to change their value when accessed, but this violates the assumptions of runtime checking. Likewise, contracts cannot yet be specified for generators. If these features are needed in contracts, Paranoid Scientist includes the Unchecked type as an alternative.

During runtime, Paranoid Scientist is able to implicitly deal with side effects relevant to the results of the computation such as modifications to global state and file IO. However, automated tests are unable to deal with these side effects. Paranoid Scientist does not have an explicit model of these or other side effects such as exceptions and printing, because a clear specification of these is seldom critical for investigative software.

Python's syntax for type annotations[4] provides a convenient way to specify types. Paranoid Scientist uses function decorators instead of type annotations. Type annotations would be suitable for the @accepts and @returns decorators, but not for the @requires or @ensures decorators, so using decorators for all of these improves syntax consistency. The use of decorators allows type annotations to be used for other purposes in the same codebase, and may avoid confusion among less-experienced Python programmers who are not used to this new syntax, or among users who run older versions of Python.

7   Related Work

Formal Methods for Scientific Software. The present focus on investigative software differs from previous work on verifying scientific software, which focuses on floating point operations [3,17] or high performance computing [18]. These tools are effective for specific types of scientific software, but the methodology they impose does not reflect the environment in which most investigative software is written and used [40]. Besides formal methods, prior work on testing scientific software does not focus on investigative software; instead, it focuses on large or collaborative software projects [5,15,41], software written by seasoned software engineers instead of researchers with limited formal training [22,29,32], software without an oracle [29], or computationally- or numerically-intensive software [9,24,49].

Testing Scientific Software. Several recognized methods exist for software testing in the scientific community, but these methods have serious limitations. One method involves rewriting a piece of software one or more times by independent parties and comparing the output for identical input [36,49]. In practice this is not feasible for most investigative software, due to the fact that it is written by a single individual for a limited number of executions. Another method is running the software with simplified parameters or artificial data for which the result is known [36,49]. This leaves the most scientifically important pieces of the code untested, and it is often difficult to determine equivalence of the software's output with the known result due to stochasticity or floating point arithmetic [30,49]. Meta-morphic testing has been proposed as an alternative means of testing software without an oracle, which involves testing specific properties which are required to hold [6,7,16,36]. This requires a deep knowledge of testing methodology and a code structure which facilitates such tests.

Python Type Systems. In recent years there has been a proliferation of static type checkers within the Python ecosystem, starting with MyPy[5] and continued

---

[4] https://www.python.org/dev/peps/pep-0484/.
[5] http://mypy-lang.org/.

by Facebook's Pyre[6], Google's PyType[7], and Microsoft's PyRight[8]. This has been further advanced by PEP 484[9], which standardized a syntax for type annotations for functions in the Python language. These type checkers introduce neither overhead nor speedups, as the types are checked before and not during runtime. Thus, the type information is not enforced during program execution.

Reticulated Python [47] includes runtime checks for annotated types using three different methods. The two bugs described in [47] which were caught using Reticulated Python would have occurred as exceptions without the runtime checks; with the present work, we are more interested in bugs which might have otherwise gone undetected. One of Reticulated Python's modes of operation can insert undetected bugs into the code by not preserving object identity, demonstrating the different objectives between Reticulated Python and the present work. Additional packages for runtime checking of static data types in Python, such as the "enforce"[10] or "typeguard"[11] packages, share many similarities to the "transient" method in Reticulated Python.

Python Contracts Libraries. While contracts were first conceived for Python in the language's infancy [37], contracts are still rare in Python code. The most popular contract library for Python is "PyContracts"[12], which embeds a domain specific language into Python for specifying properties that each argument must satisfy. It is difficult to specify complex properties or to create properties which rely on more than one argument, such as "argument 1 is greater than argument 2". PyBlame [1] provides a sophisticated contract library for Python which integrates with the debugger, but a detailed comparison could not be performed due to the lack of availability of the PyBlame source code. Data validation libraries, such as "cerberus"[13] and "voluptuous"[14], ensure that datasets satisfy particular conditions, and thus may be used in conjunction with Paranoid Scientist.

Nagini is a package which provides full static verification for a Python subset [13]. Python code is converted to an intermediate language and conditions are specified using contracts. In addition to arbitrary assertions, it can reason about exceptions, memory safety, data-race conditions, and input–output. However, approximately half of the lines of code must be devoted to the specification, and it has difficulty inferring properties about non-Python code such as C libraries.

8   Conclusions and Future Directions

It is difficult to overestimate the importance of investigative software in scientific research, but few studies have examined effective techniques for ensuring

---

[6] https://pyre-check.org/.

[7] https://google.github.io/pytype/.

[8] https://github.com/Microsoft/pyright.

[9] https://www.python.org/dev/peps/pep-0484/.

[10] https://github.com/RussBaz/enforce/.

[11] https://github.com/agronholm/typeguard.

[12] https://andreacensi.github.io/contracts/.

[13] https://docs.python-cerberus.org/en/stable/.

[14] https://github.com/alecthomas/voluptuous.

its correctness. Paranoid Scientist uses lightweight formal methods to provide correctness guarantees about this difficult-to-test class of software. It does so through a combination of contracts and refinement types in a way which is easy to use for those without explicit training in formal methods. We demonstrated that Paranoid Scientist can be used to find bugs in scientific software which would have impacted results and would have been otherwise difficult to detect.

Investigative software is built in an environment which poses two unique challenges for Hoare-style verification and static checking of preconditions and postconditions. First, the verification technique must be usable by scientists with little to no training in computer science. The state of the art techniques require a deep knowledge of formal methods to use them effectively [13]. Second, the amount of time spent verifying the software must be small compared to the amount of time spent writing the code to be verified. Current techniques are time consuming to implement. By contrast, our tool requires approximately as much time to implement as does writing function documentation.

Technical constraints of investigative software raise further challenges for formal methods. Investigative software in Python relies heavily on non-Python code such as C libraries and integrated shell commands, and thus static verification would require scaffolding for usability in practice. This scaffolding mandates more effort for verification and strong familiarity of the user with formal methods, exacerbating the previously discussed environmental challenges. Additionally, techniques such as type inference are conceptually incompatible with the present approach because the types in Paranoid Scientist often depend on the purpose of the code; for example, it may be "valid" to accept a probability less than 0 but this does not make sense on a scientific level. A gradual static verification approach, analogous to gradual typing [43], may be useful.

Lightweight formal methods may also be applied to investigative software in other programming languages. The present work targets Python due to its ubiquity in investigative software and powerful metaprogramming capabilities to simplify implementation. Besides Python, common languages for investigative software include Matlab, Julia, and R. While the bug shown in Fig. 1b may not have occurred in other languages, different programming languages have different advantages and disadvantages for the correctness of investigative software. For example, Matlab by default defines the constants i and j to be $\sqrt{-1}$, but allows these to be assigned other values by users. As a result, mistaken variable initialization or names can cause undetected bugs. Additionally, unexpected files saved to locations in Matlab's PATH can cause erroneous versions of scripts or data to be loaded, or even cause built-in functions to change their behavior. An implementation of lightweight formal methods as described here would be able to catch these and other bugs in Matlab.

It is critical to verify the correctness of investigative software, but technical and cultural constraints limit the effectiveness of conventional techniques. Lightweight formal methods as implemented in Paranoid Scientist provide a convenient and effective way to check the correctness of investigative software.

Acknowledgments. Thank you to Ruzica Piskac and Anastasia Ershova for a critical review of the manuscript; Clarence Lehman, Daeyeol Lee, and John Murray for helpful discussions; Michael Scudder for PyDDM code reviews; and Norman Lam for PyDDM development and code reviews. Funding was provided by the Gruber Foundation.

Appendix: Default types

Numerical

Numeric	A floating point or integer
ExtendedReal	A floating point or integer, excluding NaN
Number	A floating point or integer, excluding NaN and $\pm$inf
Integer	An integer
Natural0	An integer greater than or equal to zero
Natural1	An integer greater than zero
Range	A number with a value between two specified numbers, inclusive
RangeClosedOpen	A number with a value between two specified numbers, inclusive on the bottom and exclusive on the top
RangeOpenClosed	A number with a value between two specified numbers, exclusive on the bottom and inclusive on the top
RangeOpen	A number with a value between two specified numbers, exclusive
Positive0	A number greater than or equal to zero
Positive	A number greater than zero
NDArray	A Numpy `ndarray`, optionally with a given dimensionality or elements which satisfy a given type

Strings

String	A Python string
Identifier	A non-empty alphanumeric string with underscores and hyphens
Alphanumeric	A non-empty alphanumeric string
Latin	A non-empty string with Latin characters only

Collections

Tuple	A Python tuple, with elements which satisfy given types
List	A Python list, with elements which satisfy a given type
Dict	A Python dictionary, keys and values which satisfy given types
Set	A Python set, with elements which satisfy a given type
ParametersDict	A dictionary which may include only a subset of keys, with values which satisfy given types

Logical types

And	Logical AND of two or more types
Or	Logical OR of two or more types
Not	Logical NOT of a type

Special types

Boolean	Either `True` or `False`
Function	A Python function
Constant	A single specified value is accepted
Nothing	Only None, equivalent to `Constant(None)`
Unchecked	Any value (always succeeds)
Void	No value is accepted (always fails)
Maybe	Either a value of the specified type or else None
Self	The `self` argument to a method
PositionalArguments	Optional positional arguments to functions
KeywordArguments	Optional keyword arguments to functions

References

1. Arai, R., Sato, S., Iwasaki, H.: A debugger-cooperative higher-order contract system in python. In: Igarashi, A. (ed.) APLAS 2016. LNCS, vol. 10017, pp. 148–168. Springer, Cham (2016). https://doi.org/10.1007/978-3-319-47958-3_9

2. Barnett, M., Schulte, W.: Runtime verification of .NET contracts. J. Syst. Softw. **65**(3), 199–208 (2003)

3. Boldo, S., Filliatre, J.C.: Formal verification of floating-point programs. In: 18th IEEE Symposium on Computer Arithmetic (ARITH 2007). IEEE, June 2007

4. Bullmore, E., Sporns, O.: Complex brain networks: graph theoretical analysis of structural and functional systems. Nat. Rev. Neurosci. **10**(3), 186–198 (2009)

5. Carver, J.C., Kendall, R.P., Squires, S.E., Post, D.E.: Software development environments for scientific and engineering software: a series of case studies. In: 29th International Conference on Software Engineering (ICSE 2007). IEEE, May 2007

6. Chen, T., Ho, J.W., Liu, H., Xie, X.: An innovative approach for testing bioinformatics programs using metamorphic testing. BMC Bioinform. **10**(1), 24 (2009)

7. Chen, T.Y., Cheung, S.C., Yiu, S.M.: Metamorphic testing: a new approach for generating next test cases. Technical report HKUST-CS98-01, The Hong Kong University of Science and Technology (1998)

8. Chilana, P.K., Palmer, C.L., Ko, A.J.: Comparing bioinformatics software development by computer scientists and biologists: an exploratory study. In: 2009 ICSE Workshop on Software Engineering for Computational Science and Engineering. IEEE, May 2009

9. Clune, T.L., Rood, R.B.: Software testing and verification in climate model development. IEEE Softw. **28**(6), 49–55 (2011)

10. Dimopoulos, S., Krintz, C., Wolski, R., Gupta, A.: SuperContra: cross-language, cross-runtime contracts as a service. In: 2015 IEEE International Conference on Cloud Engineering. IEEE, March 2015

11. Dimoulas, C., Findler, R.B., Felleisen, M.: Option contracts. In: Proceedings of the 2013 ACM SIGPLAN International Conference on Object Oriented Programming Systems Languages & Applications - OOPSLA 2013. ACM Press (2013)

12. Duran, J.W., Ntafos, S.C.: An evaluation of random testing. IEEE Trans. Softw. Eng. **SE-10**(4), 438–444 (1984)

13. Eilers, M., Müller, P.: Nagini: a static verifier for Python. In: Chockler, H., Weissenbacher, G. (eds.) CAV 2018. LNCS, vol. 10981, pp. 596–603. Springer, Cham (2018). https://doi.org/10.1007/978-3-319-96145-3_33

14. Freeman, T.: Refinement types for ML. Ph.D. thesis, Carnegie Mellon University, Pittsburgh, PA, USA (1994)

15. Gewaltig, M.O., Cannon, R.: Current practice in software development for computational neuroscience and how to improve it. PLoS Comput. Biol. **10**(1), e1003376 (2014)

16. Giannoulatou, E., Park, S.H., Humphreys, D.T., Ho, J.W.: Verification and validation of bioinformatics software without a gold standard: a case study of BWA and bowtie. BMC Bioinform. **15**(Suppl 16), S15 (2014)

17. Goubault, E., Putot, S.: Static analysis of finite precision computations. In: Jhala, R., Schmidt, D. (eds.) VMCAI 2011. LNCS, vol. 6538, pp. 232–247. Springer, Heidelberg (2011). https://doi.org/10.1007/978-3-642-18275-4_17

18. Gunnels, J.A., van de Geijn, R.A.: Formal methods for high-performance linear algebra libraries. In: Boisvert, R.F., Tang, P.T.P. (eds.) The Architecture of Scientific Software. ITIFIP, vol. 60, pp. 193–210. Springer, Boston, MA (2001). https://doi.org/10.1007/978-0-387-35407-1_12

19. Hannay, J.E., MacLeod, C., Singer, J., Langtangen, H.P., Pfahl, D., Wilson, G.: How do scientists develop and use scientific software? In: 2009 ICSE Workshop on Software Engineering for Computational Science and Engineering. IEEE, May 2009

20. Hatcliff, J., Leavens, G.T., Leino, K.R.M., Müller, P., Parkinson, M.: Behavioral interface specification languages. ACM Comput. Surv. **44**(3), 1–58 (2012)
21. Hatton, L., Roberts, A.: How accurate is scientific software? IEEE Trans. Softw. Eng. **20**(10), 785–797 (1994)
22. Heaton, D., Carver, J.C.: Claims about the use of software engineering practices in science: a systematic literature review. Inf. Softw. Technol. **67**, 207–219 (2015)
23. Herndon, T., Ash, M., Pollin, R.: Does high public debt consistently stifle economic growth? A critique of Reinhart and Rogoff. Camb. J. Econ. **38**(2), 257–279 (2013)
24. Hochstein, L., Basili, V.: The ASC-alliance projects: a case study of large-scale parallel scientific code development. Computer **41**(3), 50–58 (2008)
25. Hook, D., Kelly, D.: Testing for trustworthiness in scientific software. In: 2009 ICSE Workshop on Software Engineering for Computational Science and Engineering. IEEE, May 2009
26. Johanson, A., Hasselbring, W.: Software engineering for computational science: past, present, future. Comput. Sci. Eng. **20**, 90–109 (2018)
27. Joppa, L.N., et al.: Troubling trends in scientific software use. Science **340**(6134), 814–815 (2013)
28. Kamali, A.H., Giannoulatou, E., Chen, T.Y., Charleston, M.A., McEwan, A.L., Ho, J.W.K.: How to test bioinformatics software? Biophys. Rev. **7**(3), 343–352 (2015)
29. Kanewala, U., Bieman, J.M.: Techniques for testing scientific programs without an oracle. In: 2013 5th International Workshop on Software Engineering for Computational Science and Engineering (SE-CSE). IEEE, May 2013
30. Kanewala, U., Bieman, J.M.: Testing scientific software: a systematic literature review. Inf. Softw. Technol. **56**(10), 1219–1232 (2014)
31. Kelly, D.: Scientific software development viewed as knowledge acquisition: towards understanding the development of risk-averse scientific software. J. Syst. Softw. **109**, 50–61 (2015)
32. Lundgren, A., Kanewala, U.: Experiences of testing bioinformatics programs for detecting subtle faults. In: Proceedings of the International Workshop on Software Engineering for Science - SE4Science 2016. ACM Press (2016)
33. Miller, G.: A scientist's nightmare: software problem leads to five retractions. Science **314**(5807), 1856–1857 (2006)
34. Paine, D., Lee, C.P.: Who has plots? Proc. ACM Hum.-Comput. Interact. **1**(CSCW), 1–21 (2017)
35. Park, I.M., Meister, M.L.R., Huk, A.C., Pillow, J.W.: Encoding and decoding in parietal cortex during sensorimotor decision-making. Nat. Neurosci. **17**(10), 1395–1403 (2014)
36. Patel, K., Hierons, R.M.: A mapping study on testing non-testable systems. Softw. Qual. J. **26**(4), 1373–1413 (2017)
37. Plosch, R.: Design by contract for Python. In: Proceedings of Joint 4th International Computer Science Conference and 4th Asia Pacific Software Engineering Conference. IEEE Computer Society (1997)
38. Ratcliff, R., McKoon, G.: The diffusion decision model: theory and data for two-choice decision tasks. Neural Comput. **20**(4), 873–922 (2008)
39. Saltelli, A., Funtowicz, S.: When all models are wrong. Issues Sci. Technol. **30**(2), 79–85 (2014)
40. Sanders, R., Kelly, D.: Dealing with risk in scientific software development. IEEE Softw. **25**(4), 21–28 (2008)

41. Sarma, G.P., Jacobs, T.W., Watts, M.D., Ghayoomie, S.V., Larson, S.D., Gerkin, R.C.: Unit testing, model validation, and biological simulation. F1000Research **5**, 1946 (2016)
42. Shinn, M., Romero-Garcia, R., Seidlitz, J., Váša, F., Vértes, P.E., Bullmore, E.: Versatility of nodal affiliation to communities. Sci. Rep. **7**(1), 1–10 (2017)
43. Siek, J., Taha, W.: Gradual typing for objects. In: Ernst, E. (ed.) ECOOP 2007. LNCS, vol. 4609, pp. 2–27. Springer, Heidelberg (2007). https://doi.org/10.1007/978-3-540-73589-2_2
44. Soergel, D.A.W.: Rampant software errors may undermine scientific results. F1000Research **3**, 303 (2015)
45. Takikawa, A., Feltey, D., Greenman, B., New, M.S., Vitek, J., Felleisen, M.: Is sound gradual typing dead? In: Proceedings of the 43rd Annual ACM SIGPLAN-SIGACT Symposium on Principles of Programming Languages - POPL 2016. ACM Press (2016)
46. Vazou, N., Seidel, E.L., Jhala, R., Vytiniotis, D., Peyton-Jones, S.: Refinement types for Haskell. In: Proceedings of the 19th ACM SIGPLAN International Conference on Functional Programming - ICFP 2014. ACM Press (2014)
47. Vitousek, M.M., Kent, A.M., Siek, J.G., Baker, J.: Design and evaluation of gradual typing for Python. In: Proceedings of the 10th ACM Symposium on Dynamic languages - DLS 2014. ACM Press (2014)
48. Vitter, J.S.: Random sampling with a reservoir. ACM Trans. Math. Softw. **11**(1), 37–57 (1985)
49. Weyuker, E.J.: On testing non-testable programs. Comput. J. **25**(4), 465–470 (1982)

SOLC-VERIFY: A Modular Verifier
for Solidity Smart Contracts

Ákos Hajdu[1(✉)] and Dejan Jovanović[2]

[1] Budapest University of Technology and Economics, Budapest, Hungary
hajdua@mit.bme.hu
[2] SRI International, New York City, USA
dejan.jovanovic@sri.com

Abstract. We present SOLC-VERIFY, a source-level verification tool for
Ethereum smart contracts. SOLC-VERIFY takes smart contracts written
in Solidity and discharges verification conditions using modular program
analysis and SMT solvers. Built on top of the Solidity compiler, SOLC-
VERIFY reasons at the level of the contract source code, as opposed to
the more common approaches that operate at the level of Ethereum
bytecode. This enables SOLC-VERIFY to effectively reason about high-
level contract properties while modeling low-level language semantics
precisely. The properties, such as contract invariants, loop invariants,
and function pre- and post-conditions, can be provided as annotations in the code by the developer. This enables automated, yet user-
friendly formal verification for smart contracts. We demonstrate SOLC-
VERIFY by examining real-world examples where our tool can effectively
find bugs and prove correctness of non-trivial properties with minimal
user effort.

1 Introduction

Distributed blockchain-based applications are gaining traction as a secure and
trustless alternative to more centralized solutions that require trusted intermedi-
aries such as banks. The focus of early blockchain implementations, such as Bitcoin [34], was to provide the infrastructure for one particular application: digital
money (cryptocurrency). Public blockchains allow arbitrary parties to transact
with each other in a secure and trustless manner, with no central authority.
In this setting a blockchain is a distributed ledger of transactions, where nodes
in a peer-to-peer network are processing and validating transactions to maintain integrity. The next step in the evolution of blockchains was to extend the
blockchain to a setting where the digital money can also be programmable. This
is achieved by generalizing the ledger to allow deployment of programs (termed
smart contracts [39]) that operate over ledger data. Blockchains with support
for smart contracts provide a general distributed computing platform and allow

---

Á. Hajdu—The author was also affiliated with SRI International as an intern during
this project.

© Springer Nature Switzerland AG 2020
S. Chakraborty and J. A. Navas (Eds.): VSTTE 2019, LNCS 12031, pp. 161–179, 2020.
https://doi.org/10.1007/978-3-030-41600-3_11

a set of mutually distrusting parties to execute and enforce their contractual terms (expressed as code) automatically. At the moment, the most popular such platform is the Ethereum blockchain [3,41].

However, smart contracts are often prone to errors with potentially devastating financial effects (see, e.g., [4] for a survey). The infamous DAO bug [16] is an illustrative example of the difficulties involved in deploying a smart contract. The DAO was a relatively small contract (2KLOC of Solidity code) that was heavily scrutinized by the wider Ethereum community before deployment. Nevertheless, an attacker managed to exploit a subtle reentrancy bug to steal $60M worth of cryptocurrency. Examples such as the DAO highlight the mission-critical nature of smart contracts. Although the code of the contract is usually small by the standards of modern software, if the contract attracts a large amount of investment, the code carries a significant amount of value per line of code. Moreover, since the contract code is stored on the blockchain, once deployed, the code is immutable and making upgrades or bug-fixes is impossible without complex solutions that involve a central authority. There has been a great interest in applying formal methods to verify smart contracts [4,23,32]. While there are ongoing projects based on identifying specific vulnerability patterns [8,13,20,22,29,35,40], theorem provers [24,25,37], finite automata [1,30] or SMT [2,26,27], they all have limitations in terms of scalability, precision, expressiveness and ease of use.

In this paper we present SOLC-VERIFY, a tool for formal verification of Ethereum smart contracts that integrates seamlessly with developer tools. SOLC-VERIFY follows the modular software verification approach (e.g., VCC [11], HAVOC [10], and ESC/Java [21]), in the context of Solidity. Given a Solidity contract, annotated with specifications, SOLC-VERIFY translates the contract into the Boogie intermediate verification language [15,28], and discharges verification conditions by SMT solvers [7]. Developers can define the expected behavior of their contracts using annotations within the contract code, including assertions, contract and loop invariants, and function pre- and post-conditions. Verification of smart contracts brings domain-specific challenges. To start with, the semantics of Solidity include Ethereum-specific constructs such as the blockchain state, transactions, and data-types not common in general programming languages. As an example, Ethereum smart contracts generally operate on 256-bit integers, making precise reasoning about low-level properties, such as the absence of overflows, infeasible with standard SMT techniques. Furthermore, some common high-level properties of smart contracts, such as "the sum of user balances is always equal to the total supply", cannot be expressed in first-order logic or in Solidity, and therefore need domain-specific treatment. SOLC-VERIFY addresses these issues through an SMT-friendly encoding of Solidity into Boogie that is expressive enough to capture the properties of interest, and takes advantage of recent advances in SMT solving to enable effective reasoning. We describe SOLC-VERIFY through examples and demonstrate how SOLC-VERIFY can both find non-trivial bugs in real-world examples and prove correctness after the bugs have been fixed (e.g., the BEC token [36] hack). As far as we know, SOLC-VERIFY is the first tool that allows specification and modular verification of Solidity smart contracts that is practical and automatic. SOLC-VERIFY is implemented as an add-on to the open-source Solidity compiler and is available on GitHub.[1]

2   Background

Ethereum. Ethereum [3,41] is a generic blockchain-based distributed computing platform. The Ethereum ledger is a storage layer for a database of *accounts* and data associated with those accounts, where each account is identified by its *address*. Ethereum contracts are usually written in a high-level programming language, most notably Solidity [38], and then compiled into the bytecode of the Ethereum Virtual Machine (EVM). A compiled contract is deployed to the blockchain using a special transaction that carries the contract code and sets up the initial state with the constructor. At that point the deployed contract is issued an address and stored on the ledger. From then on, the contract is publicly accessible and its code cannot be modified. A user (or another contract) can interact with a contract through its public API by calling public functions. This can be done by issuing a *transaction* with the contract's address as the recipient. The transaction contains the function to be called along with the arguments, and an execution fee called *gas*. Optionally, some value of Ether (the native currency of Ethereum) can also be transferred with transactions. The Ethereum network then executes the transaction by running the contract code in the context of the contract instance. During their execution, each instruction costs some predefined amount of gas. If the contract overspends its gas limit, or there is a runtime error (e.g., an exception is thrown, or an assertion is triggered), the entire transaction is aborted and has no effect on the ledger (apart from charging the sender for the used gas).

Solidity. Figure 1 shows a Solidity contract `SimpleBank` that illustrates some of the common features that Ethereum contracts use in practice. A contract can have *state variables*, which define the persistent data that the contract will store on the ledger. The state of `SimpleBank` consists of a single variable `balances`, which is a *mapping* from addresses to 256-bit integers. Further Solidity types include *value types*, such as Booleans, signed and unsigned integers (of various bit-lengths), addresses, fixed-size arrays, enums, and *reference types*, to be used with arbitrary-size arrays and structures. Once deployed, an instance of `SimpleBank` will be assigned its address and since no constructor is provided, its data will be initialized to default values (in this case an empty mapping).

Contracts define *functions* that can act on their state. Functions can receive data as arguments, perform computation, manipulate the state variables and interact with other accounts. In addition to declared parameters, functions also receive a `msg` structure that contains the details of the transaction. Our example contract defines two public functions `deposit` and `withdraw`. The `deposit` function is marked as `public` and `payable`, meaning that it can be called by anyone and is allowed to receive Ether as part of the call. This function reads

---

[1] https://github.com/SRI-CSL/solidity.

```
1  /** @notice invariant sum(balances) == this.balance */
2  contract SimpleBank {
3    mapping(address => uint256) balances;
4
5    function deposit() payable public {
6      balances[msg.sender] += msg.value;
7    }
8
9    function withdraw(uint256 amount) public {
10     require(balances[msg.sender] > amount);
11     if (!msg.sender.call.value(amount)("")) {
12       revert();
13     }
14     balances[msg.sender] -= amount;
15   }
16 }
```

```
1  /** @notice invariant x == y */
2  contract C {
3    int x;
4    int y;
5
6    /** @notice precondition x == y
7        @notice postcondition x == (y + n) */
8    function add_to_x(int n) internal {
9      x = x + n;
10     require(x >= y); // Catch overflow
11   }
12
13   function add(int n) public {
14     require(n >= 0);
15     add_to_x(n);
16     /** @notice invariant y <= x */
17     while (y < x) {
18       y = y + 1;
19     }
20   }
21 }
```

Fig. 1. An example Solidity smart contract implementing a simple bank. Users can deposit and withdraw Ether with the corresponding functions, and the contract keeps track of user balances. The top level annotation states that the contract will ensure that the sum of individual balances is equal to the total balance in the bank.

Fig. 2. An example Solidity smart contract illustrating the annotation features of SOLC-VERIFY, including contract-level invariants, pre- and post-conditions and loop invariants.

the amount of Ether received from `msg.value` and adds it to the balance of the caller, whose address is available in `msg.sender`. The `withdraw` function allows users to withdraw a part of their bank balance. The function first checks that the sender's balance in the bank is sufficient using a `require` statement. If the condition of `require` fails, the transaction is reverted with no effect. Otherwise the function sends the required amount of Ether funds by using a `call` on the caller address with no arguments (denoted by the empty string). The amount to be transferred is set with the `value` function. The recipient of the `call` can be another contract that can perform arbitrary actions on its own (within the gas limits) and can also fail (indicating it in the return value). If `call` fails, the whole transaction is reverted with an explicit `revert`, otherwise the balance of the caller is deducted in the mapping as well.

SimpleBank contains a classic reentrancy vulnerability that can be exploited to steal funds from the bank. As the control is transferred to the caller in line 11, before their balance is deducted in line 14, they are free to make another call to `withdraw` to perform a double (or multiple) spend. Although this flaw seems basic, it is the issue that lead to the loss of funds in the DAO hack [16].

3   Overview and Features

SOLC-VERIFY is implemented as an extension to the Solidity compiler. It takes a set of Solidity contracts including specification annotations and discharges verification conditions using the Boogie verifier and SMT solvers. An overview of the architecture is shown in Fig. 3.

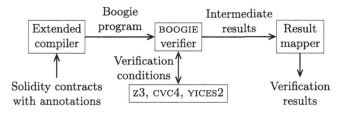

Fig. 3. Overview of the SOLC-VERIFY modules. The extended compiler creates a Boogie program from the Solidity contract, which is checked by the BOOGIE verifier using SMT solvers. Finally, results are mapped back and presented at the Solidity code level.

Specification. Solidity provides only a few error handling constructs (e.g., `assert`, `require`) for the programmer to specify expected behavior. Therefore, SOLC-VERIFY supports in-code *annotations* to specify contract properties, as illustrated in Fig. 2. Annotations are side-effect free Solidity expressions, which can reference any variable in the scope of the annotated element. *Contract-level invariants* (line 1) must hold before and after the execution of every public function and after the contract constructor. Non-public functions are inlined to a depth of one by default, but can also be specified with *pre- and postconditions* (lines 6–7). Moreover, *loop invariants* (line 16) can be attached to loops. As an extension, we also provide a special *sum* function over collections (arrays and mappings) in the specification language, as seen for example for `SimpleBank` in Fig. 1. The sum function is modeled internally by associating a ghost variable to the collection tracked by the sum: each collection update also updates the ghost variable. This encoding is a sufficient abstraction for our needs.

Correctness. SOLC-VERIFY targets functional correctness of contracts with respect to completed[2] transactions and different types of failures. An *expected failure* is a failure due to an exception deliberately thrown to guard from the user (e.g., `require`, `revert`). An *unexpected failure* is any other failure (e.g., `assert`, overflow). We say that a contract is *correct* if all transactions (public function calls) that do not fail due to an expected failure also do not fail due to an unexpected failure and satisfy their specification.

Translation to Boogie. SOLC-VERIFY relies on the Solidity compiler that parses the contracts and builds an abstract syntax tree (AST) where names, references and types are resolved. SOLC-VERIFY then traverses the internal AST and produces a Boogie [15,28] representation of the program. We discuss the details and properties of the translation in more detail in Sect. 4.

Boogie and SMT. Boogie transforms the program into verification conditions (VCs) and discharges them using SMT solvers. By default, Boogie can use z3 [33]

---

[2] Due to the usage of gas, total and partial correctness are equivalent. Furthermore, currently we do not model gas: running out of gas does not affect correctness as the transaction is reverted. However, we might model it in the future in order to verify liveness properties or to be able to specify an upper bound.

and CVC4 [6] but we also extended it to support YICES2 [18]. A notable feature of our encoding is that it allows quantifier-free VC generation, permitting to use SMT solvers that do not support quantifiers (e.g., YICES2). Boogie reports violated annotations and failing assertions in the Boogie program and SOLC-VERIFY maps these errors back to the Solidity code using traceability information. The final output of SOLC-VERIFY is a list of errors corresponding to the original contracts (e.g., line numbers, function names).

4   Translation Details and Properties

The core of SOLC-VERIFY is a translation from Solidity contracts to the Boogie IVL, supporting a majority of the Solidity language.[3]

Contracts. The input of the translation is a collection of contracts to be verified and the output is a single Boogie program with all contracts. SOLC-VERIFY can reason about single and multiple contracts as well. If the code of all contracts is available, SOLC-VERIFY can take all available annotations into account when reasoning. However, this can be unsafe as EVM addresses are not typed (any address can be cast to a contract type) and is to be used with care. SOLC-VERIFY also supports inheritance by relying on the compiler to perform flattening and virtual-call disambiguation.

Types. SOLC-VERIFY supports basic Solidity types such as Booleans, integers and addresses. Several modes are provided for modeling arithmetic operations that can be selected by the user. In the simplest mode, integers are unbounded *mathematical integers*. This mode does not capture the exact semantics of the operations (e.g., overflows) but is scalable and well supported by SMT solvers. Precise arithmetic can be provided by relying on the SMT theory of *bitvectors*. SOLC-VERIFY supports this mode but can suffer from scalability issues due to the 256-bit default integer size of Solidity. In order to provide both precision and scalability, SOLC-VERIFY provides a *modular arithmetic* mode that encodes arithmetic operations using mathematical integers with range assertions and precise wraparound semantics of all operations. Addresses are modeled with uninterpreted symbols as they can only be queried for equivalence. SOLC-VERIFY also supports mappings and arrays using SMT arrays [14,31]. Structures, enumerations and tuples are currently not supported but there are no technical difficulties in supporting them and they are planned in the future. Events (a logging mechanism) are ignored as they are not relevant for functional correctness.[4]

State Variables. State variables are mapped to global variables in Boogie. However, multiple instances of a contract can be deployed to the blockchain at

---

[3] The paper and the experiments are based on compiler version v0.4.25, but we keep SOLC-VERIFY up to date with the latest development branch.

[4] We might model events in the future to be able to specify that an event is expected to be triggered.

different addresses. Since aliasing of contract storage is not possible, SOLC-VERIFY models each state variable as a one-dimensional global mapping from contract addresses to their respective type (in essence treating the blockchain as a heap in a Burstall-Bornat model [9]). For example, the state variable x with type int at line 2 of Fig. 4 (left) is transformed to the global variable x with mapping type [address]int at line 1 of Fig. 4 (right).

```
1  contract A {                                  1  var x: [address]int;
2    int public x;                               2  procedure set(_this: address, _x: int) {
3    function set(int _x) public { x = _x; }     3    x := x[_this := _x];
4  }                                             4  }
5  contract B {                                  5  var a: [address]address;
6    A a;                                        6  procedure setXofA(_this: address, x: int) {
7    function setXofA(uint x) public { a.set(x); } 7    call set(a[_this], x);
8    function getXofA() public returns (uint) {  8  }
9      return a.x();                             9  procedure getXofA(_this: address) returns (r: int) {
10   }                                           10   r := x[a[_this]];
11 }                                             11 }
```

Fig. 4. Solidity contract (left) and its Boogie translation (right), illustrating the representation of the blockchain data as a heap and the receiver parameter of functions.

Functions. Each function in Solidity is translated to a procedure in Boogie with an additional implicit receiver parameter [5] called _this, which identifies the address of the contract instance. As an example, consider the set function of the Solidity contract A in Fig. 4. Updating x in the Boogie program becomes an update of the map x using the receiver parameter _this. Consider also the call a.set(x) in the Solidity function setXofA. The Boogie program first gets the address of the A instance corresponding to the current B instance using a[_this]. Then it passes this address to the receiver parameter of the function set.

Functions can be declared view (cannot write state) or pure (cannot read or write state), but these restrictions are checked by the compiler. Additional user-defined function modifiers are a language feature of Solidity to alter or extend the behavior of functions. In practice, modifiers are commonly used to weave in extra checks and instructions to functions. For example, the pay function in Fig. 5 (left) includes the modifier onlyOwner (defined in line 4), which performs an extra check before calling the actual function (denoted by the placeholder _). SOLC-VERIFY simply inlines statements of all modifiers of a function to obtain a single Boogie procedure (e.g., pay procedure in Fig. 5 right).

Statements and Expressions. Most of the Solidity statements and expressions can be directly mapped to a corresponding statement or expression in Boogie with the same semantics, including variable declarations, conditionals, while loops, calls, returns, indexing, unary/binary operations and literals. There are also some statements and expressions that require a simple transformation, such as mapping for loops to while loops or extracting nested calls and assignments within expressions to separate statements using fresh temporary variables. SOLC-VERIFY currently does not support inline assembly and creating new contracts from within another contract (new expressions). Furthermore, the availability of some arithmetic operations depends on the expressiveness of the underlying domain (e.g., bitwise operations).

```
1 | contract Wallet {
2 |   address owner;
3 |
4 |   modifier onlyOwner() {
5 |     require(msg.sender == owner);
6 |     _;
7 |   }
8 |   function receive() payable public {
9 |     // Actions could be performed here
10|   }
11|   function pay(address to, uint amount)
              public onlyOwner {
12|     to.transfer(amount);
13|   }
14| }
```

```
1 | var _balance: [address]int;
2 |
3 | var owner: [address]address;
4 |
5 | procedure receive(_this: address, _msg_sender: address,
              _msg_value: int) {
6 |   _balance := _balance[_this := _balance[_this] + _msg_value];
7 |   // Actions could be performed here
8 | }
9 | procedure pay(_this: address, _msg_sender: address, _msg_value:
              int, to: address, amount: int) {
10|   assume(_msg_sender == owner[_this]);
11|   assume( _balance[_this] >= amount);
12|   _balance := _balance[_this := _balance[_this] - amount];
13|   _balance := _balance[to := _balance[to] + amount];
14| }
```

Fig. 5. A simple wallet, which can receive Ether from anyone but only the owner can make transfers. This example illustrates various Ethereum and blockchain features in Solidity (left) along with their representation in Boogie (right).

Transactions. Solidity includes Ethereum-specific functions and variables to query and manipulate balances and transactions. Some examples can be seen in Fig. 5 (left) with the corresponding translation in Fig. 5 (right). Each address is associated with its balance, which can be queried using the **balance** member of the address. Correspondingly, SOLC-VERIFY keeps track of the balances in a global mapping from addresses to integers (line 1 of Fig. 5 right).

Solidity offers the **msg.sender** field within functions (line 5 of Fig. 5 left) to access the caller address. SOLC-VERIFY maps this to Boogie by adding an extra parameter **_msg_sender** of type **address** to each procedure. When a procedure calls another, the current receiver address (**_this**) is passed in as the sender.

Solidity functions marked with the **payable** keyword (line 8 of Fig. 5 left) are capable of receiving Ether when called. The amount of Ether received can be queried from the **msg.value** field. SOLC-VERIFY models this in Boogie by including an extra parameter **_msg_value** and updating the global balances map at the beginning of the corresponding Boogie procedure (line 6 of Fig. 5 right). When calling a payable function in Solidity, the amount of Ether to be transferred can be set with the special **value** function (e.g., line 11 of Fig. 1). SOLC-VERIFY translates this to Boogie by reducing the balance of the caller before making the call and passing the value as the **_msg_value** argument.

The functions **send** and **transfer** are dedicated functions to transfer Ether between addresses. SOLC-VERIFY inlines these functions by manipulating the global mapping of balances directly. If the recipient is a contract, a special fallback function is executed, but the gas passed is limited to raising events, which is irrelevant for functional correctness.[5] For example, the transfer in line 12 of Fig. 5 (left) is mapped to lines 11–13 on the right. The sender not having enough funds is an expected transaction failure, which is modeled with an assumption.

The function **call** can call a function by its name on any address and can also pass arbitrary data. Since there can be an unknown code behind the called

---

[5] Gas costs of certain write operations were about to change with Constantinople, allowing a reentrancy attack, but it was reverted with the St. Petersburg upgrade [19].

address, SOLC-VERIFY treats such cases as an external call that can perform arbitrary computation.[6] SOLC-VERIFY does not support low-level function calls such as `callcode` and `delegatecall` as it is considered dangerous and would require encoding of the EVM details (contract layout, EVM semantics).

Error Handling. Solidity exceptions will undo all changes made to the global state by the current call. Deliberately thrown exceptions (`require`, `revert`, `throw`) are therefore mapped to assumptions in Boogie, which stop the verifier without reporting an error. Assertions are mapped to Boogie assertions, causing a reported error when their condition evaluates to false.

Detection of Overflows. Neither the EVM nor Solidity performs any checking of the results of arithmetic operations by default. Due to the wraparound semantics of integers, this allows unexpected overflows and underflows to occur undetected (e.g., the infamous BEC token [36]).

In general, overflows can be detected by checking the result of every operation after it has been computed. However, reporting every such overflow would result in an overwhelming number of false alarms. For example, it is common practice for Solidity developers to perform arithmetic operations first, and then check for overflows manually after the fact (see, e.g., line 10 of Fig. 2). This practice of overflow detection is an integral part of the SafeMath library [17] that is used in almost all deployed contracts on the Ethereum blockchain and is part of Solidity best practices [12].

To reduce the number of false overflow reports, SOLC-VERIFY uses the following approach. Whenever an arithmetic computation is performed, it computes the *overflow condition* that captures whether the overflow has occurred (i.e., if the result of the computation in modular arithmetic is different from the result over unbounded integers). However, instead of immediately checking this condition, it is accumulated in a dedicated Boolean overflow-detection variable. SOLC-VERIFY then checks for overflow at the end of every basic block with an assertion. This "delayed checking" gives space to developer to perform manual checking for the overflow (in which case the assertion will not trigger) and will avoid the false alarms. For example, the potential overflow in line 9 of Fig. 2 is not reported because in the very next line the programmer guards the overflow and reverts the transaction.

5   Examples and Experiments on Real World Contracts

To demonstrate SOLC-VERIFY we first discuss the coverage of currently-supported language features and scalability by examining the (unannotated) contracts currently deployed on the Ethereum blockchain. We also pick a subset of the unannotated contracts and manually check what SOLC-VERIFY can report on them. Finally, we examine two contracts that had been exploited in

---

[6] Contract invariants are also checked before external calls as they can perform a callback to the contract.

Table 1. Etherscan results with different solvers and arithmetic encodings. Each cell represents the number of successfully processed contracts (of 7836 total) and the average execution time per contract.

Encoding	int	bv	mod	mod-overflow
Translated	4096	3919	3926	3926
CVC4	4090 (0.71 s)	3837 (0.99 s)	3921 (0.72 s)	3911 (0.79 s)
YICES2	3892 (1.15 s)	3854 (0.86 s)	3903 (0.75 s)	3859 (0.87 s)
Z3	3897 (1.24 s)	3831 (1.10 s)	3892 (0.87 s)	3894 (0.88 s)

the past, and show how SOLC-VERIFY could have found the issues, with minimal annotation burden, and prove that the fixed versions of the contracts are correct.

5.1 Language Coverage

To analyze the coverage of currently-supported language features and the scalability of SOLC-VERIFY, we collected 37531 contracts available on Etherscan.[7] These contracts were compiled with various versions of the Solidity compiler and not all of them are supported by version 0.4.25 that SOLC-VERIFY used at the time of writing the paper. We therefore selected 7836 contracts that do compile. The results of running SOLC-VERIFY on the selected contracts is shown in Table 1. Columns correspond to different arithmetic modes, with the last column representing modular arithmetic with overflow checking enabled. The first row shows that roughly 50% of the contracts can be successfully translated to Boogie in each mode. Contracts that cannot be translated contain constructs not yet handled by SOLC-VERIFY, such as structures, enumerations or special transaction and blockchain members. Some features (e.g., exponentiation) also depend on the arithmetic mode, resulting in slight differences in feature coverage. The remaining three rows show the number of contracts for which SOLC-VERIFY terminates within 10 s with a given SMT solver as a backend. Note, that the effectiveness of the different SMT solvers on this set of contracts should be taken with a grain of salt. For example, the bitvector encoding seems to be nearly as efficient as modular arithmetic. However, this is because the assertions in these contracts do not depend on complex (e.g., nonlinear) arithmetic. With more complex invariants, the bitvector encoding becomes infeasible for reasoning, as we demonstrate it with the BEC token example later in this section. The takeaway of these results is that the average execution time per contract is around a second, meaning that SOLC-VERIFY is applicable and effective for a significant amount of real-world contracts, but scalability might depend on the complexity of the properties.

5.2 Unannotated Contracts

The contracts available at Etherscan are *not annotated* and SOLC-VERIFY can only consider **assert** and **require** statements, and overflows as implicit

---

[7] http://csl.sri.com/users/dejan/contracts.tar.gz.

specification. Furthermore, the ground truth about the contracts (whether they are correct or not) is unknown. Nevertheless, we systematically selected a subset of the contracts and manually checked the results given by SOLC-VERIFY.

We took all 3897 contracts that SOLC-VERIFY could translate and process with z3 in integer mode. At the first glance we discovered that a majority of the contracts (2754) use the popular SafeMath library [17], which has just recently adopted the proper usage of **assert** and **require**.[8] We updated these contracts to properly guard against user input with **require** (instead of **assert**). Afterwards, we checked for *assertion failures* and *overflows* using SOLC-VERIFY.

Assertion Checking. Surprisingly, only 88 contracts (out of the 3897) contain assertions. SOLC-VERIFY reported an error for 80 contracts, which we all checked manually. Out of those errors, 78 are clearly false alarms caused by a bad specification – the developer wrote **assert** where **require** should have been used – and fit into one of the following categories:

- Enforcing input validity with assertion (e.g., input arrays are of equal size).
- Enforcing time locks with an assertion (e.g., `now > 100`).
- Enforcing success of functions calls with an assertion (e.g. `addr.call()`).
- Enforcing permissions with an assertion (e.g., checking `msg.sender`).
- Enforcing correct result of arithmetic operations with an assertion.

As described in the Solidity documentation [38] **assert** should only be used to check for internal errors and invariants, and all cases highlighted above should use **require** instead. After replacing the spurious assertions with **require**, SOLC-VERIFY reports no false alarms.

The 2 reported errors worth discussing in more detail are illustrated in Fig. 6. The example on the left is a pre-sale contract that accepts Ether until a sale cap is reached. The invariant of the contract, i.e. that (`raised <= max`) is enforced with a (stronger) assertion at the beginning of function. It could be argued that this fits within the mentioned prescribed usage for the **assert** construct. However, as SOLC-VERIFY performs modular analysis, and nothing is assumed about the state before a function call, it will report such an assertion as a potential error. To fix this, the invariant (`raised <= max`) should be specified as a contract invariant, and **require** should be used to check the stronger precondition at function entry (followed by an **assert** at the end of the function).

The example on the right is a token transfer function. The function checks whether the sender has enough balance, and then it transfers the tokens to the recipient. Finally, the assertion checks that no overflow has occurred using an **assert** statement on the result of the addition. As is, SOLC-VERIFY reports an error because increasing the balance of the recipient might overflow. As argued above, if the purpose of the assertion is to guard against overflows **require** should be used instead. On the other hand, one could argue that for fixed-cap tokens such an overflow should never occur since no address can hold enough

---

[8] For discussion, see https://github.com/OpenZeppelin/openzeppelin-solidity/issues/1120.

```
1  uint max     = 1000 ether;
2  uint raised = 0;
3
4  function() payable {
5    assert(raised < max);
6    require(msg.value != 0);
7    require(raised + msg.value <= max);
8    raised += msg.value;
9  }
```

```
1  mapping (address => uint) balances;
2
3  function transfer(address to, uint val) {
4    require(balances[msg.sender] >= val);
5    require(msg.sender != to);
6    balances[msg.sender] = balances[msg.sender] - val;
7    balances[to] = balances[to] + val;
8    assert(balances[to] >= val);
9  }
```

Fig. 6. Examples of failing assertions reported by SOLC-VERIFY.

tokens to trigger the overflow. This assumption can be explicitly specified, i.e., by stating a contract invariant sum(balances) <= cap. With this invariant, SOLC-VERIFY avoids the false alarm by inferring that overflow is no longer possible.

Overflow Checking. We also checked for overflows and manually verified the results for the 68 contracts (out of 3897) that have at least 100 transactions. SOLC-VERIFY reports 33 alarms of which 29 are false and 4 can be considered as real. All false alarms are due to implicit assumptions on the magnitude of used numbers. There are 20 false alarms due to missing range assumptions for array lengths causing false overflow alarms for loop counters. For example, in a loop for (uint i = 0; i < array.length; i++) {} SOLC-VERIFY reports that i++ might overflow. It is reasonable to assume that array lengths remain small due to the gas costs associated with growing an array. Other false alarms are caused by implicit assumptions on Ether balances or time. For example, it is assumed that a counter for the total amount of Ether received by a contract, or multiplying msg.value by 20000 cannot overflow because the amount of Ether is limited. Similarly, adding days or even weeks to the current timestamp will not overflow any time soon. We plan to include such implicit assumptions to a limited extent but, in general, it is best if the developer explicitly specifies them. The four issues found that could be considered real are the following:

- A pre-sale contract sets the hardCap in its constructor based on a cap provided as argument with hardCap = cap*(10**18). Although the constructor is only called once by the deployer, providing a large cap can result in an unintentional overflow.
- A crowd-sale contract sets the unit cost based on the argument perEther by calculating unitCost = 1 ether / (perEther*10**8). The problematic function is guarded so that it can only be called by the contract owner. Nevertheless, overflow can happen and can lead to an inconsistent unit price.
- A utility contract for mass distribution of tokens has a function to transfer an array of values to an array of recipients as a batch. The total amount transferred is kept accumulated in a contract counter and can overflow. However, as the counter is not used otherwise, the overflow might be benign.
- A food store contract first calculates the cost based on the bundles ordered, by computing cost = bundles * price, where bundles is provided by the caller. The function then checks if msg.value >= cost holds, but this check can be bypassed with the overflow, opening the door for a potential exploit.

```
 1  library SafeMath {
 2    function mul(uint256 a, uint256 b) internal pure returns (uint256) {
 3      uint256 c = a * b;
 4      require(a == 0 || c / a == b);
 5      return c;
 6    }
 7    // Similar for add, sub, div
 8  }
 9
10  /** @notice invariant totalSupply == sum(balances) */
11  contract BecToken {
12    using SafeMath for uint256;
13
14    uint256 public totalSupply;
15    mapping(address => uint256) balances;
16
17    function batchTransfer(address[] _receivers, uint256 _value) public returns (bool) {
18      uint cnt = _receivers.length;
19      uint256 amount = uint256(cnt) * _value; // Overflow
20      // uint256 amount = uint256(cnt).mul(_value); // Correct version
21      require(cnt > 0 && cnt <= 20);
22      require(_value > 0 && balances[msg.sender] >= amount);
23      balances[msg.sender] = balances[msg.sender].sub(amount);
24      /** @notice invariant totalSupply == sum(balances) + (cnt - i) * _value
25          @notice invariant (i <= cnt) */
26      for (uint i = 0; i < cnt; i++) {
27        balances[_receivers[i]] = balances[_receivers[i]].add(_value);
28      }
29      return true;
30    }
31  }
```

Fig. 7. Annotated part of the BECToken contract relevant for the "batchOverflow" bug [36]. While the contract uses the SafeMath library for most of its operations, there is a multiplication in line 19 that can overflow.

5.3 Annotated Contracts

While SOLC-VERIFY can find violations to implicit specifications in unannotated contracts, its main target is to allow developers to check custom, high-level properties by the means of annotations. We demonstrate this by annotating two contracts, finding bugs and proving the correctness of the fixed versions.

Reentrancy Detection (DAO). Reentrancy is a common source of vulnerabilities and the cause of the infamous DAO bug [16]. As explained in Sect. 2, the SimpleBank contract presented in Fig. 1 suffers from the same reentrancy bug. Using SOLC-VERIFY, the developer can specify the consistency of the bank contract state through a contract-level invariant, and SOLC-VERIFY can detect the bug. For example, we can annotate the contract with a property sum(balances) == this.balance. As the balance of the contract is deducted before the external call, the contract invariant is violated and SOLC-VERIFY reports a (real) error. However, if the user fixes the issue by first reducing the balance of the recipient in the mapping and then transferring the amount, the invariant will hold before making the external call and SOLC-VERIFY proves the specification successfully. For both the buggy and correct versions of the contract, the verification with SOLC-VERIFY is instant.

Overflow Detection (BEC Token). We now consider the BEC token vulnerability [36] that has been exploited and resulted in significant financial losses. The relevant part of the contract is shown in Fig. 7. The contract is a typical token contract, tracking balances of users in terms of their BEC tokens and allowing transfers of tokens between users. The function `batchTransfer` shown in the figure is intended to be used for transferring some value of BEC tokens to a group of recipients in a batch. To do so, the contract multiplies the requested value with the number of recipients. Unfortunately, this multiplication can result in an overflow (line 19), causing the total transfer amount to be invalid (e.g., 0). This allows attackers to "print" large amounts of tokens and send them to other users, while keeping their own balance constant. Running SOLC-VERIFY with the modular encoding of arithmetic successfully detects the overflow issue of BEC token and does not report any other potential overflows. After fixing the contract (line 20), SOLC-VERIFY shows that no overflows are possible. We also annotated the BEC contract with a specification that the contract maintains the correct token balances throughout the operation. As before, we add the invariant `totalSupply == sum(balances)` to the contract, and adapt it to the loop invariant. The loop invariant introduces extra complexity as it involves nonlinear arithmetic and illustrates the need for precise reasoning at large bit-sizes. Running SOLC-VERIFY on the annotated contract in the bitvector mode does not terminate regardless of the SMT solver used.[9] On the other hand, using modular arithmetic with overflow detection SOLC-VERIFY discharges all VCs (with 256-bit integers) in seconds for both the buggy and correct version of the contract (with CVC4).

Other Tools. As far as we know, SOLC-VERIFY is the only available tool that can reason effectively and precisely about Solidity code with specifications. The Solidity compiler includes an experimental SMT checker [2], which is currently limited to basic require/assert and overflow checking. For the BEC token the latest version (v0.5.10) reports every arithmetic operation as a potential overflow, including all false alarms in the `SafeMath` library. It cannot detect the reentrancy issue in the SimpleBank example because external calls and the `revert` function is not supported. Furthermore, it incorrectly reports that the condition for revert is always true (possibly because `call` is skipped and the default return value is false). ZEUS [26] is not available publicly for comparison.[10] VERISOL [27] does not support libraries (like `SafeMath`) or the `call` function, which can cause reentrancy so we could not apply it to our examples.

Two notable static analysis tools are MYTHRIL [13] and SLITHER [20]. MYTHRIL (v0.20.0) correctly reports the overflow issue with the BEC token in 200s, but it also reports all spurious overflows. MYTHRIL detects the reentrancy issue with the bank contract, but it also reports the same issue with the corrected version of the contract. SLITHER (v0.5.2), on the other hand, has a dedicated DAO-like reentrancy issue check and correctly handles both the buggy and correct version of the bank contract. However, SLITHER doesn't support overflow checking and therefore doesn't detect the BEC token issue.

---

[9] With bit-size of 16 bits, z3 can discharge the VCs in 2295 s while other solvers do not terminate.

[10] We could only obtain a spreadsheet of results from the authors.

Our goal, as demonstrated by the annotated examples, is to provide a tool that allows developers to check their own high-level annotations and business logic properties. This makes SOLC-VERIFY a good complementary to other automated verification tools that mainly target well known vulnerability patterns.

6 Related Work

The popularity of blockchain technology and many high-profile attacks and vulnerabilities have put focus on the need for formal verification for smart contracts [4, 23, 32]. We mention prominent advances relying on vulnerability patterns, theorem provers, finite automata and SMT, and relate them to our work.

Vulnerability Pattern-Based Approaches. Bhargavan et al. [8] translate a fragment of Solidity and EVM to F* and use its type and effect system to check for vulnerable patterns and gas boundedness. Grishchenko et al. [22] extend this work on EVM by checking security properties such as call integrity, atomicity, and independence from miner controlled parameters. SECURIFY [40] decompiles EVM and infers data- and control-flow dependencies in Datalog to check for compliance and violation patterns. OYENTE [29] is a symbolic execution tool that can check various patterns, including transaction ordering dependency, timestamp dependency, mishandled exceptions and reentrancy. MAIAN [35] uses symbolic analysis with concrete validation over a sequence of invocations to detect fund locking, fund leaking and contracts that can be killed. MYTHRIL [13] uses symbolic analysis to detect a variety of security vulnerabilities. SLITHER [20] is a static analysis framework with dedicated vulnerability checkers. Approaches based on vulnerability patterns, as the ones mentioned above, can be effective at discharging specific properties, but are limited to built-in patterns (or a domain specific language [40]). Furthermore, as they are mainly EVM-based it makes reasoning about more general properties difficult. Our approach focuses on Solidity and allows high-level, user-defined properties to be checked effectively.

Theorem Prover-Based Approaches. KEVM [24] is an executable formal semantics of EVM based on the K framework including a deductive program verifier to check contracts against given specifications. Hirai [25] formalizes EVM in Lem, a language used by various theorem provers and proves properties using interactive theorem proving. Scilla [37] is an intermediate language between smart contracts and bytecode, using the Coq proof assistant for reasoning. Theorem prover-based approaches offer the ability to capture precise, formal semantics of the contracts but can be cumbersome as properties also need to be formalized in the language of the theorem prover. Moreover, user interaction and assistance is usually required impeding usability for contract developers.[11] In our approach the developer can specify the properties directly within the contract, as Solidity annotations and modular verification is fully automated. Although loop invariants might be required, complex loops are rare in contracts.

---

[11] For an example of the difficulties in manually analyzing even trivial issues, see https://runtimeverification.com/blog/erc-20-verification/.

Automata-Based Approaches. FSOLIDM [30] is a finite state machine-based designer for smart contracts that can generate Solidity code. Security features and design patterns (e.g., locking, access control) can be included in the state machine. Abdellatif and Brousmiche [1] model contracts and the blockchain manually in BIP and use statistical model checking to simulate uncertainties in the environment. Such model-based approaches are orthogonal to our approach, as we are working on the source code directly. This has the advantage that the developer does not need to learn a new (modeling) language and an extra step of transformation (from model to source) is eliminated.

SMT-Based Approaches. ZEUS [26] translates Solidity to LLVM bitcode and employs existing verifiers such as SEAHORN and SMACK. Besides certain vulnerability patterns, it claims to have support for user-defined properties to some extent. However, it is not publicly available for comparison. VERISOL [27] checks for conformance between workflow policies and smart contract implementations on the Azure blockchain. While the core of their method is a translation to Boogie (similar to ours), it targets a specific problem limited in scope and does not yet support features needed for typical smart contracts (see Sect. 5.3). The Solidity compiler itself also includes a built-in experimental SMT checker [2], which executes the body of each function symbolically and checks for implicit specifications, such as assertion failures, dead code and overflows. Their approach is however, limited, by false overflow alarms and missing features (e.g., `call`, `revert`). Furthermore, it has no support for developer-supplied specification beyond `require` and `assert` statements. Some of the challenges they mention in their future work are solved by our approach, including contract level invariants and the reduced number of false overflow alarms.

7   Conclusion

We presented SOLC-VERIFY, a tool for automated verification of Solidity smart contracts based on modular program reasoning and SMT solvers. Working at the source level, SOLC-VERIFY allows users to specify high-level properties such as contract invariants, loop invariants, pre- and post-conditions and assertions. SOLC-VERIFY then discharges verification conditions with SMT solvers to verify contract properties in a modular and scalable way. The approach offers precise and scalable, yet automated and user-friendly formal verification for Solidity smart contracts. SOLC-VERIFY can already be used on real-world contracts and can effectively find bugs and prove correctness of non-trivial properties with minimal user effort.

References

1. Abdellatif, T., Brousmiche, K.: Formal verification of smart contracts based on users and blockchain behaviors models. In: 9th IFIP International Conference on New Technologies, Mobility and Security, pp. 1–5. IEEE (2018)

2. Alt, L., Reitwiessner, C.: SMT-based verification of solidity smart contracts. In: Margaria, T., Steffen, B. (eds.) ISoLA 2018. LNCS, vol. 11247, pp. 376–388. Springer, Cham (2018). https://doi.org/10.1007/978-3-030-03427-6_28

3. Antonopoulos, A., Wood, G.: Mastering Ethereum: Building Smart Contracts and DApps. O'Reilly Media, Inc., Sebastopol (2018)

4. Atzei, N., Bartoletti, M., Cimoli, T.: A survey of attacks on Ethereum smart contracts (SoK). In: Maffei, M., Ryan, M. (eds.) POST 2017. LNCS, vol. 10204, pp. 164–186. Springer, Heidelberg (2017). https://doi.org/10.1007/978-3-662-54455-6_8

5. Barnett, M., DeLine, R., Fähndrich, M., Leino, K.R.M., Schulte, W.: Verification of object-oriented programs with invariants. J. Object Technol. 3(6), 27–56 (2004)

6. Barrett, C., et al.: CVC4. In: Gopalakrishnan, G., Qadeer, S. (eds.) CAV 2011. LNCS, vol. 6806, pp. 171–177. Springer, Heidelberg (2011). https://doi.org/10.1007/978-3-642-22110-1_14

7. Barrett, C., Tinelli, C.: Satisfiability modulo theories. In: Clarke, E., Henzinger, T., Veith, H., Bloem, R. (eds.) Handbook of Model Checking, pp. 305–343. Springer, Cham (2018). https://doi.org/10.1007/978-3-319-10575-8_11

8. Bhargavan, K., et al.: Formal verification of smart contracts: short paper. In: ACM Workshop on Programming Languages and Analysis for Security, pp. 91–96. ACM (2016)

9. Bornat, R.: Proving pointer programs in hoare logic. In: Backhouse, R., Oliveira, J.N. (eds.) MPC 2000. LNCS, vol. 1837, pp. 102–126. Springer, Heidelberg (2000). https://doi.org/10.1007/10722010_8

10. Chatterjee, S., Lahiri, S.K., Qadeer, S., Rakamarić, Z.: A reachability predicate for analyzing low-level software. In: Grumberg, O., Huth, M. (eds.) TACAS 2007. LNCS, vol. 4424, pp. 19–33. Springer, Heidelberg (2007). https://doi.org/10.1007/978-3-540-71209-1_4

11. Cohen, E., et al.: VCC: a practical system for verifying concurrent C. In: Berghofer, S., Nipkow, T., Urban, C., Wenzel, M. (eds.) TPHOLs 2009. LNCS, vol. 5674, pp. 23–42. Springer, Heidelberg (2009). https://doi.org/10.1007/978-3-642-03359-9_2

12. ConsenSys: Ethereum smart contract security best practices (2018). https://consensys.github.io/smart-contract-best-practices/

13. ConsenSys: Mythril classic: security analysis tool for Ethereum smart contracts (2019). https://github.com/ConsenSys/mythril-classic

14. De Moura, L., Bjørner, N.: Generalized, efficient array decision procedures. In: Formal Methods in Computer-Aided Design, pp. 45–52. IEEE (2009)

15. DeLine, R., Leino, K.R.M.: BoogiePL: a typed procedural language for checking object-oriented programs. Technical report MSR-TR-2005-70, Microsoft Research (2005)

16. Dhillon, V., Metcalf, D., Hooper, M.: The DAO hacked. In: Dhillon, V., Metcalf, D., Hooper, M. (eds.) Blockchain Enabled Applications, pp. 67–78. Apress, Berkeley (2017). https://doi.org/10.1007/978-1-4842-3081-7_6

17. Dourlens, J.: Safemath to protect from overflows (2017). https://ethereumdev.io/safemath-protect-overflows/

18. Dutertre, B.: Yices 2.2. In: Biere, A., Bloem, R. (eds.) CAV 2014. LNCS, vol. 8559, pp. 737–744. Springer, Cham (2014). https://doi.org/10.1007/978-3-319-08867-9_49

19. Ethereum Constantinople/St. Petersburg upgrade announcement (2019). https://blog.ethereum.org/2019/02/22/ethereum-constantinople-st-petersburg-upgrade-announcement/

20. Feist, J., Greico, G., Groce, A.: Slither: a static analysis framework for smart contracts. In: Proceedings of the 2nd International Workshop on Emerging Trends in Software Engineering for Blockchain, pp. 8–15. IEEE (2019)

21. Flanagan, C., Leino, K.R.M., Lillibridge, M., Nelson, G., Saxe, J.B., Stata, R.: Extended static checking for Java. In: ACM SIGPLAN 2002 conference on Programming Language Design and Implementation, pp. 234–245. ACM (2002)

22. Grishchenko, I., Maffei, M., Schneidewind, C.: A semantic framework for the security analysis of Ethereum smart contracts. In: Bauer, L., Küsters, R. (eds.) POST 2018. LNCS, vol. 10804, pp. 243–269. Springer, Cham (2018). https://doi.org/10.1007/978-3-319-89722-6_10

23. Harz, D., Knottenbelt, W.: Towards safer smart contracts: a survey of languages and verification methods (2018). http://arxiv.org/abs/1809.09805

24. Hildenbrandt, E., Saxena, M., Zhu, X., Rodrigues, N., Daian, P., Guth, D., Rosu, G.: KEVM: a complete semantics of the Ethereum virtual machine. Technical report, IDEALS (2017)

25. Hirai, Y.: Defining the Ethereum virtual machine for interactive theorem provers. In: Brenner, M., et al. (eds.) FC 2017. LNCS, vol. 10323, pp. 520–535. Springer, Cham (2017). https://doi.org/10.1007/978-3-319-70278-0_33

26. Kalra, S., Goel, S., Dhawan, M., Sharma, S.: ZEUS: analyzing safety of smart contracts. In: Network and Distributed Systems Security Symposium (2018)

27. Lahiri, S.K., Chen, S., Wang, Y., Dillig, I.: Formal specification and verification of smart contracts for Azure blockchain (2018). http://arxiv.org/abs/1812.08829

28. Leino, K.R.M.: This is Boogie 2 (2008)

29. Luu, L., Chu, D.H., Olickel, H., Saxena, P., Hobor, A.: Making smart contracts smarter. In: Proceedings of the 2016 ACM SIGSAC Conference on Computer and Communications Security, pp. 254–269. ACM (2016)

30. Mavridou, A., Laszka, A.: Tool demonstration: FSolidM for designing secure Ethereum smart contracts. In: Bauer, L., Küsters, R. (eds.) POST 2018. LNCS, vol. 10804, pp. 270–277. Springer, Cham (2018). https://doi.org/10.1007/978-3-319-89722-6_11

31. McCarthy, J.: Towards a mathematical science of computation. In: IFIP Congress, pp. 21–28 (1962)

32. Miller, A., Cai, Z., Jha, S.: Smart contracts and opportunities for formal methods. In: Margaria, T., Steffen, B. (eds.) ISoLA 2018. LNCS, vol. 11247, pp. 280–299. Springer, Cham (2018). https://doi.org/10.1007/978-3-030-03427-6_22

33. de Moura, L., Bjørner, N.: Z3: an efficient SMT solver. In: Ramakrishnan, C.R., Rehof, J. (eds.) TACAS 2008. LNCS, vol. 4963, pp. 337–340. Springer, Heidelberg (2008). https://doi.org/10.1007/978-3-540-78800-3_24

34. Nakamoto, S.: Bitcoin: a peer-to-peer electronic cash system (2008). http://www.bitcoin.org/bitcoin.pdf

35. Nikolić, I., Kolluri, A., Sergey, I., Saxena, P., Hobor, A.: Finding the greedy, prodigal, and suicidal contracts at scale. In: Proceedings of the 34th Annual Computer Security Applications Conference, pp. 653–663. ACM (2018)

36. NIST National Vulnerability Database: CVE-2018-10299: Beauty Ecosystem Coin (BEC) issue (2018). https://nvd.nist.gov/vuln/detail/CVE-2018-10299

37. Sergey, I., Kumar, A., Hobor, A.: Scilla: a smart contract intermediate-level language (2018). http://arxiv.org/abs/1801.00687

38. Solidity documentation (2018). https://solidity.readthedocs.io/en/v0.4.25/

39. Szabo, N.: Smart contracts (1994)

40. Tsankov, P., Dan, A., Drachsler-Cohen, D., Gervais, A., Bünzli, F., Vechev, M.: Securify: practical security analysis of smart contracts. In: Proceedings of the 2018 ACM SIGSAC Conference on Computer and Communications Security, pp. 67–82. ACM (2018)
41. Wood, G.: Ethereum: a secure decentralised generalised transaction ledger (2017). https://ethereum.github.io/yellowpaper/paper.pdf

Intersection and Rotation of Assumption Literals Boosts Bug-Finding

Rohit Dureja[1](✉), Jianwen Li[1](✉), Geguang Pu[2], Moshe Y. Vardi[3], and Kristin Y. Rozier[1](✉)

[1] Iowa State University, Ames, IA, USA
{dureja,kyrozier}@iastate.edu
lijwen2748@gmail.com
[2] East China Normal University, Shanghai, China
[3] Rice University, Houston, TX, USA

Abstract. SAT-based techniques comprise the state-of-the-art in functional verification of safety-critical hardware and software, including IC3/PDR-based model checking and Bounded Model Checking (BMC). BMC is the incontrovertible best method for unsafety checking, aka *bug-finding*. Complementary Approximate Reachability (CAR) and IC3/PDR complement BMC for bug-finding by detecting different sets of bugs. To boost the efficiency of formal verification, we introduce heuristics involving intersection and rotation of the assumption literals used in the SAT encodings of these techniques. The heuristics generate smaller unsat cores and diverse satisfying assignments that help in faster convergence of these techniques, and have negligible runtime overhead. We detail these heuristics, incorporate them in CAR, and perform an extensive experimental evaluation of their performance, showing a 25% boost in bug-finding efficiency of CAR. We contribute a detailed analysis of the effectiveness of these heuristics: their influence on SAT-based bug-finding enables detection of different bugs from BMC-based checking. We find the new heuristics are applicable to IC3/PDR-based algorithms as well, and contribute a modified clause generalization procedure.

1 Introduction

Model checking techniques are widely used in proving functional correctness and have received unprecedented attention in the hardware and software design communities [6,18,22]. Given a system model M, and a property P representing a requirement, model checking proves whether or not P holds for M. A model checking algorithm exhaustively evaluates all possible behaviors (state-space exploration) of M, and returns a counterexample as evidence if any behavior violates the requirement. The counterexample gives the step-wise execution of the system that leads to property failure, i.e., a *bug*. Particularly, if P is a safety property, model checking reduces to reachability analysis, and the counterexample is of finite length. Popular reachability analysis algorithms include Bounded

© Springer Nature Switzerland AG 2020
S. Chakraborty and J. A. Navas (Eds.): VSTTE 2019, LNCS 12031, pp. 180–192, 2020.
https://doi.org/10.1007/978-3-030-41600-3_12

Model Checking (BMC) [8,10], Interpolation Model Checking (IMC) [25], Property Directed Reachability (IC3/PDR) [12,16], and Complementary Approximate Reachability (CAR). The common theme between these algorithms is that they are all SAT-based. BMC outperforms IMC on checking unsafe instances, i.e., *bug-finding*, while IC3/PDR and CAR can solve instances that BMC cannot [23]. It has been shown that better synergy between some of these algorithms and the SAT solver improves performance [14]. The continuous rapid advancement of SAT techniques also boosts the scalability of these algorithms.

Most SAT-based model checking algorithms use a CNF-based SAT solver as a *black-box*. The queries are expressed in CNF and the satisfiability result: SAT assignment, or unsat core, is used with or without modifications. Several solver management strategies: restart, clean-up, and (de)allocation, impact performance. In an ideal scenario, if the solver is aware of the verification problem then it may generate assignments or cores that help state-space exploration converge faster. However, achieving this is not trivial due to variability across different verification problems. There is a significant need to "guide" SAT search for model checking without modifying SAT solver internals, e.g. generating favorable unsat cores. This requires careful consideration of solver internals, and should have negligible overhead.

Complementary Approximate Reachability (CAR) [23,24] is a SAT-based model checking framework for reachability analysis. It can run in both forward and backward reachability modes; we focus on Backward-CAR as per previous work [23]. Contrary to reachability analysis via IC3/PDR, Backward-CAR maintains two sequences of over- and under- approximate reachable state-sets. The over-approximate sequence is used for safety checking, and the under-approximate for unsafety checking. We present clever and efficient heuristics to improve the performance of Backward-CAR on unsafety checking. The heuristics are inspired by assumption handling in modern CNF-based SAT solvers: assumptions literals are stored in a vector. The SAT solver propagates each assumption one-by-one, and therefore, the unsat core (UC) or satisfiable assignment can vary depending on the order in which literals are stored in the vector. Our heuristics, intersection and rotation aim to generate smaller UC and diverse states during search, respectively. In addition to the heuristics, we explore the effect of different state enumeration strategies in the under-approximate sequence of Backward-CAR. We argue that our heuristics are widely applicable and may improve the performance of other SAT-based model checking algorithms, like IC3/PDR. A thorough experimental evaluation on 748 single safety property benchmarks from HWMCC 2015 [2] and 2017 [3] reveals a 25% boost in the number of benchmarks that can be solved by Backward-CAR (155) compared to an earlier version in [23] (124). We also compare six implementations of Backward-CAR with varying heuristic combinations against reachability analysis algorithms (5 × BMC, 9 × IC3/PDR) in state-of-the-art model checking tools (ABC, nuXmv, IIMC, IC3Ref).

Contributions. The contributions of our work are four-fold.

1. We propose heuristics that leverage assumption handling in SAT solvers for faster convergence and scalability of Backward-CAR (Sect. 3).
2. An extensive experimental analysis on real-world benchmarks supports our performance claims, and also gives a broad comparative overview of state-of-the-art algorithms for unsafety checking (Sect. 4).
3. We make all our tools, experiment data, and analysis publicly available.
4. A modified clause generalization procedure in IC3/PDR based on our heuristics, that may help improve scalability (Sect. 5).

2   Preliminaries

A *Boolean transition system* Sys is a tuple (V, I, T), where V is a set of Boolean variables, and every state s of the system is in 2^V, the set of truth assignments to variables in V. Let V' be the set of primed variables, then T is a Boolean formula over $V \cup V'$, denoting the transition relation of the system. We say that state s_2 is a *successor* of state s_1, denoted $(s_1, s_2) \in T$, iff $s_1 \cup s_2' \models T$. The variables and their negations are called *literals*. A conjunction of literals is called a *cube*. The negation of a cube is a *clause*. A cube and clause are sets of literals we conjunct and disjunct, respectively.

A *path* (of length k) in Sys is a finite state sequence $s_1, s_2, \ldots, s_k$, where each $(s_i, s_{i+1})(1 \leq i \leq k-1)$ is in T. A state t in Sys is reachable if there exists a path such that $s_k = t$. Given a Boolean transition system $Sys = (V, I, T)$ and a safety property P, which is a Boolean formula over V, the system is called *safe* if P holds in all reachable states of Sys, and otherwise it is called *unsafe*.

Let $X \subseteq 2^V$ be a set of states in Sys. We define $R(X) = \{s' \mid (s, s') \in T \ where \ s \in X\}$, i.e., $R(X)$ is the set of successors of states in X. Conversely, we define $R^{-1}(X) = \{s \mid (s, s') \in T \ where \ s' \in X\}$, i.e., $R^{-1}(X)$ is the set of predecessors of states in X. Recursively, we define $R^0(X) = X$ and $R^i(X) = R(R^{i-1}(X))$ for $i > 0$. The notations of $R^{-i}(X)$ is defined analogously.

Let v be a vector of literals indexed from 0. We use $v[i]$ to represent the i-th element of v, $v.size$ for the size of v and $v.index(l)$ for the index of a literal $l \in v$. The intersection of two vectors $v_1 \cap v_2$ is a new vector v such that (1) $l \in v \Leftrightarrow (l \in v_1 \wedge l \in v_2)$, and (2) $v.index(l_1) < v.index(l_2) \Leftrightarrow v_1.index(l_1) < v_1.index(l_2)$. We say v_2 is a *subvector* of v_1, if $size(v_2) \leq size(v_1)$ and $\exists n.v_1[n+i] = v_2[i]$ for $0 \leq i < v_2.size$. In particular, we say v_2 is the *head* (resp. *tail*) of v_1 if v_2 is a subvector of v_1 and $n = 0$ (resp. $n = v_1.size - v_2.size$). Lastly, we say that a set of states S is *diverse* if $\bigcap_{t \in S} t = \emptyset$.

2.1   SAT with Assumptions

In our formulation, we consider SAT queries of the form $\mathsf{SAT}(A, B)$, where B is a CNF formula, and A is a cube. A query with no assumptions is simply written as $SAT(\emptyset, B)$. Essentially, the query $\mathsf{SAT}(A, B)$ is equivalent to $\mathsf{SAT}(A \wedge B)$ but the implementation is typically more efficient. If $A \wedge B$ is

Table 1. Frame sequences in Backward-CAR

	F-sequence (under)	B-sequence (over)
Init	$F_0 = I$	$B_0 = \neg P$
Constraint	$F_{i+1} \subseteq R(F_i)$	$B_{i+1} \supseteq R^{-1}(B_i)$
Safety check	-	$\exists i \cdot B_{i+1} \subseteq \bigcup_{0 \leq j \leq i} B_j$
Unsafety check	$\exists i \cdot F_i \cap \neg P \neq \emptyset$	-

1. SAT, get_assignment() returns a satisfying assignment to literals in A and B.
2. UNSAT, get_unsat_core() returns a unsatisfiable core C of the literals in A, such that $C \subseteq A$, and $C \wedge B$ is UNSAT.

We abstract the implementation details of the underlying SAT solver, and assume interaction using the above functions.

2.2 Complementary Approximate Reachability

The CAR framework performs reachability analysis in both forward and backward directions. It maintains over- and under- approximate state sequences to perform safety and unsafety checking. CAR can be implemented in both forward (Forward-CAR) or backward (Backward-CAR) modes. We focus on Backward-CAR, hereby referred to as just CAR (refer [24] for details on Forward-CAR and correctness proofs). Given $Sys = (V, I, T)$, and a safety property P, the over-approximate state frame sequence, **B**-sequence, stores states that can reach the bad states $\neg P$, while the under-approximate frame sequence, **F**-sequence, stores states reachable from the initial state I. Frame B_i is the set of states that can reach the bad states, whereas, F_i is the set of states reachable from the initial states, in i time-steps. The states in B_i and F_i are represented as a conjunction of clauses (CNF) and disjunction of cubes (DNF), respectively. Table 1 summarizes the constraints and safety checking conditions of the two sequences.

3 Algorithm and Proposed Heuristics

The CAR algorithm incrementally builds the **B**-sequence and **F**-sequence by repeated calls to the SAT solver. The system is considered: *unsafe* when a state in the **F**-sequence intersects with the bad states, and *safe* when all states that can reach the bad states have been added to the **B**-sequence. We first describe the CAR algorithm and the motivation for our heuristics, followed by the description of the proposed heuristics.

3.1 Algorithm Description

The main CAR procedure is shown in lines 1–7 of Algorithm 1. It takes as input $Sys = (V, I, T)$ and a safety property P. The procedure first checks for any

0-length counterexample (line 1). The frame sequences are then initialized per Table 1. The main loop of CAR (lines 3–7) iteratively checks both unsafety and safety. For unsafety checking, CAR picks a state s from the **F**-sequence and checks if it can reach the bad states in UNSAFECHECK (lines 4–5). The PICKSTATE function enumerates states in the **F**-sequence (line 8). Subsequently, SAFECHECK evaluates if all states that can reach the bad states have been added to the **B**-sequence (line 6).

The UNSAFECHECK procedure of lines 8–17 takes as input a state s in the **F**-sequence, and the current frame i in the **B**-sequence, and the maximum depth k of the **B**-sequence. Let's assume $\hat{s} = s$ (line 9). The procedure checks if state s can reach states in B_i using the query $SAT(s, T \wedge B_i')$ (line 10). If SAT, the assignment is a state t such that $(s, t) \in T$. If $i = 0$, then state t is a bad state (intersects B_0) and we have found a counterexample. Otherwise, t is added to the **F**-sequence, and the procedure recursively checks if t can reach a state in B_{i-1} (lines 13–14). If UNSAT, the negation of the unsat core $c \subseteq s$ is added to B_{i+1} (lines 15–16). Note that $\neg c$ represents the over-approximation of states that cannot reach the bad states and are blocked at B_{i+1}.

Alg. 1 Complementary Approximate Reachability (Backward)

1: **if** $SAT(I, \neg P)$ is satisfiable **then return** unsafe;
2: $F_0 := I$, $B_0 := \neg P$, $k := 0$;
3: **while** true **do**
4:     **while** (Cube s = PICKSTATE (F)) $\neq \emptyset$ **do**   ▷ state enumeration
5:         **if** UNSAFECHECK(s, k, k) **then return** unsafe;
6:     **if** SAFECHECK (k) **then return** safe;
7:     $k := k + 1$ and $B_k := \neg P$;   ▷ extend **B**-sequence

8: **procedure** UNSAFECHECK(s, i, k)
9:     Cube $\hat{s}$:= REORDER(s);   ▷ run proposed heuristics, by default $\hat{s} := s$
10:     **while** $SAT(\hat{s}, T \wedge B_i')$ **do**
11:         **if** $i = 0$ **then return** true;   ▷ reached bad state
12:         Cube t = get_assignment();   ▷ get SAT assignment
13:         $F_{j+1} := F_{j+1} \cup t$ supposing s is in F_j ($j \geq 0$);   ▷ extend and add to **F**-sequence
14:         **if** UNSAFECHECK $(t, i - 1, k)$ **then return** true;
15:     Cube c := get_unsat_core()   ▷ $c \subseteq s$ is the UNSAT assumptions
16:     $B_{i+1} := B_{i+1} \cap \neg c$;   ▷ add to **B**-sequence
17:     **return** false;

18: **procedure** SAFECHECK(k)
19:     $i = 0$;
20:     **while** $i < k$ **do**   ▷ no new states can be added
21:         **if not** $SAT(\emptyset, \neg(B_{i+1} \Rightarrow (\bigvee_{0 \leq j \leq i} B_j)))$ **then return** true;
22:     **return** false;

The SAFECHECK procedure of lines 18–22 takes as input the maximum depth k of the **B**-sequence. By enumerating $0 \leq i \leq k$, the safety check in Table 1 for the **B**-sequence is reduced to SAT checking of a Boolean formula (line 21). If UNSAT, all states that reach the bad states have been added to B_{i+1}, and the design is safe. Otherwise, the procedure extends the **B**-sequence (line 7) and continues by picking a new state s from the **F**-sequence.

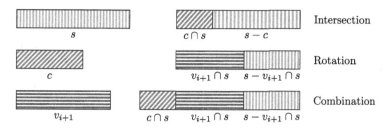

Fig. 1. Literal reordering in heuristics. We assume the SAT is $SAT(\hat{s}, T \wedge B_i')$, where $\hat{s}$ is generated by the heuristics by reordering literals in enumerated state s, $\neg c$ is the last added clause in B_{i+1} (intersection), and v_{i+1} is the vector associated with B_{i+1} (rotation).

The successive blocking of states in B_{i+1} leads to faster convergence of CAR; fewer spurious states that don't reach a bad state. We want to find a minimal unsat core (MUC) c such that $\neg c$ blocks the maximum number of states in B_{i+1}, i.e., tighten the over approximation of states that lead to a bad state. However, computing MUC is expensive [24]. A straightforward solution is to drop the literals in c one-by-one and check whether the UNSAT result is preserved. However, this solution is inefficient [23]; most attempts to find a smaller UC are unsuccessful and add to the overall runtime. Our heuristics: intersection and rotation can find smaller UC with negligible runtime overhead. Our heuristics take advantage of how modern SAT solvers handle assumption literals. Minisat [17], for example, stores the assumption literals as a vector and applies *Unit Propagation* [15] starting from the first literal in the vector. Therefore, literals that appear to the front of the vector have a higher chance of being included in the unsat core, provided the SAT query is UNSAT, compared to literals towards the end. Consider the Boolean formula of line 10 and let $c_0 \subseteq s$ be the unsat core. Let $c_1 \subset c_0$ be a smaller cube. If we order the assumption literals in line 10 such that c_1 is the head of the new vector, there is a higher chance that the UC will contain literals from c_1. This assumption literal ordering technique is the primary motivation of our heuristics.

3.2   Intersection and Rotation Heuristics

Let $\neg c_0$ be the last clause added to B_{i+1}, i.e., c_0 is a cube and $c_0 \wedge T \wedge B_i'$ is UNSAT. If c_0 is minimal we cannot reduce it. Otherwise, we can make c_0 smaller by dropping existing literals to get c_1. The clause $\neg c_1$ is weaker than clause $\neg c_0$ and therefore blocks more states at B_{i+1}. The heuristics carefully reorder the assumption literals in s (line 10) to generate $\hat{s}$ as shown in Fig. 1.

Intersection Heuristic. Given a state s and the last added clause $\neg c$ in B_{i+1}, let $\hat{s}$ be a new assumption vector such that $c \cap s$ is the head, and $s - c$ is the tail of $\hat{s}$. We pick the last added clause in B_{i+1} to avoid overhead of selection among different clauses in B_{i+1}, however, other clauses can also be used. Therefore, in $SAT(\hat{s}, T \wedge B_i)$ literals from $c \cap s$ have a higher chance to be included in the unsat query if the query is UNSAT. It is important to note that $\hat{s}$ and s have the same literals but differ in their ordering in the assumption vector, thus preserving the satisfiability result.

Rotation Heuristic. Every call to UNSAFECHECK may generate a state t reachable from the input states. Ideally, we want these states to explore disjoint parts of the state space in the quest to find a path that reaches the bad states. The rotation heuristic helps in generating such diverse states. Each B_i ($i > 0$) is associated with a vector v_i to store the assumptions literals for the most recent SAT query involving B_{i-1}. For example, v_i is equal to the enumerated state s_1 in the **F**-sequence that triggers the SAT query $SAT(s_1, T \wedge B'_{i-1})$. Subsequently, for B_{i-1} and a new enumerated state s_2, we generate $\hat{s}$ such that $v_i \cap s_2$ is the head and $s_2 - (v_i \cap s_2)$ is the tail of $\hat{v}_i$ as shown in Fig. 1. Note that $\hat{s}$ and s_2 have the same literals. Lastly, we update v_i to $\hat{s}$. The rotation heuristic generates diverse states as follows. For frame B_i in the **B**-sequence, let S be the set of generated states in the SAT queries and $C = \bigcap S$ be the set of common literals in states. Let c be the vector of literals in C. Assume x is an enumerated state in the **F**-sequence and the query $SAT(\hat{x}, T \wedge B'_{i-1})$ is UNSAT. Based on rotation literal reordering, c is the head of $\hat{x}$. The returned unsat core u is added to B_i. For a subsequent enumerated state y and frame B_i, a new state t is generated if the query $SAT(\hat{y}, T, B_i)$ is SAT. The new state satisfies $t \not\supseteq u$. Ideally, if $c \supseteq u$ is true, it is guaranteed that $t \cap c \neq c$. The state t is added to S, and therefore $\bigcap(S \cup \{t\}) \subset C$, i.e. the number of common literals is reduced. After several satisfiable SAT calls with different enumerated states and B_i, we will have $C = \emptyset$.

Combination of Intersection and Rotation Heuristics. The intersection and rotation heuristics have complementary strengths: intersection minimizes spurious state hits that do not reach bad states, while rotation generates diverse states reachable from the initial states. We use a combination to take advantage of their strength. For an enumerated states s we generate $\hat{s}$ as shown in Fig. 1. Let $\neg c$ be the last added clauses in B_{i+1} (intersection) and vector v_{i+1} is associated with B_{i+1} (rotation). Then $c \cap s$ is the head of $\hat{s}$, and $\hat{s}_I$ is the tail where $\hat{s}_I$ is generated from s by the rotation heuristic. Note that $\hat{s}$ may contain redundant literals but will preserve the satisfiability result of s.

4   Performance Evaluation

We incorporate the proposed heuristics in SimpleCAR [23]. Recall state enumeration in line 10 of Algorithm 1. As the number of states stored in the **F**-sequence increase, the order of selection of state s becomes vital. We evaluate two simple strategies for state enumeration in the PICKSTATE procedure: begin selects states from the first element in F_0 to the last element in F_n, and end selects state from the last element in F_n to the first element in F_0. Therefore, we consider six different implementations of CAR with varying assumption ordering heuristics and state enumeration strategies.

Table 2. Tools and algorithms (with category) evaluated in the experiments.

Tool	Algorithm	Configuration flags
ABC	BMC (abc-bmc)	-c 'bmc'
	BMC (abc-bmc2)	-c 'bmc2'
	BMC (abc-bmc3)	-c 'bmc3'
	PDR (abc-pdr)	-c 'pdr'
IIMC	BMC (iimc-bmc)	-t bmc --bmc_timeout 3600
	IC3 (iimc-ic3)	-t ic3
	Quip [21] (iimc-quip)	-t quip
	Backward IC3 (iimc-ic3r)	-t ic3r
IC3Ref	IC3 (ic3-ref)	-b
Simplic3	BMC (simplic3-bmc)	-a bmc
	IC3 (simplic3-best1)	-s minisat -m 1 -u 4 -I 0 -O 1 -c 1 -p 1 -d 2 -G 1 -P 1 -A 100
	IC3 (simplic3-best2)	-s minisat -m 1 -u 4 -I 1 -D 0 -g 1 -X 0 -O 1 -c 0 -p 1 -d 2 -G 1 -P 1 -A 100
	IC3 (simplic3-best3)	-s minisat -m 1 -u 4 -I 0 -O 1 -c 0 -p 1 -d 2 -G 1 -P 1 -A 100 -a aic3
	Avy [27] (simplic3-avy)	-a avy
SimpleCAR	Backward CAR (simpcar-bb)	-b -begin
	Backward CAR (simpcar-be)	-b -end
	Backward CAR (simpcar-bbi)	-b -begin -intersection
	Backward CAR (simpcar-bei)	-b -end -intersection
	Backward CAR (simpcar-bbr)	-b -begin -rotation
	Backward CAR (simpcar-ber)	-b -end -rotation
	Backward CAR (simpcar-bbir)	-b -begin -intersection -rotation
	Backward CAR (simpcar-beir)	-b -end -intersection -rotation

4.1 Experiment Set-Up

We compare our additions to SimpleCAR with ABC 1.01 [13], IIMC[1], IC3Ref [4] and Simplic3 [19]. The evaluated checkers algorithms together with the respective running configurations are listed in Table 2. All checkers use the Minisat [5,17] solver. There are three implementations of BMC in ABC: bmc and bmc2 for static and dynamic unrolling, respectively, and bmc3 for dynamic unrolling plus the termination after exhausted state exploration.[2] The BMC in Simplic3 and IIMC has the same functionality as bmc2 and bmc3 in ABC, respectively.

We evaluate all tools against 748 benchmarks in the *aiger* format [9] from the SINGLE safety property track of the HWMCC in 2015 [2] and 2017 [3]. We primarily focus on unsafety checking in our analysis. We check correctness in two ways: (1) We use the aigsim [1] to check whether the counterexample generated for unsafe instances is a real counterexample by simulation, and (2) For inconsistent results (safe and unsafe for the same benchmark by at least two different tools) we attempt to simulate the unsafe counterexample, and if successful, report an error for the tool that returns safe. The experiments were performed

---

[1] We use version 2.0 available at https://ryanmb.bitbucket.io/truss/ [7]– similar to the version available at https://github.com/mgudemann/iimc with addition of Quip [21] and Backward IC3/PDR.

[2] From personal communication with Alan Mishchenko.

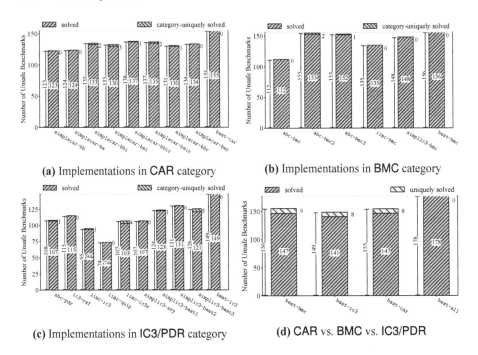

(a) Implementations in **CAR** category   (b) Implementations in **BMC** category

(c) Implementations in **IC3/PDR** category   (d) **CAR** vs. **BMC** vs. **IC3/PDR**

Fig. 2. Number of unsafe benchmarks solved. The "category-uniquely solved" benchmarks are not solved by any other implementation in the same category. The "uniquely solved" benchmarks are not solved by any other algorithm category.

on Rice University's DavinCI cluster[3], which comprises of 192 nodes running at 2.83 GHz, 48 GB of memory and running RedHat 6.0. We set the memory limit to 8 GB with a wall-time limit of an hour for each benchmark. Each model checking run had exclusive access to a node. All artifacts for reproducibility and detailed experimental results for both safety and unsafety checking are available on the paper website at http://temporallogic.org/research/VSTTE19/.

4.2   Experimental Results

Performance of CAR. We compare the performance of six versions of CAR from this paper, and 2 from [23]: `simpcar-bb` and `simpcar-be`. The results are summarized in Fig. 2a. `simplecar-bbir` solves the most number of unsafe instances (138) than any other CAR implementation, while the virtual best CAR (`best-car`), which includes the six CAR implementations proposed in this paper, solves 155 instances. In contrast, the CAR implementations from [23] solves 124 instances; these instances are solved by all six CAR implementations from this paper, and on average take ~**30% less time**. We also measure the average size of unsat cores generated by all CAR implementations at each frame in **B**-sequence.

---

[3] https://oit.rice.edu/davinci.

For the same benchmark, `best-car` generates on average ∼**14% smaller UC** compared to [23]. `simpcar-bbir` that uses a combination of intersection and rotation heuristics achieves the highest compression in UC size: on average ∼**20% smaller** UC. This supports our claim that smaller UC in the **B**-sequence lead to faster convergence, and validates the effectiveness of our heuristics in generating smaller unsat cores and diverse states with negligible runtime overhead.

Performance of BMC. The performance of five different BMC implementations is summarized in Fig. 2b. `abc-bmc2` solves all instances that are solved by `abc-bmc`, `iimc-bmc` and `simplic3-bmc` for a total of 155. `abc-bmc3` is able to solve one instance not solved by `abc-bmc2`. The virtual best BMC (`best-bmc`, which includes all five BMC implementations, solves 156 instances.

Performance of IC3/PDR. We found an error in `simplic3-best3` on the instance "6s309b034", for which `abc-bmc3` returns unsafe (the counterexample passes the check of `aigsim`) but `simplic3-best3` returns safe. The performances of nine different IC3/PDR implementations is summarized in Fig. 2c. `simplic3-best2` solves the most number of unsafe instances (131) than any other IC3/PDR implementation, while the virtual best IC3/PDR (`best-ic3`), which includes all nine IC3/PDR implementations, solves 149 instances.

Comparison of CAR *and* BMC. The `best-bmc` and `best-car` implementations solve 156 and 155 instances, respectively. However, `best-bmc` solves 15 instances not solved by `best-car`, and `best-car` solves 14 instances not solved by `best-bmc`. The virtual best of BMC and CAR solves 170 instances.

Comparison of CAR *and* IC3/PDR. There are 20 instances solved by `best-car` that are not solved by `best-ic3`, whereas, `best-ic3` solves 14 instances not solved by `best-car`. Both Reverse-IC3/PDR (`iimc-ic3r`) and Backward-CAR perform reachability analysis in the reverse direction. `iimc-ic3r` solves four instances not solved by any other IC3/PDR implementation; all implementations of CAR solves these 4 instances. The virtual best of IC3/PDR and CAR solves 169 instances.

The three algorithm portfolios complement each other as summarized in Fig. 2d. BMC can solve 7 "6s" instances not solved by CAR and IC3/PDR, whereas, CAR can solve four "6s" and three "oski" instances not solved by IC3/PDR and BMC. Overall, the virtual best of BMC, IC3/PDR, and CAR solves 170 unsafe instances. Our heuristics have negligble runtime overhead and significantly boost the performance of CAR making it an integral part of any algorithm portfolio for unsafety checking.

5   Discussion and Future Work

Invariant checking algorithms, like IC3/PDR, maintain a frame sequence $F_0, F_1, \ldots, F_i$ to store over-approximate states reachable in up to i steps. The sequence is refined iteratively by tightening the over-approximation for every step, i.e., blocking unreachable states. IC3/PDR terminates when an inductive invariant is found. For more details on IC3/PDR, we refer the reader to [12,16,19]. Several techniques [11,20] for faster IC3/PDR convergence try to block more than one state, instead of directly using the UC from the SAT solver, by clause *generalization*.

The intersection heuristic can also benefit IC3/PDR by improving the efficiency of generalization. Algorithm 2 describes a procedure to perform iterative generalization [13,19] using intersection. The literals in the clause to generalize are reordered (line 5). The last added generalized clause $\neg c$ in F_i can be used for intersection to generate the head and tail for vector $\hat{s}$. Note that the reordering of s to $\hat{s}$ in repeated iterations of the loop (lines 2–10) mimics the same behavior as dropping literals from g, albeit, cleverly. The literal reordering may generate a smaller inductive clause $\neg b$ compared to $\neg c$ that tightens the over-approximation F_i, hence, leading to faster convergence of IC3/PDR.

Alg. 2 IC3/PDR Generalization

GENERALIZE-ITER(**Clause** g, i)
1: done := False; **Cube** $s = \neg g$;
2: **for** iter := 1 **to** max_iter **do**
3:     **if** done **then break**
4:     done := True;
5:     Cube $\hat{s}$ = REORDER(s);
6:     **if not** $SAT(\emptyset, I \wedge \hat{s})$ **and**
        not $SAT(\hat{s}', F_i \wedge T \wedge \neg \hat{s})$ **then**
7:         **Cube** b := get_unsat_core()
8:         **while** $SAT(\emptyset, b \wedge I)$ **do**
9:             pick $l \in \hat{s} \setminus b$; set $b := b \cup \{l\}$;
10:        $s := b$; done = False; **break**

SAT solvers use the VSIDS [26] heuristic to score variables in a SAT query. The variables with high scores are preferred over variables with low scores for branching. Our heuristics implicitly perform variable scoring by picking literals from recently added clauses to the **B**-sequence, however, are external to the SAT solver. A better synergy between VSIDS in the SAT solver and our heuristics may generate even smaller UC. The state enumeration strategy also impacts performance. Quip [21] also suffers from this bottleneck: the algorithm discards states it cannot afford.[4] VSIDS can help generate diverse states by enumerating diverse satisfying assignments. CAR implementations with the intersection and rotation heuristics perform comparably, but disjointly; for example, `simpcar-beir` is unable to solve six instances solved by `simpcar-bei`. Evaluating model structure, and clausal learning as CAR progresses to better utilize the combination of the two heuristics is a promising research direction.

Acknowledgments. We thank the anonymous reviewers for their valuable comments. We thank Alan Mischenko and Alexander Ivrii for answering several queries during early phases of this work. This work is supported by NSF CAREER Award CNS-1664356, NASA ECF NNX16AR57G, NSF grants CCF-1319459, and NSFC grants 61572197 and 61632005. Geguang Pu is also partially supported by MOST NKTSP Project 2015BAG19B02 and STCSM Project No. 16DZ1100600. The experimental platform is supported by the Data Analysis and Visualization Cyberinfrastructure funded by NSF under grant OCI-0959097 and Rice University.

---

[4] Discussion with Alexander Ivrii.

References

1. AIGER Tools. http://fmv.jku.at/aiger/aiger-1.9.9.tar.gz
2. HWMCC 2015. http://fmv.jku.at/hwmcc15/
3. HWMCC 2017. http://fmv.jku.at/hwmcc17/
4. IC3Ref. https://github.com/arbrad/IC3ref
5. Minisat 2.2.0. https://github.com/niklasso/minisat
6. Bernardini, A., Ecker, W., Schlichtmann, U.: Where formal verification can help in functional safety analysis. In: 2016 IEEE/ACM International Conference on Computer-Aided Design (ICCAD), pp. 1–8 (November 2016)
7. Berryhill, R., Ivrii, A., Veira, N., Veneris, A.: Learning support sets in IC3 and Quip: the good, the bad, and the ugly. In: Formal Methods in Computer Aided Design (FMCAD), pp. 140–147 (October 2017)
8. Biere, A., Cimatti, A., Clarke, E.M., Fujita, M., Zhu, Y.: Symbolic model checking using sat procedures instead of BDDs (1999). https://doi.org/10.1145/309847.309942
9. Biere, A.: AIGER Format. http://fmv.jku.at/aiger/FORMAT
10. Biere, A., Cimatti, A., Clarke, E., Zhu, Y.: Symbolic model checking without BDDs. In: Cleaveland, W.R. (ed.) TACAS 1999. LNCS, vol. 1579, pp. 193–207. Springer, Heidelberg (1999). https://doi.org/10.1007/3-540-49059-0_14
11. Bradley, A.R., Manna, Z.: Checking safety by inductive generalization of counterexamples to induction. In: Formal Methods in Computer Aided Design (FMCAD 2007), pp. 173–180 (November 2007)
12. Bradley, A.R.: SAT-based model checking without unrolling. In: Jhala, R., Schmidt, D. (eds.) VMCAI 2011. LNCS, vol. 6538, pp. 70–87. Springer, Heidelberg (2011). https://doi.org/10.1007/978-3-642-18275-4_7
13. Brayton, R., Mishchenko, A.: ABC: an academic industrial-strength verification tool. In: Touili, T., Cook, B., Jackson, P. (eds.) CAV 2010. LNCS, vol. 6174, pp. 24–40. Springer, Heidelberg (2010). https://doi.org/10.1007/978-3-642-14295-6_5
14. Cabodi, G., Camurati, P.E., Mishchenko, A., Palena, M., Pasini, P.: Sat solver management strategies in IC3: an experimental approach. Formal Methods Syst. Des. **50**(1), 39–74 (2017). https://doi.org/10.1007/s10703-017-0272-0
15. Dowling, W., Gallier, J.: Linear-time algorithms for testing the satisfiability of propositional horn formulae. J. Logic Program. **1**(3), 267–284 (1984)
16. Een, N., Mishchenko, A., Brayton, R.: Efficient implementation of property directed reachability. In: Proceedings of the International Conference on Formal Methods in Computer-Aided Design, FMCAD 2011, pp. 125–134. FMCAD Inc., Austin (2011). http://dl.acm.org/citation.cfm?id=2157654.2157675
17. Eén, N., Sörensson, N.: An extensible SAT-solver. In: Giunchiglia, E., Tacchella, A. (eds.) SAT 2003. LNCS, vol. 2919, pp. 502–518. Springer, Heidelberg (2004). https://doi.org/10.1007/978-3-540-24605-3_37
18. Golnari, A., Vizel, Y., Malik, S.: Error-tolerant processors: formal specification and verification. In: IEEE/ACM International Conference on Computer-Aided Design (ICCAD), pp. 286–293 (November 2015)
19. Griggio, A., Roveri, M.: Comparing different variants of the IC3 algorithm for hardware model checking. IEEE Trans. Comput.-Aided Des. Integr. Circuits Syst. **35**(6), 1026–1039 (2016)
20. Hassan, Z., Bradley, A.R., Somenzi, F.: Better generalization in IC3. In: Formal Methods in Computer-Aided Design, pp. 157–164 (October 2013)

21. Ivrii, A., Gurfinkel, A.: Pushing to the top. In: Proceedings of the 15th Conference on Formal Methods in Computer-Aided Design, FMCAD 2015, pp. 65–72, FMCAD Inc., Austin (2015). http://dl.acm.org/citation.cfm?id=2893529.2893545
22. Jhala, R., Majumdar, R.: Software model checking. ACM Comput. Surv. **41**(4), 21:1–21:54 (2009). https://doi.org/10.1145/1592434.1592438
23. Li, J., Dureja, R., Pu, G., Rozier, K.Y., Vardi, M.Y.: SimpleCAR: an efficient bug-finding tool based on approximate reachability. In: Chockler, H., Weissenbacher, G. (eds.) CAV 2018. LNCS, vol. 10982, pp. 37–44. Springer, Cham (2018). https://doi.org/10.1007/978-3-319-96142-2_5
24. Li, J., Zhu, S., Zhang, Y., Pu, G., Vardi, M.Y.: Safety model checking with complementary approximations. In: Proceedings of the 36th International Conference on Computer-Aided Design, ICCAD 2017, pp. 95–100. IEEE Press, Piscataway (2017). http://dl.acm.org/citation.cfm?id=3199700.3199713
25. McMillan, K.L.: Interpolation and SAT-based model checking. In: Hunt, W.A., Somenzi, F. (eds.) CAV 2003. LNCS, vol. 2725, pp. 1–13. Springer, Heidelberg (2003). https://doi.org/10.1007/978-3-540-45069-6_1
26. Moskewicz, M.W., Madigan, C.F., Zhao, Y., Zhang, L., Malik, S.: Chaff: engineering an efficient SAT solver. In: Proceedings of the 38th Design Automation Conference, pp. 530–535 (June 2001)
27. Vizel, Y., Gurfinkel, A.: Interpolating property directed reachability. In: Biere, A., Bloem, R. (eds.) CAV 2014. LNCS, vol. 8559, pp. 260–276. Springer, Cham (2014). https://doi.org/10.1007/978-3-319-08867-9_17

Author Index

Printed in the United States
By Bookmasters